PREFACE

This report assesses conditions that contribute to or are potentially hospitable to transnational criminal activity and terrorist activity in selected regions of the world during the period 1999-2002. Although the focus of the report is on transnational activity, domestic criminal activity is recognized as a key foundation for transnational crime, especially as the forces of globalization intensify.

The report has been arranged geographically into the following major headings: Africa, the former Soviet Union and Eastern Europe, South Asia, Southeast Asia, Western Europe, and the Western Hemisphere. Within the geographical headings, the report addresses individual countries with particularly salient conditions. Cases such as the Triborder Area (TBA) of South America and East and West Africa, where conditions largely overlap national borders, have been treated as regions rather than by imposing an artificial delineation by country. The bibliography has been divided into the same geographical headings as the text.

The major sources for this report are recent periodical reports from Western and regional sources, Internet sites offering credible recent information, selected recent monographs, and personal communications with regional experts. Treatment of individual countries varies according to the extent and seriousness of conditions under study. Thus some countries in a region are not discussed, and others are discussed only from the perspective of one or two pertinent activities or conditions. Because they border the United States, Canada and Mexico have received especially extensive treatment.

I0448260

TABLE OF CONTENTS

INTRODUCTION

As organized crime and terrorist groups have globalized and diversified their operations in the past decade, they have based their activities in countries offering conditions most favorable to survival and expansion. Mobility, an important new characteristic of most such groups, has given groups a wider selection of operational bases and the ability to respond faster to changes that are unfavorable to their operations.

The main domestic elements making a nation "hospitable" to transnational crime and terrorism are official corruption, incomplete or weak legislation, poor enforcement of existing laws, non-transparent financial institutions, unfavorable economic conditions, lack of respect for the rule of law in society, and poorly guarded national borders. In some cases, several of those conditions arise together from a lack of political will to establish the rule of law. In turn, such a lack can derive from weak national institutions or from high-level corruption. A failing national economy often is an influential background factor that increases domestic and transnational criminal activity in a country. Such purely domestic factors often are exacerbated by a nation's geographic location (along a key narcotics trafficking route or in a region where arms trafficking is prolific, for example), or the influence of regional geopolitical issues such as a long-standing territorial dispute.

The reach of transnational crime and terrorism is increasing for many of the same reasons that the reach of legitimate business is expanding. Many of the regions discussed in this report are touched by criminal or terrorist activity from other regions of the world. For example, the starting point of arms trafficking in Africa often is weapons supplies in Eastern Europe and the former Soviet Union, and the trafficking of narcotics and human beings covers long distances from Asia and Africa to Western Europe and North America. Intermediary agents often are involved in transit countries along the routes. This globalization has brought about greatly increased cooperation and sophistication among criminal groups based in different parts of the world. In recent years, terrorist groups also have proven that their reach is worldwide, as they benefit from some of the same conditions that make nations hospitable to organized crime. Evidence shows, for example, that terrorist groups based in the Middle East have established connections in several other continents.

This report uses the term "trafficking" to refer to two categories of illegal transnational movement of people: the buying and selling of women and children for illegal labor and for the sex trade, and the movement of illegal migrants through or into countries without fulfilling the documentation requirements of those countries. Although the second activity often is called "smuggling," transnational criminal groups view both activities as the movement of a profit-bearing commodity. For that reason, this report refers to all transnational movement of illegal people or goods as "trafficking."

AFRICA

Introduction

In the past decade, the continent of Africa has been the scene of violent acts and planning operations by terrorist groups, as well as many types of "conventional" transnational crimes. In December 2000, an interagency law enforcement working group in the U.S. Government issued a report, *International Crime Threat Assessment,* that described the African climate for international organized crime and terrorism as follows:

> Porous borders, ample routes for smuggling drugs, weapons, explosives, and other contraband, and corruptible police and security forces make Sub-Saharan Africa an inviting operational environment for international criminals, drug traffickers, and terrorists. Major Sub-Saharan cities with extensive commercial, financial, and sea and air transportation links to Europe, the Middle East, and Asia are hubs for international criminal activity. . . . These include Nairobi and Mombasa in Kenya, Addis Ababa in Ethiopia, Abidjan in Côte d'Ivoire, Johannesburg in South Africa, and Lagos in Nigeria.[1]

Several other factors, common to almost every country on the continent, could also be cited. In the most general terms, these are the endemic weaknesses of state institutions and loyalties, transnational ethnic networks, and widespread poverty.[2] Other factors come into play on a regional or country basis.

Most states in Africa offer multiple opportunities and provide few constraints on criminal behavior, whether that behavior is displayed by traditional criminal organizations or by corrupt

---

[1] U.S. Government, *International Crime Threat Assessment* (Washington: 2000), 34. <http://clinton4. nara.gov>
[2] These factors are discussed in any number of sources on contemporary Africa. This discussion is based largely on Phil Williams and Doug Brooks, "Captured, Criminal , and Contested States: Organised Crime and Africa in the Twenty-First Century," *South African Journal of International Affairs*, 6, no. 2 (Winter 1999), 86-96.

political elites. Nation-states in Africa are almost all multi-ethnic entities in which local populations affect at best only embryonic allegiance to the nation as opposed to clan, tribe, or kin. In such states, integrative national institutions tend to be poorly developed, and they are often conceived of as "prizes" to be won and exploited rather than as forums for national government. There is often limited or no capacity to effect policy intervention in economy and society. Criminal justice systems are also often inadequate with respect to legislation to control or prevent racketeering and money laundering and to mandate punishment requisite to the crime committed. Police capacity and commitment to fight crime may be similarly limited.

Corruption is particularly pervasive and entrenched in many African states. This condition manifests itself many ways, often in collusive relationships between criminals and the elites in control of the state. In many cases, corruption is a natural outgrowth of the social and cultural practices that characterize the patrimonial state in Africa—a type of organization in which personal and/or patron-client ties, rather than prescriptive criteria or elections, determine the allocation of resources (and often of public office).

Another manifestation of weak states is porous borders and weak border controls. The extensive land and sea boundaries of many African states often are virtually unpatrolled. Many points of entry cannot be monitored by states with limited resources, resulting in opportunities for illegal immigration and constituting entry points for organized criminals. Customs and immigration services generally are poorly developed, trained, equipped, and paid. As such, they are readily circumvented or intimated by the relatively sophisticated methods employed by drug dealers and others who can offer bribes and have access to speedboats and overwhelming firepower.

Transnational ethnic networks are a natural outgrowth of artificial, colonial-era borders that divide ethnic groups in virtually all African countries. Local populations move back and forth freely across such borders. The resulting transnational networks readily transport stolen or illicit goods. Foreign communities resident in a given country also may form networks that often control legal commerce, but they may also protect well-established trafficking networks that channel illegal commodities between the host country in Africa and the home country abroad. Such networks exist among Chinese, Indian, Nigerian, and Russian communities in southern Africa and among Indian and Middle Eastern groups in East and West Africa. Such networks have come to characterize religious communities that may be ethnically based or trans-ethnic in composition, such as Muslims in coastal East Africa and in large parts of West Africa.

A final factor is poverty in the starkest economic sense. By Western standards, most Africans are incredibly poor. Vast areas of the continent are poorly endowed with natural resources; soils often are infertile and difficult to work, and the climate of many countries offers unpredictable and insufficient rain. In such conditions, legal economic activity may offer limited opportunities for wealth and upward mobility. The temptation to turn to various forms of illicit activity to earn a living or simply to survive can become overwhelming. This temptation is made even greater by the extremes of wealth and poverty that exist between a small elite and the impoverished majority in all African countries, particularly in cities. Such illicit activity includes individual and organized fraud, robbery, and illegal trafficking, all of which provide fertile ground for transnational exploitation and connections. At least some members of the continent's elite acquired their wealth by following this path.

North Africa

With the exception of Egypt and Morocco, the nations at North Africa's "corners" closest to the Middle East and Europe respectively, North Africa has not included important transit, origination, or destination points for the transnational trafficking of arms, narcotics, or people. In recent years, Morocco has suffered rapid expansion of its narcotics export activity, which has become linked with Islamic fundamentalist groups. In recent years, Algeria, Egypt, and Morocco have been the most fertile countries of the region for terrorist groups.

Algeria

Algeria has a rich history of activity by terrorist groups, dating to the country's bloody war for independence from France between 1956 and 1962. According to the U.S. Department of State, since the early 1990s government enforcement has effectively reduced the level of terrorist-related violence in Algeria, although individual acts still occur outside Algiers, the capital city.[3]

---

[3] U.S. Department of State, *Patterns of Global Terrorism 2002*.
<http://www.usis.usemb.se/terror/rpt2002/middle_east_overview.html>

The main terrorist group emanating from the revolutionary years is the Armed Islamic Group (Groupe Islamique Armé, GIA), a loosely organized movement that surfaced in 1992 as a radical branch of Algeria's main Islamic party, the Islamic Salvation Front. The overall aim of the organization, which is made up of highly autonomous cells, is to replace the secular government of Algeria with an Islamic state, using violent means if necessary. After a spate of terrorist killings in the mid-1990s, the GIA has been credited with occasional bombings in recent years, including a series of attacks in Paris in the mid-1990s. Current membership is estimated at between several hundred and several thousand individuals. Some members are believed to have joined other Islamic extremist groups, but current information about the GIA is scarce.[4]

No direct link between the GIA and al Qaeda has been identified, although al Qaeda has some Algerian operatives. In addition, some GIA leaders may have been in contact with Osama bin Laden in the 1980s, during the campaign against Soviet occupation of Afghanistan. GIA's goals and activities seem to be confined mainly to Algeria. However, some terrorism experts have speculated that a national Islamist movement such as the GIA would be a likely source for al Qaeda to reinvigorate its operations.[5]

In 1998 GIA was eclipsed by the Salafist Group for Call and Combat (GSPC) as the largest and most active terrorist organization in Algeria. The size and structure of the GSPC's membership and support networks are unknown. Attacks mainly focus on government and military targets in rural areas. For such attacks, the GSPC reportedly receives weapons and equipment from Islamic extremist groups in southern Algeria and has links with traffickers within and outside Algeria. GSPC members reportedly maintain contact in Europe with other North African Islamic groups sympathetic to al Qaeda.[6]

Egypt

Two major Islamic terrorist groups, Jamaat al-Islamiyya and Islamic Jihad, have been based in Egypt since the 1970s. Both groups have contributed members and leaders to al Qaeda, including top functionaries Ayman al-Zawahiri and Muhammad Atef, and many members of the

---

[4] Council on Foreign Relations and Markle Foundation, "Armed Islamic Group: Algeria, Islamists." <http://www.terrorismanswers.com/groups/gia.htm>
[5] Council on Foreign Relations and Markle Foundation, "Armed Islamic Group: Algeria, Islamists."
[6] U.S. Department of State and Federation of American Scientists, Intelligence Resource Program, "Salafist Group for Call and Combat (GSPC)." <http://www.fas.org/irp/world/para/salaf.htm>

two groups attended Taliban training facilities in Afghanistan. Jumaat al-Islamiyya has a worldwide membership; within Egypt the group has observed a 1999 cease-fire with the government, but the activity of individual members has continued in other countries. Islamic Jihad carried out the 1981 assassination of Egyptian president Anwar Sadat and attempted to assassinate government officials in the early 1990s. The organization has operated mainly outside Egypt in recent years; it was implicated in the attacks of September 11, 2001. The Muslim Brotherhood, from which both Jamaat al-Islamiyya and Islamic Jihad sprang, is a 70-year-old, grassroots Islamic social and political organization based in Egypt. The Muslim Brotherhood has not been linked with recent terrorist activity, and several members represent their organization in the national parliament.[7]

Beginning in the late 1990s, the activity of terrorist groups in Egypt has been limited substantially by harsh reprisals, mass arrests, and financial crackdowns instituted by the Mubarak government.[8] The last major terrorist attack occurred at Luxor in November 1997. However, the government has not dealt effectively with Egypt's long-term economic crisis, which combines with a high birth rate to foster social unrest and yield new recruits for the terrorist ranks. Some experts have argued that, under those conditions, Mubarak's "iron fist" policy against terrorism in fact exacerbates conditions that produce violent measures against the government. The terrorist acts of the 1990s themselves worsened economic conditions by severely damaging Egypt's vital tourism industry.[9]

Morocco

Morocco's participation in transnational narcotics trafficking is based on the country's status as the world's largest exporter of cannabis. In 2002 an estimated 75 percent of Morocco's total output of 2,000 tons was trafficked into Europe, accounting for an estimated 70 percent of the cannabis products entering Europe. Experts believe that cannabis cultivation, which already

---

[7] Council on Foreign Relations and Markle Foundation, "Jamaat al-Islamiyya, Egyptian Islamic Jihad: Egypt, Islamists." http://www.terrorismanswers.com/groups/jamaat.htm>

[8] Council on Foreign Relations and Markle Foundation, "Jamaat al-Islamiyya, Egyptian Islamic Jihad: Egypt, Islamists."

[9] Marc David Turetzky, "Egypt, Mubarak, and the Rise of Islamic Fundamentalist Terrorism, 1981-1994: An Empirical Analysis of the Mubarak Regime's Punitive Counter-Terrorist Policy," *Michigan Journal of Political Science*, no. 24 (Winter 1998). <http://www.umich.edu/~mjps/archives/issue24/turetzky24.htm>

is the most important economic activity in northern Morocco, is expanding rapidly.[10] The trade in hashish resin and oil that is prepared from cannabis is Morocco's largest single source of foreign currency. The high profitability of cannabis cultivation compared with cultivation of legal crops is a strong stimulus for growers to continue cultivating and for the government to tolerate such enterprises. In Morocco cannabis also has the advantage of being a highly drought-resistant crop.[11]

According to international narcotics trade expert Alain Labrousse, Morocco's cannabis exporters constitute one of Africa's two well-organized narcotics trafficking networks (the other is Nigeria's).[12] Cannabis products move from Morocco to Spain, thence into the rest of Europe, via the Mediterranean ports of Oued Lalou, Martil, and Bou Ahmed. Vehicles containing cannabis also reach Spain by ferry from the Spanish enclaves of Ceuta and Melilla. Some cannabis also moves overland to ports in Western Africa.[13]

The government's role in the narcotics trade occasionally has extended beyond benign neglect. In 2000 a Moroccan newspaper linked the head of King Hassan's security services with a Moroccan trafficker arrested in Spain, and the bribing of local police and customs officials is an accepted procedure for traffickers.[14] International pressure on Morocco's government to curtail transnational cannabis trafficking is mitigated by Morocco's role as a primary bulwark against Islamic fundamentalism in the Muslim world.

Meanwhile, northern Morocco's drug trade is the nucleus of a dangerously autonomous and lawless enclave. Narcotics traffickers have entered symbiotic relationships with Islamic groups in and around the port of Tangier. Although they remain organizationally separate, the traffickers and the religious extremists share tactics and a deep distrust of the secular government, which opposes Muslim participation in government (Islamic groups have been repressed harshly) and has attempted to manipulate rival narcotics trafficking groups. According to a 2001 *Middle East Report*:

---

[10] For example, international narcotics trade expert Alain Labrousse says Morocco's area of cannabis cultivation "has increased enormously," interview by Frederic Dorce, reported in *Jeune Afrique Economie* [Paris], 16 December 2002-19 January 2003 (FBIS Document AFP20030108000224).

[11] U.S. Department of State, Bureau for International Narcotics and Law Enforcement Affairs, *International Narcotics Control Strategy Report 2003* (Washington, D.C.: Department of State, 2003), X-37-38.

[12] Labrousse, in Dorce interview.

[13] U.S. Department of State, Bureau of International Narcotics and Law Enforcement Affairs, X-37-38.

[14] James Ketterer, "Networks of Discontent in Northern Morocco," *Middle East Report*, no. 218 (Spring 2001). <http://www.merip.org/mer/mer218/218_ketterer.htm>

Drug traffickers, contraband smugglers, prostitution rings, the chronic unemployed, Islamists and other groups in Tangier have built up elaborate networks based on illegal commerce, political opposition, corruption and violent protest that have infiltrated the local political system and now challenge the state's power in northern Morocco. Periodic attempts to control these informal networks have largely been unsuccessful…. Although informal, these networks are highly organized.[15]

Morocco is a transit point and a destination for transnational trafficking of women into the sex industry, as well as a starting point for trafficking illegal migrants into Europe. The eight-mile distance across the Mediterranean from Morocco to Spain is a key geographical factor, as Spain is the first step for both types of trafficking in people. In 2001 the government of Morocco claimed to have dismantled 400 networks that were smuggling illegal migrants, but the government of Spain has asserted that Morocco's enforcement measures are insufficient to stop the illegal entries.[16] According to the U.S. Department of State, in 2002 Morocco did not have a law specifically prohibiting trafficking in people. The country's resources for dealing with such crimes are limited, border controls are insufficient, and police complicity in cross-border trafficking has been observed.[17] Morocco also has been unable to reduce the substantial incidence of domestic forced prostitution, often run by criminal groups, that is concentrated around tourist centers and military bases.[18] An estimated 200,000 women work as prostitutes in Morocco.[19]

Morocco's status as a relatively terror-free nation was shattered in May 2003, when a series of bomb attacks in Calcutta killed 41 people. Authorities attributed the attacks to a little-known domestically based Salafist organization having links to al Qaeda. This was the first such attack in Morocco since 1995.[20]

---

[15] Ketterer.

[16] "A Human Rights Report on Trafficking of Persons, Especially Women and Children: Morocco." <http://209.190.246.239/ver2/cr/Morocco.pdf>

[17] U.S. Department of State, *Trafficking in Persons Report 2002*. <http://www.state.gov/g/tip/rls/tiprpt/2002>

[18] Global March, "Worst Forms of Child Labour Data 2002: Morocco." www.globalmarch.org/worstformsreport/world/morocco.html.

[19] "A Human Rights Report on Trafficking of Persons, Especially Women and Children: Morocco."

[20] Adrian Croft, "Radical Muslim Link to Morocco Blast," *The Age* [Melbourne], 19 May 2003. <http://www.theage.com.au/articles/2003/05/18/1053196472643.htm>

Sub-Saharan Africa

Eastern Africa

In the past decade, Eastern Africa has been the scene of several major terrorist acts, and populations in the region reportedly support terrorist planning and supply cells. Several forms of transnational crime are rampant in the region as well. The countries of Eastern Africa offer all of the advantages to international criminals and terrorists mentioned in the general overview of Africa: weak state institutions, corrupt politicians and law enforcement personnel, porous borders, ethnic groups with ties in neighboring and foreign states, and high levels of poverty. Of all such factors, however, the most important element may be the region's geographical position along the eastern coast of Africa, on trade routes that for more than a millennium have linked South Asia with the African continent.

Contributing Factors

In recent years, many nations of East Africa have been plagued by domestic and transnational upheavals that have destabilized borders and weakened law enforcement in both the nations directly affected and their more stable neighbors. Sudan has endured a lengthy insurgency, Somalia is an agglomeration of rival groups without a national government, Ethiopia and Eritrea have been at war often, and the Great Lakes District has been plagued by inter-tribal brutality in Rwanda and Burundi and insurgent movements in eastern Congo. International traffickers in narcotics, human beings, and arms have found this environment favorable for their enterprises. The more stable nations of the region—Kenya, Tanzania, and Uganda—have suffered from the instability surrounding them as well as from domestic corruption and law enforcement insufficiencies. Smugglers and terrorists are attracted to East Africa because of its geographic proximity to the Middle East and South Asia, its long coastline that is difficult to control, regular airline service to Europe and North America, and sizeable and increasingly radicalized Muslim communities.

Poverty is a major factor in all the countries of the region. Most of Somalia is arid or semi-arid desert that provides few natural resources. Most Somalis are shepherds; sedentary agriculture is practiced in some areas, but no industry has functioned since the breakdown of civil order in the early 1990s.[21] The lack of gainful employment causes the young to enroll in local militias or leave to find work in neighboring countries or in the Middle East.

In 1997 a survey by the government of Kenya showed that more than one-half of the population was below the government's standard for absolute poverty, and that in the 1990s poverty was spreading from rural areas into urban centers.[22] This trend has been accelerated by Kenya's very high birth rate, especially in the 1980s. The large age cohorts produced during that decade now are coming of age, finding no employment, and contributing to an environment of rising street crime and desperation in Kenya society. Said a resident of one of Nairobi's Muslim neighborhoods, "If a bomber came to my house and asked to stay, I would say, 'A salaam aleikum' [peace be with you], my brother, especially I if it might help us out, financially speaking."[23] British terrorism expert Danna Harman has predicted that as Kenya's economic woes persist, the Muslim population probably will become more susceptible to Islamic radicalization, a situation that in turn may facilitate yet more acts of terrorism.[24] Tanzania shares many of Kenya's economic problems. It is economically underdeveloped and more than one-third of the population falls below the government-defined poverty line.[25]

Somalia, Kenya, and to a lesser extent Tanzania, lie astride one of the most convenient transit routes between South and Southeast Asia on the one hand and Europe and North America on the other. The coasts of those countries are perhaps the most attractive stretch of an age-old 2,000-mile commercial arc that stretches from India along the Arabian and African coasts as far as Mozambique and the Comoro Islands.[26]

The East African coast is open, poorly patrolled, and easily accessible to small watercraft that can make landfall almost at will. Together with the population, urban settlements, and infrastructure of the mainland, the coast offers great advantages for legitimate traders as well as smugglers seeking access to world markets with a minimum of risk.

---

[21] Economist Intelligence Unit, *Eritrea, Somalia, Djibouti: Country Profile 2001* (London: 2001), 36-40; Ken Menkhaus, "Political Islam in Somalia," *Middle East* Policy, 9, no. 1 (March 2002), 121-122.

[22] Kenya, Ministry of Finance and Planning, *Second Report on Poverty in Kenya. Vol. I: Incidence and Depth of Poverty* (Nairobi: 2000), 46.

[23] Danna Harman, "Why Radicals Find Fertile Ground in Moderate Kenya," *Christian Science Monitor*, December 6, 2002, 8.

[24] Harman.

[25] Economist Intelligence Unit, *Tanzania, Comoros: Country Profile 2002* (London: 2002), 14-17, 20ff.

[26] U.S. Department of State, *International Narcotics Control Strategy Report 2003*, X-25, X-27, X-61, and X-62.

Kenya has long and porous land borders, which offer easy entry and exit for legitimate merchants as well as traffickers and terrorists. The border with Somalia is a case in point. That unmarked frontier runs through semi-desert territory that is virtually impossible to patrol. Police and customs posts are quite easily circumvented by detouring through adjacent scrub cover. The boundaries with Tanzania and Uganda are better demarcated but still difficult to patrol in their entirety.

Tanzania's coast, which has numerous natural harbors that facilitate trade and smuggling, is even more poorly patrolled than Kenya's. Tanzania also suffers from long and porous land borders. The country has minimal institutional capacity to combat narcotics trafficking and other criminal activity. Few resources are available to law enforcement agencies, and Tanzania's police and coastal defense forces are poorly trained and equipped.[27]

Kenya and some of its East African neighbors have based their national economies heavily on the tourist industry, attracting large concentrations of Westerners who present inviting targets for Islamic fundamentalist terrorists.[28] Kenya's beaches and game parks attract nearly 500,000 foreign visitors annually. Nairobi alone has an estimated 50,000 permanent residents from Western countries, of whom about 5,000 are Americans.[29] Because East Africa is relatively close to the Middle East and the East African nations do not effectively control passage into and out of their jurisdictions, such concentrations of Westerners are targets of convenience.

Somalia has the weakest law enforcement infrastructure in the region. Since the early 1990's, it has had no national executive or administration, no national army, no organized police forces in urban areas or in the countryside, and no centralized control of seaports. Somalia's coastline, which extends nearly 1,500 miles along both coasts of the Horn of Africa, includes the points of the African continent closest to South Asia and to the southern coast of the Arabian peninsula. That coastline likewise is without effective controls.

Kenya has an increasingly restive Muslim population that accounts for at least 5 percent of the country's total population. Kenyans whose ancestors migrated from South and Southwest Asia maintain a network of commercial and family ties with their countries of origin. These ties

---

[27] U. S. Department of State, *International Narcotics Control Strategy Report 2003*, X-62.
[28] "Attentats anti-israéliens: pourquoi le Kenya?" [Anti-Israeli Attacks: Why Kenya?], *Marchés Tropicaux et Mediterranéens* [Paris], no. 2978 (6 December 2002).
[29] Emily Wax, "Marines Comb Borders As Worries Rise in Kenya," *Washington Post*, 17 May 2003, A16

involve trade in hashish and heroin as well as in legitimate goods.[30] In recent decades, the Swahili-speaking Muslim population along Kenya's eastern coast has voiced resentment against perceived religious discrimination by the central government in Nairobi. That population has viewed government authorities with suspicion and businessmen from the central highland as unwanted intruders.[31] This sense of alienation and the growth of pro-Palestinian sympathies provide a receptive environment and a recruiting ground for terrorist groups such as al Qaeda.

Tanzania also has a sizeable Muslim population, which is situated along the mainland coast and on Zanzibar, Pemba, and smaller offshore islands. Tanzania's Muslims traditionally have been occupied primarily with commerce rather than religious zealotry or militancy. However, they, like their Kenyan counterparts, have provided a hospitable environment for their co-religionists from Middle Eastern and Southwest Asian countries, whatever the newcomers' agendas.

Kenya's infrastructure makes the country attractive to businessmen, travelers, and international traffickers.[32] Although roads and telecommunications have deteriorated in recent years, Kenya's air and sea transport systems are in good condition, especially in comparison with neighboring African states. Nairobi's Jomo Kenyatta International Airport is the major air hub for all of eastern Africa, providing air links from other continents to much of Central and Southern Africa. International air routes connect to Europe, the Middle East, and South Asia. For ocean transport, the port of Mombasa, one of the busiest ports on the east coast of Africa, handles a large annual volume of trade, and a transnational network of roads and railroads connects Mombasa with Tanzania, Uganda, and Central Africa. West and East Africans and South Asians predominate in the trafficking of heroin through Kenya, normally by air.[33]

Arms Trafficking

In the past decade, trafficking in small arms has increased substantially in Kenya, Somalia, Sudan, and Uganda. Livestock is commonly exchanged for firearms in a process that

---

[30] Yaroslav Trofimov, "In Mombasa Streets, Bin Laden Is 'Hero,' And U.S. Is Hated," *Wall Street Journal*, December 2, 2002, A1.

[31] Trofimov.

[32] Information on Kenya's infrastructure may be found in Economist Intelligence Unit, *Kenya: Country Profile 2001* (London, 2001), 25-27, 29-40, and in "Kenya: Communications," *Africa South of the Sahara 2003* (London: Europa, 2003), 527-28.

[33] U.S. Department of State, *International Narcotics Control Strategy Report 2003*, X-25.

has become an accepted part of life in East Africa. In Kenya, government demands to surrender illegal firearms have gone unheeded. Throughout the Horn of Africa, small arms are exacerbating conflicts over natural resources, cattle rustling, and urban crime rates. According to a 2002 report, illegal arms in the region "filter beyond armies and police forces to criminal organizations, private security forces, vigilante squads, and individual citizens."[34]

Unstable political conditions throughout the area minimize government controls and ease the contribution of illegal arms to a vicious cycle of violence and disorder. Authorities attribute much of the chronic unrest in parts of the region to the easy availability of firearms, which come from transnational and domestic traffickers and indigenous rebel organizations such as the Sudan-based Lord's Resistance Army, the Allied Democratic Forces of Uganda, and the Sudan People's Liberation Army (SPLA). An estimated 25 percent of the small arms come from the United Kingdom, which is the largest non-African source country. Another 30 percent comes from other countries in the European Union.[35] The Sudanese government's policy of arming tribal groups against the insurgent SPLA also has contributed to this problem. In the 1990s, the Toposa tribe in southern Sudan reportedly received 50,000 AK-47 rifles from the government,[36] but they also reportedly received substantial amounts of arms from the SPLA during that period.[37]

Arms traffickers are able to move easily from Sudan, which has no controls on such activity, into Uganda. A wide variety of arms are available in Kenya, Uganda, and Somalia.[38] A 2001 study estimated that black marketers sell 11,000 guns in Kenya annually, most of which arrive via Uganda, Somalia, Ethiopia, and Sudan. Viktor Bout, the notorious Russian arms dealer based in the United Arab Emirates, is known to have sold weapons in Kenya, Sudan, and

---

[34] Lynne Griffiths-Fulton, "Small Arms and Light Weapons in the Horn of Africa," *Ploughshares Monitor*, Summer 2002. <http://www.ploughshares.ca/content/MONITOR/monj02a.htm>

[35] International Action Network on Small Arms, "Kalashnikovs for Chickens: Small Arms Boom in East Africa," 7 May 2001. <http://www.iansa.org/news/2001/may_01/chicken.htm>

[36] Cathy Majtenyi, "Small Arms: Only a Regional Approach Can Stop the Trade," *The East African* [Nairobi], 26 November 2001. <http://www.nationaudio.com/News/EastAfrican/03122001/Regional/Regional2.htm>

[37] United Nations, Office for the Coordination of Humanitarian Affairs, "East Africa: Small Arms Exacerbating Regional Insecurity," Integrated Regional Information Network report, 30 November 2001. <http://www.reliefweb.int/w/rwb.nsf/s/23C43ACB12FDC40085256B14005B3462>

[38] International Action Network on Small Arms.

Uganda. Tanzania reportedly also is a major arms transit country in the region.[39] Middlemen in Tanzania supply arms to rebels in Uganda and to both competing factions in Burundi.[40]

An important center of illegal arms distribution in Kenya is the Dadaab refugee camps near Nairobi, from which arms reportedly reach all parts of Kenya as well as Rwanda, Burundi, Uganda, and Sudan. Arms from these camps also reach terrorists belonging to the fundamentalist al Itihaad group, which the United States accused of having supplied bases in Africa to al-Qaeda before the embassy bombings of August 1998.[41] Arms traffickers reportedly have a sophisticated smuggling system that links Somalia with the camp and with Nairobi. U.S. arms proliferation expert Kathi Austin reports that corruption among local Kenyan officials is a major contributing factor. Another cause is the central government's neglect of the border region between Kenya and Somalia, where a substantial share of illegal arms shipments transit.[42] Kenyan officials have identified lax customs controls at designated entry points and the political instability of Somalia, southern Sudan, and the Great Lakes region (eastern Congo, Burundi, and Rwanda) as the major factors in the large-scale influx of arms.[43]

Substantial amounts of arms reach competing factions in Somalia through sources in neighboring Eritrea and Ethiopia, as well as from Kenya, Yemen, Russia, and Italy. Eritrea and Ethiopia flaunt a United Nations arms embargo by buying arms from outside sources for themselves and for customers in Somalia. Somalians then sell arms to rebels and criminals in Tanzania, Uganda, and Kenya as well as to customers in neighboring Rwanda and Burundi.[44]

Narcotics Trafficking

The trafficking of cocaine, heroin, mandrax, and marijuana has flourished in coastal East Africa. The Kenyan port of Mombasa is a key point of entry for transnational narcotics moving from Asian sources to Europe and from India to South Africa. Mandrax from India moves

---

[39] Solomon Muyita, "Uganda Major Point in Arms Trafficking," *New Vision* [Kampala], 15 July 2001. <http://allafrica.com/stories/200107150067.htm>
[40] Robert E. Sullivan, "Burgeoning Small Arms Trade Has High Profits and Losses," *Earth Times*, March 2001. <http://www.globalpolicy.org/security/smallarms/2001/03sc.htm>
[41] "Arms Trafficking Networks out of Kenya and Somalia, Including Links to Terrorists, Exposed in Fund for Peace Investigation," Fund for Peace news release, 5 December 2002. <http://www.fundforpeace.org>
[42] Kevin J. Kelley, "Africa News Service: Daadab an 'Arms Centre,'" Fund for Peace report, 19 November 2000. <http://www.fundforpeace.org/media/inthenews/itn10001119.php>
[43] "Mombasa Main Conduit for Drug Trafficking," International Action Network on Small Arms report, 18 June 2001. <http://www.iansa.org/news/2001/jun_01/mombasa.htm>
[44] Sullivan.

overland through Kenya, Tanzania, and Zambia. Since 1993 large amounts of hashish from Pakistan and Afghanistan have been entering Kenya through Mombasa and the border point of Namanga. Sea routes for heroin begin in Pakistan and Sri Lanka. [45] Traffickers use trucks, oil tankers, conventional merchant ships, and airplanes to move narcotics and arms into the region. The narcotics trade has brought with it money laundering and other organized crime activities. Most drug confiscations occur at Kenya's airports, although it is known that the majority of traffic passes overland or by sea.[46] As in the case of arms trafficking, lax customs controls and corrupt officials have promoted the role of Kenya and its neighbors as a narcotics transit center. Kenya also is handicapped by rampant cultivation of domestic marijuana (promoted by corrupt officials) and a growing domestic market for narcotics.[47]

In 2002 Ethiopia, which is located on the route between Asian heroin production countries and major West African narcotics trafficking networks, was ranked first among African nations in volume of heroin trafficking.[48] As a hub for flights from Southeast and Southwest Asia into Africa and Europe, Bole Airport in Addis Ababa is a major transit point for this trade. Frequent two-day layovers for transcontinental flights offer an opportunity for marketing in Addis Ababa. Nigerian and Tanzanian traffickers are especially active in Ethiopia. Government interdiction personnel have been poorly trained and equipped, although some improvements were made in 2002.[49]

Like Kenya and Ethiopia, Tanzania is located along natural narcotics trafficking routes from east to west and offers traffickers numerous accessible points of entry by sea, land, and air. The major points of entry are the airports at Dar es Salaam, Zanzibar, and Kilimanjaro; major seaports at Dar es Salaam and Zanzibar; and smaller ports at Tanga and Mtwara. Traffickers also use small boats on inland waterways. Heroin from Afghanistan enters Tanzania from Pakistan and is smuggled further to Europe and North America by various traffickers, particularly Nigerians, utilizing air routes. In recent years, the use of less central access points has increased

---

[45] Observatoire Géopolitique des Drogues, "Kenya," in 1997 annual report.
<http://www.ogd.org/rapport/gb/RP11_7_KENYA.htm>
[46] Ken Opala, "The Case for a More Effective Approach," *Daily Nation* [Nairobi], 1 August 2002.
<http://www.mapinc.org/ccnews/v02/n1429/a05.html?347>
[47] Opala.
[48] Opala.
[49] U.S. Department of State, Bureau for International Narcotics and Law Enforcement Affairs, *International Narcotics Control Strategy Report 2002*. <http://www.state.gov/g/inl/rls/nrcrpt/2002/html/17950.htm>

as government enforcement measures at airports have improved.[50] However, it is widely believed that corrupt officials at airports facilitate the transshipment of narcotics through Tanzania.[51] Criminal organizations in Tanzanian communities provide in-country support for drug smugglers from Afghanistan and Pakistan[52]

Trafficking in Humans

Jomo Kenyatta International Airport in Nairobi is a central transit point for transnational trafficking in human beings. Large numbers of illegal migrants from Somalia, Ethiopia, China, India, and Sri Lanka pass through the airport's weak customs barriers en route to Western Europe and the United States. According to a Kenyan immigration officer, the routes involving Kenya include more than four countries. Common stops after Nairobi are Mumbai (Bombay) and Dubai. An estimated 500 to 750 Somali migrants per month arrive at Wilson Airport, from where they travel by road to Nairobi.[53] A 2002 investigation by the *Nairobi Daily Nation* found that Kenya's trafficking syndicate was run by high-ranking and wealthy Kenyans in collusion with unscrupulous immigration, intelligence, and police officials at the airport and in the Immigration Department. A separate investigation revealed that 3,000 to 4,000 Somalis a year were purchasing Kenyan identity and travel documents and one-way air tickets to their destination of choice. [54] Immigration personnel lack the skill and equipment to stay ahead of sophisticated document counterfeiters.

The International Organization for Migration has reported large numbers of Ethiopian women working as low-paid domestic servants in the Middle East and the Gulf States, after having been delivered there by traffickers. In 1999, the number of such cases in Lebanon was estimated at between 12,000 to 20,000. Some Ethiopian women also have been trafficked as nude dancers in Mongolia.[55]

---

[50] U.S. Department of State, Bureau for International Narcotics and Law Enforcement Affairs, *International Narcotics Strategy Report 2002*..

[51] U. S. Department of State, *International Narcotics Control Strategy Report 2003*, X-61-X62.

[52] "East Africa: Terrorism's Ties to Drugs," *Strategic Forecast* [Austin, Texas], Daily Global Intelligence Report, October 5, 2001. < http://www.stratfor.com>; U. S. Department. of State, *Narcotics Control Report, 2003*, X-61.

[53] Stephen Muiruri, "How Illegal Migrants Use Kenya's Airports," 13 August 2002. <http://fpmail.friends-partners.org/pipermail/stop-traffic/2002/002266.htm>

[54] Ibid.

[55] International Organization for Migration, "New IOM Figures on the Global Scale of Trafficking: Africa," *Trafficking in Migrants*, special issue, April 2001.

Corruption

Kenya's level of corruption among public officials has been extremely high for several decades. In its June 2001 survey, Transparency International ranked Kenya 84th out of 91 countries in publicly perceived corruption.[56] The corruption problem has come to permeate Kenyan society from bottom to top; it ranges from the exactions demanded by police on the street to the open embezzlement of funds from state coffers, institutions, and organizations. In the 1990s, pervasive corruption came to be regarded simply as a way of life.

The most visible level of Kenya's corruption was the administration of President Daniel arap Moi (in office 1978–2003), whose officials were widely known as seeking personal profit at the country's expense. More than once in the 1990s, the World Bank and the International Monetary Fund suspended development aid because of allegations of misspent funds.[57] Such large-scale graft and corruption in the public sector have contributed to an environment of permissiveness that accommodates and even encourages other forms of criminal behavior, including organized crime and terrorism. In early 2003, newly elected President Mwai Kibaki characterized Kenya's pervasive corruption as the root cause of all the country's problems. Kibaki announced an immediate attack on corruption in government and elsewhere.[58] However, experts remained skeptical that Kenya's ingrained power relationships would yield to such an attack.

Money Laundering

The hawwalat system, the main method of credit transfer in Somalia, has the potential to provide cover for money laundering operations that support crime and terrorism.[59] Based on that potential, in November 2001 the United States government closed the international offices of al-Barakaat, the largest of the Somali hawwalat offices. However, as of early 2002, allegations of involvement in funding terrorism had not been confirmed, and the issue remained unresolved. The Somali hawwalat is not intrinsically hospitable to outside manipulation because the system's

---

[56] Economist Intelligence Unit, *Kenya: Country Profile 2001* (London: 2001), 15.
[57] Economist Intelligence Unit, *Kenya: Country Profile 2001*, 6.
[58] Martin Mutua, "Kibaki Opens Parliament, Vows to Fight Corruption," *The East African Standard* [Nairobi], 19 February 2003. <http://allafrica.com/stories/200302190693.html>
[59] U.S. Department of State, *International Narcotics Control Strategy Report 2003*, XII-29.

norms of reciprocity are based on relationships of trust embedded in clan and familial structures.[60]

Nairobi, which serves as a regional banking and trade center for Eastern, Central, and Southern Africa and Kenya, has a large informal economic sector and large amounts of unrecorded cash-based international transfers. However, as of 2002 the U.S. Department of State had not found that the international financial transactions of Kenyan banks include a significant amount of money laundering.[61]

Terrorist Activity

Like other parts of the continent, East Africa offers terrorists porous borders, interethnic and intertribal conflict, lax financial systems, and easily available weapons.[62] Sudan is a terrorist haven because the government of Omar el-Bashir is run by the National Islamic Front, whose goal is to install fundamentalist Islamic government throughout the country. In 1995 an assassination attempt was launched from Sudan against Egyptian President Hosni Mubarak.[63] In 1998 al Qaeda terrorists attacked U.S. embassies in Nairobi, Kenya and Dar es-Salaam, Tanzania. In 2001 the U.S. Department of State identified al Qaeda, the Egypt-based Muslim Brotherhood, and the Palestinian Islamic Jihad and Hamas as terrorist groups having safe havens in Sudan.[64] Kenya, the scene of major terrorist attacks in 1998 and 2002, seems to harbor shadowy terrorist networks, the nature of which remains unclear. Some of the perpetrators of the 1998 American embassy attacks were foreign Muslims who occupied safe houses in Mombasa, using small businesses and relief organizations to subsidize and conceal their activities.[65] In

---

[60] For these points as well as a detailed discussion of Somali *sharikat hawwalat*, see Khalid M Medani, "Financing Terrorism or Survival? Informal Finance and State Collapse in Somalia, and the US War on Terrorism," *Middle East Research & Information Project (MERIP)*, 32, no. 223 (Summer 2002), 3-6.

[61] Medani.

[62] U.S. Department of State, *Patterns of Global Terrorism 2001*. <http://www.state.gov/s/ct/rls/pgtrpt/2001/html/10236.htm>

[63] Council on Foreign Relations and Markle Foundation, "Terrorism: Questions and Answers: Sudan," 2002. http://www.terrorismanswers.com/sponsors/sudan.htm>

[64] U.S. Department of State, *Patterns of Global Terrorism 2001*.

[65] "East Africa" Terrorism's Ties to Drugs"; Benjamin Weiser, "Details Given, and 5 More Charged, in Tanzania Bombing," *New York Times*, December 17, 1998; Marc Lacey and Benjamin Weiser, "After Attack, Kenya Traces Qaeda's Trail in East Africa, *New York Times*, 1 December 2002, A1.

Tanzania local Muslims helped plan and carry out the 1998 attack on the American embassy in Dar es Salaam.[66]

In Uganda, an Islamist terrorist group, the Allied Democratic Forces (ADF), opposed to the Ugandan government, allegedly has sent fighters to train in al Qaeda camps in Sudan and Afghanistan. In 2001, the ADF sought financial support and training from Iraq for a terrorist campaign in Africa, but apparently little came of these efforts.[67]

Somalia's fragmented political situation makes a government-based antiterrorist program impossible. However, other factors have discouraged long-term implantation of terrorist groups in that country. In general, Somalis (nearly all of whom are Muslim) have not been receptive to non-Somali Muslims with political agendas, in part because the pragmatic Somali view of Islam and the dominance of the clan structure in society are not compatible with a politicized form of religion.[68] In addition, Somalia's decrepit communications and transportation infrastructures cannot support an effective transnational organization.[69]

The only terrorist group known to operate in Somalia is al-Ittihad al-Islamiya, ("Islamic Unity," AIAI), which is believed to have links with al Qaeda and was implicated as a transit agent in the American embassy bombings of 1998[70] and the November 2002 attacks against Israeli targets in Mombasa.[71] In early 2002, experts estimated that as many as 25 militants with links to al Qaeda were resident in Somalia.[72]

Southern Africa

Southern Africa in a narrow geographical sense encompasses six countries at the southern end of the continent—Botswana, Lesotho, Mozambique, Namibia, South Africa, and Swaziland. These countries tend to have large geographical areas and long national boundaries and coastlines that are difficult or impossible to patrol and leave the interior of the countries

---

[66] Benjamin Weiser, "Details Given and Five More Charged in Tanzania Bombing," *New York Times*, 17 December 1998.

[67] Philip Smucker and Faye Bowers, "Iraq Regime Linked to Terror Group," *Christian Science Monitor*, 18 April 2003, 1, 9.

[68] "Al Qaeda Suspect Handed to FBI," "World in Brief*," Washington Post,* Thursday, March 20, 2003, A26.

[69] Economist Intelligence Unit, *Eritrea, Somalia, Djibouti: Country Profile 2001*, 38, 42.

[70] Lacey and Weiser.

[71] Dexter Filkins and Marc Lacey, "Kenya's Porous Border Lies Open to Arms Smugglers," *New York* Times, 4 December 2002, A18.

[72] Donald G. McNeil, Jr., "A New Scrutiny of Somalia as the Old Anarchy Reigns," *New York Times*, 10 February 2002.

vulnerable to penetration by criminal groups. South Africa is the most economically developed of the region's countries, followed by Botswana. The remainder of the region is poor and underdeveloped, with meager resources available to develop effective programs relating to education, health, or law enforcement. As of the late 1990s, some countries were in a process of political and economic transition, rendering state structure fragile and ineffective. In Angola and the Democratic Republic of Congo, on-going civil wars promoted instability and trafficking in arms, narcotics, gold, diamonds, and other natural sources throughout the region. Bribery and corruption involving government officials, law enforcement personnel, and border guards were also major problems.

By the 1980s, indigenous criminal networks existed in most if not all of the countries of Southern Africa. Such groups often were linked with each other in cross-border networks that trafficked in stolen vehicles, narcotics, and arms among other items. In the early 1990s, international criminal organizations began to converge upon the region, where most counties were extremely vulnerable to illicit activities. In the 1990s, both Mozambique and South Africa emerged from drastic political transitions that left them vulnerable to a variety of transnational groups. South Africa, which possesses by far the richest natural resources and the most developed infrastructure in the region, was the favorite target of such groups, both terrorist and criminal, from a wide variety of countries. Criminal activities based in South Africa have spread across the borders into neighboring countries. Mozambique has become involved mainly as a transit country whose banking system promotes the money laundering of transnational traffickers.

Mozambique

After Mozambique emerged from a prolonged period of civil war in 1992, the movement of people and goods increased. With that increased movement has come a new role for Mozambique as a major transit country for narcotics. There are two main routes: heroin moves from South Asia via Dubai and Tanzania and is sent on to Europe, and cocaine arrives from Colombia and Brazil and goes on to Europe and East Asia. Mandrax (methaqualone), imported from South Asia and manufactured domestically, is destined for South Africa. Hashish is smuggled from Southeast Asia in huge quantities, averaging an estimated 200 tons per year in the mid-1990s. In May 2001, a single shipment of six tons of hashish was seized. It is processed and re-exported to Europe and North America.[73]

The drug trade has grown in Mozambique as major drug syndicates have sought new routes that international agencies do not monitor as effectively as more traditional routes through neighboring countries. Mozambique's ports are entry points for hinterland countries of Southern Africa, and the 1,550-mile coastline is impossible for resource-poor Mozambican maritime authorities to patrol. The country's extreme poverty, low salaries, and climate of corruption foster bribery and corruption of police, border guards, and government officials. One provincial governor allegedly received $500,000 for each large shipment of cocaine that passed through his territory. International experts claim that the Mozambican police are almost totally corrupted, and that Maputo airport is easily available to narcotics couriers.[74]

Other established forms of transnational crime in Mozambique are vehicle theft and gun running. Since the late 1990s, counterfeiting, bank fraud, money laundering, and trade in ivory and precious stones have made their appearance.[75] Like South Africa, Mozambique has a network of willing locals who facilitate these activities, often in conjunction with cross-border criminal networks in South Africa.

The country's financial institutions may be heavily involved in money laundering. One investigative reporter notes that, as of mid-2001, Mozambique has far more banks and foreign exchange bureaus than can possibly be justified by the size of the legal economy and the need to exchange sizable foreign aid funds. Therefore, authorities suspect that these institutions are involved the laundering of proceeds from the narcotics industry, although officials of the Bank of Mozambique deny such charges. Other outlets for converting illegal profits in Mozambique include conspicuous consumption, investment in real estate, and the purchase of stocks and bonds, which can be executed with few questions asked.[76]

---

[73] Antonio Paulo Namburete, "Organised Crime in Mozambique and Its Impact Within the Regional and International Context," in M. Hough and A. Du Plessis, eds., *The Grim Reaper: Organised Crime in the 1990s— Implications for South and Southern Africa,* Institute for Strategic Studies, Monograph no. 36, 1999), 28; U. S. Department of State, Bureau for Narcotics and Law Enforcement Affairs, *International Narcotics Control Strategy Report 2001.* <http://www.state.gov/g/inl/rls/nrcrpt/2001/html/17950.htm>

[74] Joseph Hanlon, "*Metical* Special Investigation: Drugs Now Biggest Business," *Metical* [London], 28 June 2001. <mozambique-news@geo2.poptel.org.uk>

[75] Namburete, 27, 29-31.

[76] Hanlon; Namburete, 32-33.

Mozambican authorities have attempted to restrict illicit activities. The country is a signatory to several international conventions aimed at narcotics control, has enacted legislation of its own, and has conducted operations against drug lords and the trade in stolen vehicles.[77] Nonetheless, even when legislation is on the books, officials lack the financial resources and often, it seems, the will to enforce it. The country is too poor to make crime interdiction a priority, and corruption reaches into the highest echelons of law enforcement and government. For instance, a former director of investigative operations of the Criminal Investigative Police was himself recently detained for allegedly distributing hashish and heroin (he was released without charges being filed), and a high-profile trial that concluded on January 31, 2003, involving charges of illegal imports, currency dealings, and murder, implicated even President Joaquim Chissano's son.[78]

South Africa

Several factors create a favorable environment for international organized crime and terrorism in South Africa. In terms of geography, it is situated midway on communication routes that connect South America, South and Southeast Asia, the Middle East, and Europe. South Africa has a long coastline that requires a constant effort to patrol. The well-equipped deep-water ports at Cape Town, Durban, and Port Elizabeth invite a high rate of seagoing commerce that complicates effective import-export control. Land borders are also long and often unpatrolled. They are crossed daily by criminals trafficking in many forms of contraband, including but not limited to narcotics, stolen cars, illegal firearms, diamonds, and precious metals. An indigenous and radicalized Muslim community provides protection and support for Islamic fundamentalist groups.

Until the late 1980s, South Africa had remained largely isolated from the international developments that affected organized crime, both domestic and international. The authoritarian and security-conscious environment fostered by the apartheid regime made aggressive activity in South Africa quite risky for international crime syndicates. However, as the state's law enforcement agencies focused their attention on political opponents, indigenous criminal groups

---

[77] Namburete, 35; U.S. Department of State, *International Narcotics Control Strategy Report 2001.*
[78] U.S. Department of State, *International Narcotics Control Strategy Report 2001*; "Mozambique: A Flood of Mud," *Africa Confidential* [London], 43, no. 25 (20 December 2002): 2-3; "Carlos Verdicts Taint Chissano's Son," 1 February 2003. <http://allAfrica.com>

increased their activities significantly during the 1980s. Despite relatively strict border controls, cross-border organized crime between South Africa and its neighboring states also expanded, forming smuggling networks that crisscrossed the southern cone of Africa.[79]

The political changes that occurred in 1994 when apartheid was replaced by constitutional democracy created opportunities for both indigenous and international organized criminal groups to exploit the new low-risk environment that South Africa now provided. The country entered an era of political transition during which state structures, including security services, were undergoing substantive reform that weakened them. Border controls relaxed at the same time that international trade and tourism expanded. South Africa gradually became more accessible to the international community, including the criminal underworld. By the late 1990s, many of the uncertainties caused by the transition had subsided, but organized crime had gained a firm foothold in South Africa. Belatedly recognizing the danger that both internal and international organized crime posed, the new democratic government began taking steps to counter both.[80]

South Africa has the most developed transportation, communications, and banking infrastructure in sub-Saharan Africa. This infrastructure is an essential attraction for criminals both inside and outside the country. Air connections across the Atlantic to South American drug sources are excellent, telecommunications connections across the world are instantaneous and reliable, and an efficient banking system, well integrated into the global economy, offers opportunities for money laundering. South Africa is also rich in commodities, such as gold, diamonds, and platinum, that can be used to fund criminal or terrorist activities and to transfer wealth from one place to another. Since the mid-1990s, the country has become a relatively stable and open society with broad civil liberties that permit easy movement of people and money, both legal and illegal.[81] The situation in South Africa, particularly as concerns terrorism, was summarized by Gideon Jones, former head of the Criminal Intelligence Unit of SAPS: "It's a perfect place to cool off, regroup, and plan your finances and operations. The communications

---

[79] Peter Gastrow, "Main Trends in the Development of South Africa's Organised Crime," *African Security Review*, 3, no. 6 (1999), 1.

[80] Gastrow, "Main Trends," 1; Mark Shaw and Peter Gastrow, "Crime and Its Impact in Post-Apartheid South Africa," Daedalus, 130, no. 1 (Winter 2001): 250-51.

[81] South Africa's attractions for international crime and terrorism are mentioned in a number of sources: Gastrow, "Main Trends," 7; Williams and Brooks; U.S. State Department, *International Narcotics Control Strategy Report 2001*, "Africa: South Africa" (Washington, 2002), <http://www.state.gov>

and infrastructure are excellent, there is a radical Muslim community, and our law enforcement is overstretched."[82]

Two additional factors contribute to South Africa's profile of criminal attraction. A large and well-organized criminal network or syndicate exists within the country, composed of a number of notorious street-gangs. The street gangs control local narcotics distribution and have established a mutually advantageous arrangement to divide up the domestic narcotics market with their international suppliers. The gangs, already engaged in internal and cross-border vehicle theft, gun-running, and trade in cannabis and mandrax, presented dealers from outside South Africa with contacts and ready-made networks that offered the opportunity to develop a more sophisticated narcotics industry. In return, the gangs have learned new techniques of the trade from their international mentors. Gang membership and criminality is promoted by high rates of poverty and unemployment, particularly among the black segment of the population.[83]

According to the South African Police Service (SAPS), international criminal organizations involving, among others, Nigerians, Russians, Chinese, Moroccans, and Italians, have been operating in South Africa since at least the early 1990s.[84] Nigerian groups were perhaps the first to arrive, establishing themselves in Johannesburg during the late 1980s. By the late 1990s, Nigerian crime syndicates dominated the illicit trade in cocaine in South Africa, which had become a transit country for narcotics shipments into Europe and the Middle East. The Nigerians also had begun to trade in locally produced cannabis and some heroin, which also was shipped to Europe, and to engage in kidnapping and ransoming schemes.[85]

By the mid-1990s, SAPS became aware that Russian organized criminals were present and active in South Africa. While the scope of their activities was difficult to discern, they appeared to be involved in arms smuggling, fraud, car theft, narcotics trafficking, and possibly trafficking in uranium. Russian criminals were suspected of conducting their activities, including money laundering, behind the cover of legitimate business operations.[86]

Chinese criminal groups, linked to Chinese triad organizations in Hong Kong and Taiwan, have been active at least since the early 1990s. Operating largely from Johannesburg

---

[82] Block, "In South Africa," A7.
[83] Kinnes, "From Urban Street Gangs--National and Local Trends," 1-2; Shaw and Gastrow, "Crime and Its Impact," 250-53;
[84] Gastrow, "Main Trends," 3.
[85] Gastrow, "Main Trends," 4.
[86] Gastrow, "Main Trends," 5-6.

and Pretoria, they deal in the illicit trade in rhino horn and ivory, money laundering, contraband, and the trafficking of Chinese migrants into South Africa. Chinese gangs also dominate the illegal harvesting and trade in abalone, an edible mollusk with a mother-of-pearl shell that is in high demand in the Far East. This is a low-risk activity because South African authorities give little attention to the depletion of marine resources. Chinese narcotics traffickers specialize in mandrax, which is the overwhelming choice of South African narcotics users. Mandrax is manufactured in South Africa and neighboring Mozambique, but substantial quantities of mandrax tablets are imported from Asian sources by Chinese, Indians, and Pakistanis in South Africa.[87]

During the 1990s, senior Italian mafia operatives are known to have penetrated middle and upper government echelons. The reputed mafia "boss" Vito Palazzolo, who was arrested in 1998, gained a reputation for corrupting government officials. Palazzolo allegedly suborned a cabinet minister, a security force general, a top immigration official, and many policemen.[88] Indian and Pakistani groups in South Africa are involved mainly in narcotics, illegal migrants, and smuggling of contraband. Portuguese crime groups have been involved in truck-hijackings and the smuggling of illicitly obtained diamonds and gold. Moroccans in the Cape Town engage in extortion rackets and the narcotics trade.[89]

During the 1990s, Muslim-based groups inclined toward vigilantism, and urban terrorism appeared in the Muslim communities of South Africa, whose total population is estimated at 600,000. Among these are Muslims Against Global Oppression (MAGO), Muslims Against Illegitimate Leaders (MAIL), and People Against Gangsterism and Drugs (PAGAD).[90] The last group, based in the Western Cape, is perhaps the most notorious and the best known outside South Africa. Dedicated originally to the elimination of drug dealers and street gangs in former colored townships, PAGAD has evolved into a full-fledged terrorist organization with alleged support and training from Iran, Libya, and Sudan. Its militants have resorted to violence, including bombings, directed against police, businessmen, religious leaders, and foreign interests, particularly those of the United States. For example, PAGAD operatives bombed the

---

[87] Gastrow, "Main Trends," 5-6.
[88] Gastrow, "Main Trends," 6-7.
[89] Gaatrow, "Main Trends," 7.
[90] Irvin Kinnes, "From Urban Street Gangs to Criminal Empires: The Changing Face of Gangs in the Western Cape, National and Local Trends," Institute for Strategic Studies, Monograph no. 48, 2000), 2.

Planet Hollywood restaurant in Cape Town in July 1998, causing two deaths and injuring dozens. PAGAD is known for militantly anti-American and anti-Israeli views.

Several international Muslim terrorist organizations also are present in South Africa. According to South African intelligence sources, the militant Palestinian group Hamas has been active since at least 1992, raising funds and enlisting recruits for military training. The Lebanese-based Hizballah group allegedly maintains a presence in South Africa as well. After establishing a foothold in 1997, al Qaeda seems to view South Africa as a source of funds as well as a place of refuge for fugitive militants. These groups are aided by local radicals in the indigenous Muslim population.[91]

Mandrax, imported from production sources in India, Kenya, and Pakistan, is rated as South Africa's most serious narcotics problem. The problem is most serious in Cape Town, where competition among thousands of drug dealers and the high cost of supporting addicts' habits are responsible for most of the serious crime that occurs. Dubai and Mumbai (Bombay) are the main transit points from which traffickers move mandrax into South Africa.[92]

The final factor is quite peculiar to South Africa: effect of the apartheid legacy on law enforcement agencies. Under apartheid, the police and legal systems were intended to control and to suppress dissent among the black population, not to investigate crime per se. Because the police enjoyed little legitimacy with the majority of the population, the law and its enforcement was not the object of public respect. Under these circumstances, a "culture of violence" characterized South African society. For its part, the SAPS has had to undergo a reorientation of mission and attitudes since 1994. The SAPS has expanded and reorganized to emphasize enforcement of the new democratic order. As entire segments of the population remain suspicious of the police and the courts, law enforcement officials are now learning to deal with criminal and terrorist groups of far greater sophistication than those of the apartheid era.[93] In this atmosphere of mistrust and transition, organized criminals and terrorist elements have flourished in recent years.

---

[91]Robert Block, "In South Africa, Mounting Evidence of al Qaeda Links," *Wall Street Journal*, Tuesday, December 10, 2002, A1, A7.

[92] "Mandrax," *Electronic Doctor* [South Africa]. <http://www.edoc.co.za/drughelp/mandrax>

[93] Peter Gastrow and Mark Shaw, "In Search of Safety: Police Transformation and Public Responses in South Africa," *Daedalus*, 130, no. 1 (Winter 2001): 262-72; George Govender, "Prevention and Combating of Organised Crime in South Africa," in M. Hough and A. Du Plessis, eds., *"The Grim Reaper: Organised Crime in the 1990s— Implications for South and Southern Africa,"* Institute for Strategic Studies Publication no. 36 (1999), 52-59.

Western Africa

Introduction

Like other regions of the continent, West Africa suffers from chronic armed conflict, extremely high rates of poverty, porous border security, and governmental inefficiency and corruption. These conditions have permitted the growth of numerous armed insurgent groups, an extensive narcotics trafficking network centered in Nigeria; trafficking in women and children originating in many countries of the region; misallocation of natural resources such as timber, precious metals, and diamonds; and an enormous arms trafficking industry that is supplied from Eastern Europe and the former Soviet Union and regionally centered in Liberia. A strong driver of criminal conduct in West Africa is the region's rich supply of natural resources, which has attracted unscrupulous entrepreneurs from Europe and financed criminal and terrorist activity. Reportedly, al Qaeda has established at least tenuous links in parts of the region.

Narcotics Trafficking

In recent years, Nigerian and Ghanaian trafficking groups have established strong links with heroin sources on the Indian subcontinent, in the Golden Triangle, and in the Golden Crescent. An extensive transnational network of narcotics traffickers has extended from Nigeria, which has become the West African center for that type of crime and for money laundering. That network extends into neighboring countries and as far as Kyrgyzstan and South America. Already in 1999, authorities estimated that Nigerian groups were active in 60 countries, and ties have been established with criminal groups in the United States, Europe, South America, Asia, and South Africa.[94] Lomé, the capital of nearby Togo, has been described as "a spoke in the Nigerian hub of narcotics trafficking and money laundering."[95] In recent years, Nigerian narcotics groups also have migrated into neighboring Benin, Chad, and Niger.[96] A significant proportion of heroin arriving in the United States from Asia has passed through Nigeria, and Nigerian agents in South America move cocaine to points in Europe, North America, and South

---

[94] U.S. Department of State, *International Narcotics Control Strategy Report 2003*, X-43.
[95] U.S. Department of State, *International Narcotics Control Strategy Report 2003*, X-43.
[96] "New Ambitions in the Fight Against Drugs," *Geopolitical Drug Newsletter* [Paris], October 2001. <http://www.geodrugs.net/mini-lettres/AEGD6GB.pdf>

Africa. Nigerian narcotics traffickers also are involved in counterfeiting documents, trafficking in migrants, and financial fraud.[97]

Drug enforcement in Nigeria has been hindered by chronic corruption (Nigeria consistently is rated one of the most corrupt nations in the world) and by under-funding of law enforcement agencies. Corruption is compounded by the low salaries received by civil servants and by a poorly trained and motivated police force. The populace of Nigeria distrusts the police force, making citizens vulnerable to manipulation by criminals in urban centers such as Lagos, Enugu, Port Harcourt, Jos, Kano, and Kaduna.[98]

National drug interdiction agencies have not effectively shut down large-scale dealers, who benefited from declines in the national infrastructure to establish strong footholds during a long series of military dictatorships ending in 1999. Interagency cooperation for drug interdiction has not been effective, and the corrupt court system has not backed law enforcement efforts. The Nigerian Customs Service has resisted interdiction measures of the National Drug Law Enforcement Agency. In 2002 the Obasanjo government reportedly made progress in limiting the money laundering activity that stems directly from narcotics trafficking and related crime.[99]

The volume of narcotics transiting through Ghana has increased sharply in recent years, mainly under the direction of Nigerian traffickers. Cocaine moves via Ghana from South America to Europe, and heroin moves via Ghana from Southeast and Southwest Asia to Europe. Narcotics destined for South Africa and North America also move through Ghana. Major factors in this trend are Ghana's proximity to Nigeria and its increasing role as an international transportation hub. Accra's Kotoka International Airport is a major transit point, as are the ports of Tema and Sekondi and the border towns of Elubo, Aflao, and Sampa. Customs officials have complained that the national judicial system does not back their interdiction efforts with timely prosecution.[100]

Human Trafficking

Because the poverty of the region has created a widespread state of desperation, trafficking in women from West Africa has become a major transnational crime. The majority of

---

[97] U.S. Department of State, *International Narcotics Control Strategy Report 2003*, X-64.
[98] U.S. Department of State, *International Narcotics Control Strategy Report 2003*, X-43.
[99] U.S. Department of State, *International Narcotics Control Strategy Report 2003*, X-43-45.
[100] U.S. Department of State, *International Narcotics Control Strategy Report 2003*, X-14.

the victims are poor women who are promised money-earning jobs in the country of destination but find themselves instead in the sex trade or working as virtual slaves. The primary European end points are Belgium, Italy, and the Netherlands; other women are moved to Lebanon, Libya, and the United States as well as to Nigeria and other countries in West Africa.[101] The connection between Nigeria and Italy, one of the most frequent destinations, began in the 1980s, when Nigerian women began traveling to Italy as agricultural laborers.[102] Mali also sends significant numbers of women as domestic servants to Kuwait and Saudi Arabia.[103]

Large numbers of West African children also are trafficked as agricultural and domestic workers and for the sex trade. Mali and Benin are primary sources of this trade, in which poverty is a major factor. In recent years, the cacao plantations of Ivory Coast have come under investigation for allegedly using thousands of child laborers from Mali and Burkina Faso. Cultural and legal factors also play a part, as parents often send their children to be raised by others who then sell them to traffickers. Ghana has no laws against child trafficking or child labor,[104] and its laws protecting women have been described as "woefully outdated" in dealing with the relatively new transnational forms of trafficking.[105] The International Labor Organization also has identified significant trafficking in humans in Burkina Faso and the Ivory Coast.[106]

The U.S. Department of State has identified Senegal as both a source and a transit point for trafficking in women. According to the 2002 report, Senegal's weak border controls and official corruption have made the capital city, Dakar, a transit point for Nigerian traffickers moving women from Nigeria to the sex trade in European cities. Senegal's light legal penalties for such crimes are a contributing factor.[107]

---

[101] International Organization for Migration.
[102] The Advocacy Project, "Girls for Sale: Building a Coalition to Fight Trafficking in Nigeria." <http://advocacynet.autoupdate.com/cpage_view/nigtraffick_girlsforsale_6_25.htm>
[103] International Organization for Migration.
[104] "Trafficked Children Registered," report of AllAfrica.com, 4 February 2003. <http://allafrica.com/stories/200302040508.htm>
[105] "ECOWAS Experts Discuss Action Plan Against Human Trafficking," *News in Ghana* [Accra], 2001. <http://www.newsinghana.com/politics/archive/ECOWAS-experts-discuss-action.htm>
[106] International Labour Organization, "ILO Reports on Child Trafficking in West and Central Africa," 15 June 2001. <http://www.ilo.org/public/english/bureau/inf/pr/2001/21.htm>
[107] U.S. Department of State, *Trafficking in People Report 2001*. <http://www.state.gov/g/tip/rls

Arms Trafficking

Because of persistent insurgencies and weak governments, the region has absorbed large amounts of illegal arms in the past two decades. Small arms (conventionally, those that can be carried by an individual or on a small vehicle) are attractive in such a region because they are durable and the newest models offer high firepower at a relatively low price. In 2002, Nigeria's defense minister warned that the proliferation and illegal trafficking of small arms into that country was intensifying criminal activity in the country and raising the danger of violent clashes among Nigeria's several ethnic groups.[108] Liberia has gained a reputation as a center of government corruption and high-volume trafficking in arms, diamonds, and timber. Since the early 1990s, European-based large-scale arms dealers have taken advantage of unstable regional conditions to trade arms for diamonds with a variety of rebel groups in West Africa and elsewhere on the continent. Liberia has been the arbiter of many such deals, opportunities for which are perpetuated by the political fragility of post-conflict societies. The World Bank's African economics expert Paul Collier has called this fragility the "legacy of induced polarizing grievance."[109] At the point of origin, dealers provide falsified end-user documents that usually declare Guinea as the end point for arms shipments. Those documents seldom have been verified by authorities in Central and Eastern Europe.[110]

Some of the dealers also have been identified as providers of arms to terrorist groups such as al Qaeda. Beginning in 2002, reports indicated the presence in Mali, Mauritania, and Niger of Mokhtar Belmokhtar, an Algerian arms dealer with connections to the extremist Islamic group Call to Combat, which has received funding from al Qaeda. According to a Voice of America report, al Qaeda could take advantage of the sparse population and limited law enforcement capability of those countries to establish a foothold in the interior of Western Africa.[111] Until at least 2001, Russian arms trafficker Victor Bout sold large amounts of small

---

[108] "Nigeria: Defence Minister Denounces Increased Number of Small Arms in Country," BBC report, 14 January 2002. <http://www.clw.org/atop/newswire/nw011402.htm>

[109] Paul Collier, "Economic Causes of Civil Conflict and Their Implications for Policy." http://www.worldbank.org/research/conflict/papers/civilconflict.htm, quoted in Lansana Gberie, "War and Peace in Sierra Leone: Diamonds, Corruption and the Lebanese Connection," Diamonds and Human Security Project, *Occasional Paper* no. 6, November 2002, 1.

[110] Joost Hiltermann, "Liberia: New Arms Embargo Failing: Weak Export Controls Largely to Blame," Human Rights Watch report, 5 November 2001. <http://www.hrw.org/press/2001/11/liberia1105.htm>

[111] "Washington Possibly Examining Militancy Threat in West Africa," Stratfor report, 14 November 2002. <http://www.stratfor.com>

arms, helicopters, missiles, and armored vehicles to the insurgent Revolutionary United Front (RUF) in Sierra Leone through the government of Liberia.[112] Many of those arms presumably still are in circulation in the region.

The Liberia Problem

The government of Liberian president Charles Taylor, who abdicated and went into exile in August 2003, was linked with several forms of transnational crime including arms trafficking. Although an international peacekeeping force entered Liberia as he was abdicating, regional analysts agreed that Taylor's extensive regional contacts could enable him to preserve the extensive network of transnational criminal activities that he had established in West Africa. Because Taylor's departure left a divided country lacking any central authority, Liberia still offers an attractive base for such activities.

A 2003 report linked Liberia's European-owned timber industry with the trafficking of arms to rebel groups in nearby Ivory Coast and Sierra Leone. According to that report, arms shipments arrive in Liberia from Eastern Europe every two or three weeks, via Nigeria and Libya, then are dispersed to client groups. Arms arrive at the two port cities that are controlled by the timber industry, demonstrating the interdependence of government-supported arms trafficking with timber companies. Under Taylor, the Liberian government also has directly controlled insurgent groups that have caused full-scale civil war in Ivory Coast in the past year and continue to threaten stability in Sierra Leone.[113]

Taylor is known to have very large bank accounts in Switzerland and elsewhere that were fed by embezzlement of government funds.[114] The government's timber policy ignored international logging restrictions by permitting timber companies to clear-cut large expanses of protected West African rain forest. Taylor's regime also was identified as the intermediary in cut-rate sales of diamonds from insurgents in Sierra Leone to al Qaeda operatives, who raised

---

[112] Steve Park, "'Victor B' Watched for Taliban Ties," *Washington Times*, 22 July 2002.
<http://www.washtimes.com/world/20020722-330000642.htm>
[113] "West African Arms Trafficking and Mercenary Activities Supported by the Liberian Government and Logging Companies," Global Witness press release, 13 March 2003.
<http://www.globalwitness.org/text/press_releases/display2.php?id=186>
[114] "West African Arms Trafficking and Mercenary Activities Supported by the Liberian Government and Logging Companies."

money by selling the diamonds at higher prices in Europe.[115] In December 2002, the *Washington Post* reported that the Taylor government had accepted US$1 million to provide refuge for al Qaeda members after the September 11 attacks, and that while in Liberia those individuals bought missiles and other arms.[116] In June 2003, a United Nations-backed war crimes court found Taylor guilty of crimes against humanity because various trafficking activities of the president prolonged and promoted the civil war in Sierra Leone.[117]

FORMER SOVIET UNION AND EASTERN EUROPE

Introduction

Several countries of the former Soviet Union have been bases for or victims of terrorist activity within the past three years. Those countries include Georgia, Kyrgyzstan, the Russian Federation, Tajikistan, and Uzbekistan. In addition, ethnic Albanian insurgent groups have been active in the vicinity of Kosovo, including parts of Macedonia and Serbia. The states of the former Soviet Union and Central and Eastern Europe also demonstrate characteristics that make them inviting targets for transnational criminal groups seeking favorable territory from which to operate. A wide range of criminal activities in those countries includes trafficking in arms, drugs, and persons; money laundering; and bribery. Particularly vulnerable to criminal activity are the states that emerged from the former Socialist Federal Republic of Yugoslavia (with the exception of Slovenia) and the states that emerged from the former Soviet Union (increasingly, with the exception of the Baltic states).

The prospect of closer contact with Western institutions such as the European Union has motivated the Baltic states and most of the former Warsaw Pact countries of Eastern and Central Europe to substantially strengthen their laws and border enforcement. The same stimulus has acted less forcefully in the new nations of Central Asia and the Caucasus. However, recent reforms in those countries have not necessarily eliminated them from the list of "nations

---

[115] Michael Barone, "Dirty Diamonds," *U.S. News and World Report* online report, 12 November 2001. <http://www.usnews.com/usnews/opinion/baroneweb/mb_011112.htm>
[116] Douglas Farah, "Report Says Africans Harbored al-Qaeda: Terror Assets Hidden in Gem-Buying Spree," *Washington Post*, 29 December 2002, A1.
[117] Douglas Farah, "Taylor Charged with War Crimes During Long Conflict in Sierra Leone," *Washington Post*, 5 June 2003, A22.

hospitable"; in all cases, well-established patterns and routes can be expected to remain until legislation is backed by substantive action.

In the former Soviet states, progress toward the rule of law has been hindered by the sudden disappearance of national authority (the Soviet state) in areas having no individual tradition of state authority or civil society but having very well developed traditions of underground criminal activity. As is the case with the former Yugoslav republics, some of the former Soviet states have fared better than others in making themselves inhospitable venues for criminal activity. In general, in this respect the Baltic states have done best, Moldova and Tajikistan worst.

In their progress toward the rule of law, the former Warsaw Pact nations of Eastern and Central Europe have geographical disadvantages (being located on the trafficking routes between East and West and adjacent to states with severe criminal problems), economic disadvantages (facing the upheaval of complete economic transition), and geopolitical advantages (proximity to the well-developed West European community and prospective membership in West European organizations). Together, these factors have yielded substantial but mixed progress in warding off criminal and terrorist activities. Bulgaria, Hungary, and Romania have faced difficulties associated with their location along main east-west trafficking routes; the Czech Republic, Poland, and Slovakia have less diversified forms of criminal activity. Because of its weak political and law-enforcement systems, Albania has presented a uniquely hospitable gateway to the West for various criminal groups.

Albania

Since 1992, ethnic Albanian organized crime groups have profited greatly from instability and war in the Balkans to become the fastest growing ethnic criminal presence in Europe. With operations reaching as far as Australia and the United States, Albanian groups are the direct distributors of an estimated 40 percent of heroin in West European markets and may have an indirect role in as much more. Experts disagree about the degree to which Albanian groups have abandoned the traditional clan-based structure of their predecessors as they recruit outside their communities and cooperate with a variety of foreign criminal groups. Some restructuring undoubtedly has occurred, and the transnational cooperation of Albanian groups has increased dramatically.

Although Albanian government and law enforcement are not as unstable as they were in the 1990s, they are not yet strong enough to combat clan-based banditry, which has a long tradition in Albania, or the new forms of organized crime that have flourished in the past decade. Observes transnational crime expert Mark Galeotti: "In much of the country, local clans and allied criminal organizations are more powerful than the state. Cities such as Vlorë and Gjirokaster and regions including Gramsh, Elbasan, and Dirba remain virtual bandit homelands."[118] In many cases, the frontier between activities of Albanian political and criminal organizations is very unclear because both forms of activity retain roots in Albania's clan system and at least part of the corruption that permeated the political system in the 1980s and 1990s has remained.[119] The police are poorly equipped and poorly paid, and specialized units such as the financial crimes division receive no training.

The influence of government corruption has been obvious in several instances. In March 2002, two officials with major responsibilities in the Albanian government's recent anti-narcotics campaign were found to be themselves participating in a heroin trafficking operation.[120] In mid-2002, a leak compromised a major trafficking interdiction operation of the Albanian army and police. That operation, in cooperation with Italian, Greek, and Yugoslav authorities, was expected to confiscate as many as 30 boats crossing the Adriatic from the port of Vlorë, but most of the smugglers escaped.[121] Authorities often link police personnel with various types of smuggling. Aside from corruption, special police interdiction units are hampered by poor equipment. The judiciary's policy of quickly releasing narcotics suspects does not support police apprehension efforts, and traffickers are adept at changing their routes to avoid detection.[122]

Lawless conditions in Albania are promoted by the domination of criminal organizations in neighboring Kosovo, where the population is about 90 percent Albanian, and in the adjoining region of northwestern Macedonia, which also has an Albanian majority. In Albania and the two

---

[118] Mark Galeotti, "Albanian Gangs Gain Foothold in European Crime Underworld," *Jane's Intelligence Review*, 1 November 2001.
[119] Galeotti.
[120] Zylyftar Bregu, Albania: Authorities Rocked by Drugs Scandal," Institute for War and Peace Reporting report, 22 March 2002. <http://www.iwpr.net>
[121] "Smuggling Continues Despite Multinational Efforts," *RFE/RL Crime and Corruption Watch*, 2, no. 30 (30 August 2002). <http://www.rferl.org/corruptionwatch/2002>
[122] Bregu.

Albanian regions nearby (the respective borders of which are not meaningful for law enforcement), extreme economic disorder, the substantial displacement of Albanian populations by war, and nationalist aspirations combine to promote the recruitment of young people for the illicit activities of organized crime groups. In this process, for example, Albanians in all three jurisdictions have played an increasingly vital role in transporting heroin across the Balkan region for the Turkish and Kurdish organizations that dominate the wholesale heroin trade.[123] The so-called Italian Route, one variant of the Balkan Route, moves heroin from Kosovar bases in Peč and Prizren across the border into the lawless Tropoje region of Albania, controlled by the Haklaj clan. Shipments then move to the ports of Vlorë, Sarande, and Durrës.[124]

In the 1990s, Albanians began as couriers for established Italian smuggling organizations, offering familiarity with routes that avoided border patrols during the Yugoslav conflicts of 1992-95. From that beginning, the Albanians gradually acquired their own heroin processing and distribution systems and diversified their smuggling operations to include illegal migrants, stolen cars, cigarettes, and other commodities. Reportedly, the trade in counterfeit cigarettes is so profitable that Albanian and Macedonian groups have fought for market control.[125]

As they diversified their products, Albanian groups also were able to reach cooperative agreements with several Italian mafia organizations, which had resisted the incursion of foreign elements into their territory. Eventually the Albanians shared operations with major Italian mafia groups in Calabria, Apulia, and Naples. The ongoing migration of Albanians into Italy has formed a bridgehead of increasingly independent Albanian criminal groups that have penetrated northern Italy, where no single Italian group has been dominant. The activities of new Albanian groups have been especially profitable in the wealthy cities of Milan and Florence[126] (see Western Europe).

From Italy, Albanian criminal groups have spread to other parts of Europe. Albanians now dominate the heroin market in Switzerland and have gained substantial shares of the money laundering and arms smuggling businesses. In North America, Albanians occupy dominant positions in the so-called YACS (Yugoslav-Albanian-Croatian-Serb) gangs that now engage in a variety of crimes. Recently, Albanian groups have been seeking to establish relations with

---

[123] Galeotti.
[124] Galeotti.
[125] Galeotti.
[126] Galeotti.

Georgian and Armenian organizations in order to shorten the heroin supply line from Central Asia. However, both expansion and ethnic integration tend to weaken the structure and solidarity of the traditional ethnic Albanian criminal organizations, and expansion into markets such as Hungary has brought resistance from groups such as the Russian Solntsevo organization.[127]

Besides narcotics, the routes through Albania also carry large numbers of women for the illegal sex trade and illegal arms. As in other East European societies, the sex trade is fueled by the availability of large numbers of women lacking economic prospects at home and seeking employment in the West. If they become prostitutes, society condemns them if they return to Albania, and border guards treat them as criminals. Thus, even women who return to Albania after being smuggled out seek to once again find work in a Western country, because they see no other choice.[128]

The illegal arms trade has been fed by an estimated 550,000 military weapons, nearly 1 billion rounds of ammunition, and 16 million explosive devices that were removed from military stockpiles during the rioting of 1997. Although only 200,000 of the weapons have been recovered in the government's guns-for-money swap programs, in August 2002 the government abolished the special police unit assigned to collect weapons. Despite urging by international agencies, and despite the fact that criminal organizations are believed to have gained possession of a large share of the unaccounted-for equipment, the Albanian parliament has passed no new national legislation on the subject.[129]

Former Warsaw Pact European Nations

Although Bulgaria, the Czech Republic, Hungary, Poland, Romania, and Slovakia exhibit significant diversity in domestic conditions hospitable to organized crime and terrorist organizations, some strong similarities also exist. First, none of these countries is known to have been a significant host or victim of terrorist organizations. Second, four of the six have been accepted for membership in the next expansion of the European Union (probably in 2004), and the remaining two, Bulgaria and Romania, had the status of candidate countries in mid-2003. In

---

[127] Galeotti.

[128] Agim Kanani, "Albania: Breaking the Cycle of Prostitution," Institute for War and Peace Reporting, Balkan Crisis Report, 19 April 2002. <http://www.iwpr.net>

[129] Agim Kanani, "Albania: Cash-for-Guns Plan Misfires," Institute for War and Peace Reporting report, 4 November 2002. <http://www.iwpr.net>

November 2002, Bulgaria, Romania, and Slovakia were accepted to join the North Atlantic Treaty Organization in 2004 (the other three gained membership in 1999). Membership or candidate status in one or both organizations has been a strong incentive for these countries to take such measures as strengthening border controls and arms export controls. Border controls are especially important to reduce trafficking in states bordering the former Soviet Union and the Balkans. In the 1990s, all six countries sold arms on the world market rather indiscriminately, having inherited large amounts of surplus military equipment and production capability from the Warsaw Pact era and experiencing severe economic crises in the painful post-Soviet readjustment period of the 1990s. Hungary, which played a different role in the defense structure of the Warsaw Pact alliance,[130] was not left with as large a concentration of arms as the other five. Although since that time the five principal holders of military equipment have taken significant steps toward controlling the destination and conditions of such sales, in 2002 most still had gaps in legislation or enforcement that made them potential source countries for illegal arms traffickers. Contributing to this situation is the economics of surplus military equipment: to maintain or destroy such equipment requires large amounts of money, making resale a much more attractive option. Accordingly, in 2002 the defense ministries of all five nations announced the availability of large numbers of tanks, artillery systems, and smaller weapons.[131] Such availability has led inevitably to illegal arms transactions.

Bulgaria

Like other states emerging from communist dictatorship in the early 1990s, Bulgaria experienced rampant corruption and organized crime in the first half of that decade. Declining economic conditions combined with a class of powerful former communist officials and weak domestic law enforcement and civil institutions to allow a deluge of narcotics and arms smuggling, money laundering, and other forms of criminal activity. Lax law enforcement encouraged the formation of organized crime groups. Based on Bulgaria's very close relations with the Soviet Union, the post-Soviet connection with Russian criminal groups has been

---

[130] Stephen R. Burant, ed., *Hungary: A Country Study* (Washington, D.C.: GPO, 1990), 236.
[131] Human Rights Watch, "Arms Trade, Human Rights, and European Union Enlargement: The Record of Candidate Countries," 8 October 2002. <http://www.hrw.org>

especially strong.[132] Government corruption, which was a key element in the growth of criminal activity in the early and mid-1990s, has decreased somewhat in recent years. Transparency International's 2002 Corruption Perception Index placed Bulgaria 45th among the 102 nations evaluated, marginally higher than the previous rating.[133] The 2002 corruption index of the U.S. Agency for International Development rated corruption in Bulgaria as unchanged from the previous evaluation.[134]

Wars and ensuing sanctions in the nearby former Socialist Federal Republic of Yugoslavia provided opportunities for smuggling fuel, arms, cigarettes, alcohol, and stolen cars from Bulgaria into Yugoslavia. Aided by the non-existence of financial laws, groups laundered money by fictitious investments in a variety of offshore firms, including banks. Laundered money often returned to Bulgaria in investments in privatized state enterprises. By the late 1990s, Bulgaria's aspirations to membership in West European organizations promoted stricter law enforcement, including stronger border controls and cooperation with international law enforcement agencies. However, Bulgaria's geographic position, its close cultural affinity with Russia, and remaining gaps in law enforcement have promoted a more sophisticated but still widespread range of organized criminal activities, most of which have a significant transnational component.[135]

Security analyst Elizabeth Konstantinova describes transnational crime in Bulgaria thus: "Over the past decade organized crime networks in the country have evolved as an essential link supporting global criminal groups operating the Balkan transit route for smuggling drugs from Asia to the European Union. Their activities have increasingly extended into areas affecting domestic and regional security, namely illicit traffic of human beings, money laundering, and arms smuggling."[136]

Many of those activities involve cooperation with international crime organizations. According to Deputy Minister of the Interior Boiko Kotzev, "Bulgarian organized crime groups mostly serve as auxiliary units to powerful Turkish and Albanian networks, which dominate the

---

[132] Elizabeth Konstantinovna, "Bulgarian Gangs Provide Key Link in European Trafficking Chain," *Jane's Intelligence Report*, 1 November 2002; and Robert Kaplan, "Crime and Democracy in Bulgaria," *The Globalist*, 23 June 2001 <http://www.theglobalist.com>
[133] *Balkan Times*, 29 August 2002 <http://www.balkantimes.com>
[134] Southeast European Legal Development Initiative, "Corruption Indexes: Regional Corruption Monitoring in Albania, Bosnia and Herzegovina, Bulgaria, Croatia, Macedonia, Romania, and Yugoslavia," April 2002, 14.
[135] Konstantinova.
[136] Konstantinova.

drug traffic from Asia and Afghanistan through the Balkans into the EU."[137] Bulgarian groups also are known to cooperate with criminal networks from the former Yugoslavia, Ukraine, Russia, Greece, Italy, the Czech Republic, Germany, Spain, Norway, and Brazil in smuggling narcotics, arms, cigarettes, alcohol, and people as well as the sexual exploitation industry, counterfeiting, and credit card fraud. For narcotics traffic, Bulgaria is the shortest route between the Black Sea and the republics of the former Yugoslavia. In trafficking operations, Bulgarian groups usually are limited to domestic activities.[138]

In the 1990s, Russian narcotics groups cultivated some markets in Bulgaria, but their main goal was control of the transit routes via Bulgaria toward the West, which carry as much as 90 percent of the heroin passing from Turkey to the West. That dominant position has been disturbed by turf struggles and the commitment of the Bulgarian government to dislodge Russian organized crime from Bulgarian soil.[139] However, it is likely that domestic criminal groups such as the Security Insurance Company and the Power Insurance Company (whose names derive from the term that protection rackets adopted to conceal their true activities from government investigation in the 1990s),[140] have maintained their traditional close connections with their Russian equivalents. Those "companies," which in the 1990s were the two largest criminal groups in Bulgaria,[141] have declined in power in recent years.

Although the domestic demand for drugs is relatively small, illicit Bulgarian laboratories have begun manufacturing synthetic drugs. Materials for such production are readily available from the country's well developed pharmaceuticals industry. Some of the laboratories discovered by authorities were run by Arabs, indicating a connection with markets in the Middle East.[142]

Experts rate trafficking in women as the second most profitable activity of Bulgarian organized crime groups, next to narcotics trafficking. The same geographical factors promote all forms of smuggling in Bulgaria. Efforts to curtail trafficking have been hampered by limited resources, the complicity of law and government officials in trafficking operations, and the lack of a specific law prohibiting trafficking in humans. In 2002 the Bulgarian government considered

---

[137] Quoted in Konstantinovna.

[138] Konstantinovna.

[139] "Drug War for $1.2 Billion," *Trud* [Sofia], 6 February 2001 (FBIS Document EUP20010206000047).

[140] Jovo Nikolov, "Crime and Corruption After Communism: Organized Crime in Bulgaria," *East European Constitutional Review*, 6, no. 4 (Fall 1997). <http://www.law.nyu.edu/eecr/vol6num4/feature/organizedcrime.htm>

[141] Denis Ryabtsev, interview with Emanuil Yordanov, minister of the interior of Bulgaria, *Segodnya* [Moscow], 6 December 2000 (FBIS Document CEP20001206000268).

[142] Konstantinovna.

establishing a national committee to establish policy on human trafficking.[143] However, in April 2003 a report by the U.S. Agency for International Development stated that the Bulgarian government had no trafficking prevention programs.[144] The IOM continues its trafficking awareness campaign that began in 2000. The capacity of the Bulgarian public institutions in the area of trafficking in persons is still weak, the inter-agency coordination and the cooperation with the non-governmental sector is in its initial stage. The governmental institutions and non-governmental entities on central and local levels require support in terms of technical expertise and funding. In the meantime, the government has not provided direct protection to victims of trafficking, and convictions under existing laws have been few. Women originating in Bulgaria or transited through Bulgaria most often go to France, Spain, the Netherlands, and Greece. In 2001 and 2002, authorities uncovered a total of 48 organized crime groups trafficking in women or involved in coercive prostitution. As Bulgaria's tourist industry grows, the country is gradually becoming a destination point as well as a source for these activities. Bulgarian authorities expect that the country's location will increase connections with international trafficking lines.[145] In 2002, improved controls on Romania's eastern border forced the flow of human trafficking southward, to the border between Bulgaria and Romania, which in July 2002 was described as an "uncontrolled territory." The main concentration of illegal movement was the Lom region of northwestern Bulgaria, where trafficking groups were able to cross the Danube into Romania with ease.[146]

Foreign and Bulgarian criminal groups also take advantage of Bulgaria's location to move stolen vehicles from Western Europe (especially Spain and Germany) to Turkey, Greece, Albania, and Macedonia, as well as across the Black Sea into Ukraine, Russia, and Georgia. An elaborate system of Bulgarian "chop shops" removes vehicle identifications. Some vehicles are resold in Bulgaria.[147]

Other large-scale organized criminal activities are currency counterfeiting and compact disc (CD) piracy. In 2000-01, authorities discovered five counterfeit printing shops in which counterfeiting rings were manufacturing United States, German, and Greek currency and false

---

[143] Report from Bulgarian Press Agency (BTA), 15 August 2002 (FBIS Document EUP20020815000210).
[144] U.S. Agency for International Development, "Combating Human Trafficking in Bulgaria," 25 April 2003. <http://www.usembassy.bg/prog/aps.htm>
[145] U.S. Department of State, *Trafficking in Persons Report*, June 2002. <http://www.state.gov/g/tip/rls/tiprpt/2002>
[146] Report in *Adevarul* [Bucharest], 25 July 2002 (FBIS Document EUP20020725000182).
[147] Konstantinova.

credit cards. In 1997 international watchdog organizations threatened to blacklist Bulgaria because of the huge volume of pirated CDs that were emanating from that country as a result of weak commercial copyright laws and lax law enforcement. Although the blacklist threat brought stricter enforcement and some operations moved to "greener pastures" in republics of the former Soviet Union, in 2001 authorities confiscated 188,000 pirated CDs. That volume indicates that Bulgaria is not yet able to control this form of commercial crime.[148]

Bulgaria's defense industry, a major source of arms and ammunition in the Soviet era, continues to manufacture assault rifles and guided weapons systems. Bulgaria also has an estimated 700 each of surplus tanks, artillery pieces, and armored personnel carriers and 160,000 tons of ammunition, all remaining from the Soviet era. In recent years, Bulgarian authorities have identified 29 criminal groups using these stocks to participate in the international illegal arms trade. Although arms export controls have been improved gradually since the mid-1990s, in recent years large amounts of illegally shipped weapons and ammunition and 25 containers of radioactive substances have been confiscated.[149] In mid-2002, new arms trade legislation failed to establish mandatory minimum export criteria, improve transparency in arms transactions, or provide for destruction rather than resale of surplus weapons.[150] In part, a shortage of financial resources explains Bulgaria's failure to destroy surplus heavy conventional arms because it lacks financial resources. In mid-2002, the Bulgarian government reported the intention to export nearly 200 large-caliber artillery systems.[151]

In the late 1990s, Bulgaria passed money-laundering legislation in recognition of the vulnerability of its financial system to the laundering of illegal money from narcotics sales and commercial crimes. However, in 2000 the Financial Action Task Force of the Organisation for Economic Coordination and Development found that the new legislation had significant loopholes such as the lack of coverage of negligent laundering, the inability to enforce foreign confiscation orders, and the inability to try a legal entity for laundering.[152] In early 2002, a

---

[148] Konstantinova.

[149] Konstantinova and International Action Network on Small Arms, "Central and Eastern Europe Remains Important Source and Transit Route for Arms: Country Analysis." <http://www.saferworld.org.uk>

[150] Human Rights Watch, "Arms Trade, Human Rights, and European Union Enlargement: The Record of Candidate Countries."

[151] Human Rights Watch, "Arms Trade, Human Rights, and European Union Enlargement: The Record of Candidate Countries."

[152] Organisation for Economic Cooperation and Development, Financial Action Task Force on Money Laundering, "Members and Observers, PC-R-EV Committee." <http://www1.oecd.org/fatf>

corruption index found that corruption was continuing to spread in Bulgaria at the same rate as it had in the 1990s, mainly because of socio-economic factors and the low legitimacy of the state in the view of the public.[153]

Beginning in 1997, Bulgaria joined international and regional efforts such as the Southeast European Cooperative Initiative (SECI), which is aimed at reducing illegal trafficking in women. In 2002 the SECI established a regional center to combat various types of cross-border crime. The government of Prime Minister Simeon Saxe-Coburg has passed legislation criminalizing bribery, participation in criminal groups, and money laundering.[154] However, as in other countries in the region, the efficacy of those laws will depend on the resources and training available to enforcement agencies.

The Czech Republic

The Czech Republic's arms trade legislation has left the country vulnerable to some trafficking in illegal weapons. According to Czech intelligence sources, arms traffickers have moved illegal shipments through the Czech Republic by submitting false documents and by obtaining licenses in partnership with legitimate arms companies.[155] Economic crime and corruption also have grown substantially in recent years. According to a federal authority, instances of bribe taking by public officials increased from 6 in 1993 to 53 in 2000.[156] In mid-2002, the European-Czech Forum, a multinational business watchdog agency, called for drastic reform of the Czech Republic's judicial and regulatory procedures in order to reduce economic crime. Public attention focused on corruption at that time because a former Foreign Ministry official confessed to collecting bribes from companies seeking contracts from the ministry.[157]

---

[153] Southeast European Legal Development Initiative.

[154] Konstantinova.

[155] Human Rights Watch, "Arms Trade, Human Rights, and European Union Enlargement: The Record of Candidate Countries."

[156] "Top Attorney Calls for Radical Solution to Widespread Corruption," *RFE/RL Crime and Corruption Watch*, 2, no. 13 (4 April 2002). <http://www.rferl/corruptionwatch>

[157] "Suspected Accomplice Says She Spent Years Collecting Bribes Related to Ministry Contracts," *RFE/RL Crime and Corruption Watch*, 2, no. 27 (27 July 2002). <http://www.rferl/corruptionwatch>

Hungary

In the past decade, organized crime has concentrated in Hungary because of that country's fast-growing commercial ties with the West, its well-developed transportation and communications infrastructure, and its geographical location in the center of Europe. In a 2001 report, *Jane's Intelligence Review* estimated that 160 to 180 criminal organizations were active in Hungary, with particular concentration in Budapest. At that time, organized crime controlled an estimated 60 percent of Hungarian enterprises, including major financial institutions. These organizations, which participate in a wide variety of criminal activities, often have links with groups in Russia, for whom Hungary has been a vital connection with the West. In 2000 the activities of the Russian Solntsevo group reportedly increased in Hungary, and Semen Mogil'yevich, head of the rival Russian Solomon group, is known to have pursued various business and smuggling activities from Budapest in recent years.[158] The recent influx of foreign groups has caused considerable instability and violence in Hungary's criminal underworld, while diminishing the ethnic homogeneity of individual criminal operations.[159]

Hungary is the next step after Bulgaria and Romania on the main narcotics route from Southwest Asia to Western Europe. According to Interpol, in 2000 Hungary had the third-largest amount of transited narcotics in the world; as many as 64 groups were involved in this traffic. In 2000 the Hungarian Customs Authority reported sharp increases in seizures of heroin, marijuana, hashish, and opium.[160] In September 2002, Hungarian authorities uncovered a very large operation smuggling cocaine from Columbia, allegedly run by a Hungarian-Italian company based in Italy.[161] Hungary also has been an important transit country for the smuggling of arms, vehicles, and stolen works of art. In the 1990s, conflicts in Yugoslavia increased the smuggling of arms.

Hungary is both a destination and a transit country for illegally trafficked migrants as well as women moving into the sex industries of Austria, Germany, Spain, the Netherlands, Italy, France, Switzerland, and the United States. The main source countries for such women are

---

[158] Daša Matejickova, "Ivan I. Miško on His Contacts with S. Mogilyevich, Strong Man of the Ukrainian Mafia in the World," *SME* [Bratislava], 11 January 2000 (FBIS Document FTS20000115000458).
[159] Kelly Hignett, "Hungary Takes On the Mafia," *Jane's Intelligence Review*, 1 January 2001.
[160] Hignett.
[161] "Major Busts Made by Hungarians, Russians, Romanians," *RFE/RL Crime and Corruption Watch*, 2, no. 35 (4 October 2002). <http://www.rferl.org/corruptionwatch/2002>

Romania, Ukraine, Moldova, Poland, Yugoslavia, and China. Hungary has not actively prosecuted traffickers, although anti-trafficking laws exist. Police in eastern Hungary, the entry area for a high percentage of such traffic, are not well equipped to deter traffickers, and police reportedly treat individual victims as criminals.[162]

The relative success of Hungary's economic liberalization in the 1990s has combined with the secrecy provided by Hungary's banking laws to promote money-laundering activities. The scale of those activities has increased with the scale of illegal trafficking and other activities, particularly those of Russian groups. In 1999 and 2000, Hungarian financial institutions were implicated in two major international money- laundering schemes.[163] Money laundering has been promoted by the fact that luxury cars and real estate often are purchased with cash in what still is largely a cash-based economy. Hungary's 2,000 bureaus of exchange also have been vulnerable to money laundering because such institutions (and all other enterprises in Hungary's non-financial sectors) have not been monitored for such activity. Until legislation stopped the practice in 2002, anonymous savings passbooks were permitted for Hungarian citizens and foreign nationals.[164] Following the passage of major new money laundering legislation in November 2001, Hungary was removed from the Organization for Economic Cooperation and Development (OECD)'s list of noncompliant countries in mid-2002.[165]

Poland

According to a 2002 estimate, 80 percent of the 13.5 million people who cross Poland's eastern borders with Belarus and Ukraine annually are engaged in some form of smuggling. This regular process mainly moves illegal alcohol, cigarettes, and migrants into Białystok and other urban centers of eastern Poland. In 2000 this activity cost Poland an estimated US$4 billion in revenue. In 2001 the amount of smuggled goods doubled and confiscated narcotics increased by a factor of ten; in mid-2002, Polish authorities again reported substantial increases in illegal immigration and smuggling across the Poland-Ukraine border.[166] Poland also is a transit country

---

[162] U.S. Department of State, *Trafficking in Persons Report 2002.*
[163] Hignett.
[164] Ulrika Lomas, "Hungary Bans Anonymous Accounts in Response to FATF Listing," *Tax-News.com* [Brussels], 3 September 2001. <http://www.tax-news.com/asp/story/story_print.asp?/storyname=5188>
[165] U.S. Department of State, International Information Programs, "Hungary, Israel Removed from Money Laundering Blacklist," report of 21 June 2002. <http://usinfo.state.gov/topical/econ/mlc/02062101.htm>
[166] Report from UTI Television, Kiev, 12 July 2002 (FBIS Document CEP20020713000058).

for illegal trafficking in women, most of whom come from the former Soviet Union, Bulgaria, and Romania. Local police corruption is a major contributing factor to domestic prostitution, especially in the western province of Zielona Góra.[167]

Lax controls on Poland's eastern border also are a factor in the presence in Poland of numerous criminal gangs from Belarus and Russia, which are able to maintain connections with their homeland. Local conditions in Warsaw have enabled Polish gangs to establish relations with and protect such groups. According to a 2002 report, several important Russian gang leaders smuggle narcotics and vehicles and launder large amounts of money through real estate transactions in Warsaw.[168] In December 2002, the Ministry of Finance estimated that between US$1.5 billion and US$8 billion of illegal profits from narcotics, theft, prostitution, gambling, and trafficking in persons is laundered in Poland annually. Poor cooperation from financial institutions, insufficient police resources, and legal restrictions on dissemination of information by prosecutors have hindered enforcement of Poland's money-laundering laws, which theoretically comply with European standards.[169]

An important factor supporting this activity is that, in support of an informal "central European community," which includes the Baltic states, Belarus, and Ukraine, Poland requires no entry visas. That situation will change in July 2003, when Poland plans to begin requiring visas in preparation for its entry into the European Union in 2004.[170] Another factor in the porosity of the eastern border has been the use of as many as 3,000 conscripts in the Border Guard Service.[171]

Romania

Trafficking in migrants and women is a major activity of transnational criminal groups active in Romania. Romania lies on the natural westward route of refugees from Afghanistan, Iraq, and other eastern points of origin. The Romanian Border Police identify two trafficking

---

[167] United Nations, Office for Drug Control and Crime Prevention, "The Case of Poland," 1 October 2002 <http://www.undcp.org>

[168] Rafal Pasztelanski, "You Should Not Mess Around with 'Wolf,'" *Zycie* [Warsaw], 28 August 2002 (FBIS Document EUP20020830000246).

[169] "Poland: Country Used to Launder Large Amounts of Money," *RFE/RL Crime and Corruption Watch*, 2, no. 41 (3 December 2002). <http://www.rferl.org/corruptionwatch>

[170] Bernard Osser, "In the East, Specter of Another Iron Curtain," *Le Figaro* [Paris], 8 March 2002 (FBIS Document EUP20020310000003).

[171] "Up to Code," *The Polish Voice*, no. 21 (2002). <http://thepolishvoice.pl>

routes. The first, used mainly by Iraqis, passes from Turkey into Romania via Bulgaria. Migrants then use neighboring Hungary as the transit point to enter the European Union countries. The second route is used primarily by Afghan and African migrants, who fly to Moscow, then enter Romania via Moldova or Ukraine. Faulty border controls are a major factor in illegal trafficking: parts of Romania's border are not well patrolled, and the Border Police have not cooperated effectively with their Bulgarian and Moldovan counterparts.[172]

In 2001 and 2002, Romania improved its compliance with international standards for eliminating trafficking in persons by improving cooperation with neighboring states and among domestic agencies and strengthening border security measures. However, the 2002 U.S. Department of State trafficking report found limitations in the prosecution of public officials involved in trafficking. Because Romania passed its first law criminalizing trafficking only in December 2001,[173] the enforcement process was not yet fully developed as of the end of 2002.

Romania has been a primary Central European transit point for narcotics arriving from Turkey along the "Balkan route." Large amounts of precursor chemicals also travel through Romania in the other direction, from Western Europe to Turkey. The narcotics divisions of Romania's law enforcement have not been sufficient to deal with this movement, and the main anti-narcotics agency, the Directorate for Combating Organized Crime and Anti-Drug Operations, has itself been implicated in the drug trade. The low pay of law enforcement officials remains an incentive for corruption that prevents enforcement of narcotics and other laws.[174]

Slovakia

From the Warsaw Pact era, Slovakia retains substantial research-and-development capability to produce major weapons.[175] The nation's arms export controls have a legislative loophole that inhibits effective monitoring of arms transiting the country; as of 2002, no government license was required for arms remaining in Slovakia for less than seven days. In mid-2002, new arms trade legislation failed to correct this loophole and failed to improve the

---

[172] Paul Christian Radu, "Romania Tackles Human Traffickers," Institute for War and Peace Reporting, *Balkan Crisis Report*, no. 9 (9 August 2002). http://www.iwpr.net>
[173] U.S. Department of State, *Trafficking in Persons Report 2002*.
[174] U.S. Department of State, Bureau for International Narcotics and Law Enforcement Affairs.
[175] International Action Network on Small Arms.

transparency of the arms trade.[176] In recent years, international authorities have observed a number of questionable arms transfers through Slovakia, including major shipments to Liberia (as a point of origin) and to Angola (as a transit point from Iran).[177] Arms export control will become a more important issue in the following decade, as Slovakia's military modernization program makes an estimated 200 tanks and 300 armored personnel carriers redundant.[178]

The process of privatizing Slovakia's economy has resulted in substantial amounts of economic crime, notably tax evasion, larceny, embezzlement, and fraud. A substantially cash-based economy, combined with dispersed and non-transparent banking and financial institutions and casinos, have made Slovakia a hospitable environment for laundering profits from the narcotics traffic that passes through the country.[179]

Nations of the Former Soviet Union

The Baltic States

The Baltic States—Estonia, Latvia, and Lithuania—have similar problems in a number of areas, including the presence of transnational crime organizations and the domestic conditions that invite such a presence. However, no major terrorist presence or activities have been reported. The three countries are located between Russia, home of one of the world's largest networks of organized crime, and the West European countries that often are the primary markets for goods and services sold by transnational crime groups. In the late Soviet period, the "Baltic Corridor," which already had existed for many years for both legal and illegal trade, became an important pathway for an "illegal economic free-for-all as goods and people passed through from east to west and west to east."[180] By economic necessity, the Baltic states have continued many of their Soviet-era commercial ties with Russia along their segment of the Baltic Corridor, inhibiting efforts to curtail illegal traffic on the existing corridor.

---

[176] Human Rights Watch, "Arms Trade, Human Rights, and European Union Enlargement: The Record of Candidate Countries."
[177] Human Rights Watch, "World Report 2002." <http://www.hrw.org>
[178] Human Rights Watch, "Arms Trade, Human Rights, and European Union Enlargement: The Record of Candidate Countries."
[179] Council of Europe, European Committee on Crime Problems, Select Committee of Experts on the Evaluation of Anti-Money Laundering Measures, "Second-Round Evaluation Report on Slovak Republic," 8 April 2003. <http://www/coe.int>
[180] Paddy Rawlinson, "Russian Organized Crime and the Baltic States: Assessing the Threat," Centre for Comparative Criminology and Criminal Justice, *Working Paper* 38/01, 8.

Among the republics of the former Soviet Union, the Baltic countries have made the most progress in eliminating conditions that promote transnational criminal activity. In 1996 the Baltic countries organized the Task Force on Organized Crime in the Baltic and established crime units to combat specific types of crime. In 2002 the Task Force continued to evaluate progress, issue reports, and act as an information clearing-house for the member countries. The most frequent types of transnational crime in the region have been illegal immigration, vehicle theft, money laundering, contract murders, narcotics trafficking, and other types of smuggling.[181] In general, the Baltic states have not had sufficient resources or personnel training to enforce new legislation dealing with trafficking in human beings or narcotics.[182] As in other parts of Europe, improvements in financial systems (rapid communications, computer use, and electronic transfer of funds) have facilitated money laundering in the Baltics.[183]

Estonia

According to the U.S. Department of State's most recent narcotics report, the activity and international connections of Estonian narcotics traffickers have expanded significantly in recent years, and domestic demand for narcotics has increased in proportion. The Ministry of Internal Affairs of Estonia estimated in 2001 that narcotics transit generated 70 percent of the income of domestic criminal groups, with domestic sales accounting for 30 percent. Although staffing of police narcotics specialists has increased, the U.S. Department of State reported in 2001 that as presently constituted the police force was unable to reduce the flow of narcotics or associated crimes.[184] In recent years, Estonian and Russian narcotics groups have gained a firm foothold in the narcotics markets of Finland, although Estonia's strict monitoring of its Russian minority has reduced the Russian presence in this activity. Estonia's successful prosecution of Russian crime bosses Boris Malinovskiy and Nikolay Bleskov in 1996 was the first stage of this process.[185] Experts predict that Estonia's imminent membership in the European Union will intensify

---

[181] Jan K. Collins, "Doing Business in the Baltic." <http://research.moore.sc.edu/Research>

[182] "Trafficking in Women in the Baltic States: Legal Aspects," *Trends in Immigration*, special issue, 2001.

[183] Sabrina Adamoli, "Organised Crime and Money Laundering Trends and Countermeasures: A Comparison Between Western and Eastern Europe, in Petrus C. van Duyne, Vinzenzo Ruggiero, Miroslav Scheinost, and Wim Valkenburg, eds., *Cross-Border Crime in a Changing Europe* (Huntington, New York: Nova Science Publishers, 2001), 187.

[184] U.S. Department of State, Bureau for International Narcotics and Law Enforcement Affairs, *International Narcotics Control Strategy Report 2001*. <http://www.state.gov/g/inl/nrcrpt/2001>

[185] Patricia Rawlinson, "Baltic States Battle Organised Crime," *Jane's Intelligence Review*, 1 November 2001.

interdiction of the smuggling of items such as cigarettes and liquor, which authorities often have ignored. Smuggling of those commodities has been concentrated in Estonia's coastal islands, which present a difficult target for enforcement.

The manufacture of amphetamines and methamphetamines now constitutes the majority of Estonia's illegal narcotics trade. The Finnish market, where most of this production is sold, is promoted by the price differential between Estonia and Finland and the large numbers of Finnish tourists in Estonia. As the Russian presence has receded, Estonian criminal groups have established new links with groups in Finland and in South America.[186] Some narcotics traffickers eventually expanded their activities to include trafficking in human beings. That form of trafficking most often brings people from Russia to Scandinavian countries; the main organizers of such activity have been Scandinavians rather than Estonians.[187] This activity took advantage of the failure of Estonian law to cover specifically trafficking in persons. Although Estonia had upgraded its legislation by 1999, trafficking continued in 2002.

Beginning in the late 1990s, organized economic crime expanded in Estonia as new activities such as a black market in mobile telephones emerged. The activities of remaining Russian groups concentrated on racketeering, theft, vehicle trade, and violent crime as domestic groups delved into the profitable new areas in addition to narcotics trafficking. In the late 1990s, organized crime also moved into the real estate industry, taking advantage of corruption among municipal officials to gain large profits on bogus transactions that sometimes also involve money laundering.[188] Some Finnish and Swedish groups also are active in the production and trafficking of narcotics and the recruiting of prostitutes.[189]

Latvia

The chaos that followed Latvia's independence in 1991 saw the development of especially strong relations between Latvian and Russian crime groups, in part because Latvia had the largest Russian minority population of the three Baltic states. The leading criminal

---

[186] Patricia Rawlinson.

[187] Jüri Mois, "Organized Crime and Illegal Immigration in Estonia," speech to 14th session of Baltic Assembly, May 27, 1999. <http://www.baltsam.org/activity/documents>

[188] Mois.

[189] University of Exeter, Department of Politics "Organised Crime in Estonia," 2001. <http://www.ex.ac.uk/politics/pol_data/undergrad/jaakko/caseestonia>

associations that appeared in Latvia in the 1990s were based on athletic clubs, as were some of the contemporaneous Russian groups (see Russia). Russian leaders of major Latvian groups include Ivan Kharitonov (now in prison) and Boris Raygorodskiy, who retained close contact with their counterparts in Russia.[190] Relations between the Latvian and Russian groups were especially evident in Riga, the regional financial center, where Russian crime leaders such as Aleksandr Lavent and Vladimir Leskov became dominant figures in Latvia's developing financial system.[191]

In the first post-Soviet years, a major activity of organized crime was the smuggling of precious metals from Russia through Estonia to the West, in what became known as Estonia's "Metal Age." Some of the trafficking lines from that era remain in existence, and the smuggling of narcotics, alcohol, and other illegal and highly taxed items remains a central part of Estonia's organized crime activity.[192] In the 1990s, organized crime in Latvia moved into more "businesslike" activities such as banking, and the protection rackets that had flourished under Russian leadership in the early 1990s evolved into private security agencies. In the mid-1990s, the U.S. Department of State characterized Latvia's banking system as vulnerable to the laundering of narcotics money. The reasons for this evaluation were the lack of money laundering legislation, the absence of strict banking accountability, the lack of currency reporting requirements, and the loose regulations under which many of Latvia's banks had been founded.[193] Some of those problems have been addressed in subsequent years.

The thriving post-Soviet black market spawned high levels of official graft. The United States considered high levels of corruption in Latvia's government and security forces a substantial obstacle to sharing security information with this prospective NATO member.[194] In 2000-02, under pressure from the public and from West European multinational institutions to reduce corruption and conflicts of interest among government officials, the Latvian government passed significant legislation on those subjects. In November 2001, the chair of Transparency International's Latvian branch rated that legislation as meeting the West European standard.

---

[190] Paddy Rawlinson, 16.
[191] Paddy Rawlinson, 14.
[192] "Organised Crime in Estonia."
[193] U.S. Department of State, Bureau for International Narcotics and Law Enforcement Affairs, *International Narcotics Control Strategy Report 1996.* <http:www.state.gov.g/inl/rls/nrcrpt/1996>
[194] Fred Weir, "Baltics Step from Russia's Shadow into Western Club," *The Christian Science Monitor*, 20 November 2002, 13.

However, she also noted that the laws had not yet been implemented and that Latvia still needed laws requiring political parties to report donations.[195] In Transparency International's 2002 Corruption Perceptions Index, Latvia was rated 52d out of 102 countries evaluated.[196] Reporting on legislative developments, Latvian journalist Valts Kalnins has observed that the new laws leave significant loopholes and that Latvia still has no effective law against money laundering. Kalnins noted that Latvia has no institutional experience in the control and investigation of such crimes; corrupt officials have been apprehended in a haphazard way, mainly at lower levels of responsibility. Conflict-of-interest legislation does not specify precisely what actions by a government official constitute a conflict of interest.[197]

In controlling money laundering, Latvia currently has no organized accounting system by which to compare previously existing assets with current assets. Authorities have not enforced existing legislation that prohibits the establishment of anonymous bank accounts, and Latvia has no legislation against negligent laundering.[198] Fully anonymous accounts are illegal, but numbered accounts, which can substantially reduce access to suspicious transactions, are legal.[199] A report on Latvia by the Council of Europe's Anti-Corruption Group found, except for the Security Police, "nothing to suggest that complex police methods are being used. It appeared that there is a lack of imagination and officially organized training in the fight against corruption."[200] Another 2001 Council of Europe report faulted Latvia for insufficient reporting requirements for banks and exchange houses. In 2001 the head of the Environmental State Inspectorate, the deputy chief of the economic police, 12 police officers, 2 border guards, and 14 employees of the Ministry of Interior were arrested for accepting bribes.[201]

International narcotics officials have identified Latvia as primarily a narcotics transit country, although the production of synthetic illicit drugs increased in the 1990s. As in the other

---

[195] "Latvia's Anticorruption Effort Gets High Marks," *RFE/RL Crime and Corruption Watch*, 1, no. 6 (6 December 2001). <http://www.rferl.org/corruptionwatch/2001>
[196] Transparency International, "Corruption Perceptions Index 2002." <http://www.transparency.org/cpi/2002/cpi2002en.html>
[197] Valts Kalnins, "Corruption: The Battle Is Not Finished," *Diena* [Riga], 30 August 2002 (FBIS Document CEP20020830000048)
[198] Latvia, Ministry of Justice, "Status Report of the Republic of Latvia Under the Baltic Anti-Corruption Initiative," April, 2002. <http://www.nobribes.org/Documents/Latvia_BACIReport_2002.doc>
[199] Council of Europe, European Committee on Crime Problems, Select Committee of Experts on the Evaluation of Anti-Money Laundering Measures, "First Evaluation Report on Latvia," 19 January 2001. <http://www.coe.int>
[200] Kalnins.
[201] "New Bribery Scandal," *RFE/RL Crime and Corruption Watch*, 1, no. 6 (6 December 2001). <http://www.rferl.org/corruptionwatch>

Baltic states, transit activity increased in the 1990s as the "Balkan route" was disrupted by war. Latvian and Russian groups have primarily carried out that transit. In recent years, the Solntsevo group, one of Russia's largest criminal organizations, has increased its activity in Latvia.[202] The general trafficking route extends from Central Asia, through Russia and Belarus, then through the Baltic States into Scandinavia. Most of Latvia's narcotics trafficking is done by organized crime groups that began with cigarette and alcohol smuggling, although recently some groups have specialized in narcotics. Although the volume of trafficking is small compared with larger European countries, it has increased significantly in recent years; in 2000 and 2001, the annual volume of large narcotics interdictions doubled compared with the volumes of previous years.[203]

Cooperation between Latvia's Ministry of Finance and the Ministry of Interior, the two agencies responsible for narcotics control at the borders, has not been effective at the working level. Coordination with the other Baltic states also is weak. The resource base (human, material, and financial) for customs inspections is not adequate to overcome the sophisticated concealment methods used by today's narcotics traffickers. Inspectors limit their searches of potential drug-containing vehicles because they fear being held responsible for damage. Latvian border authorities continue to emphasize inspection for smuggled taxable items such as cigarettes and alcohol.[204] Nevertheless, the weaknesses in border control have promoted the smuggling of counterfeit goods, particularly cigarettes, through Latvia and to the West. In December 2001, authorities destroyed 25 million fake cigarettes that had been confiscated by customs police.[205]

In recent years, Latvia's roles as a source and transit country for trafficking in prostitutes to Scandinavia and Western Europe have increased as domestic groups have established links with international systems trafficking in women. As of mid-2002, Latvia did not have a comprehensive law against trafficking in humans, although trafficking for sexual exploitation is illegal. According to Interpol, prostitutes on the Latvian route also become involved in money laundering, document counterfeiting, and narcotics sales.[206]

---

[202] "Latvian Officials May Have Interest in Russian Criminal Group," *Neatkariga Rita Avize* [Riga], 22 February 2001 (FBIS Document CEP20010222000055).

[203] United States Department of State, *International Narcotics Control Strategy Report 2001.*

[204] U.S. Department of State, *International Narcotics Control Strategy Report 2001.*

[205] Coalition for Intellectual Property Rights, "Latvian Government Incinerates 25 Million Counterfeit Cigarettes," press release, 10 December 2001. <http://www.cipr.org/activities>

[206] "Trafficking in Prostitutes Is Urgent Problem in Latvia—Interpol," *Leta* [Riga], June 7, 2002 (FBIS Document CEP20020607000086).

Lithuania

Like Estonia and Latvia, Lithuania underwent a strong wave of organized crime in the chaotic years following the dissolution of the Soviet Union. In 1993 an estimated 30 criminal groups in Lithuania had international links. Despite Lithuania's relatively small Russian minority, Russian groups were very active during the early 1990s. Lithuania's proximity to Kaliningrad, a Russian enclave designated as a depository for superfluous military equipment, made it a center of illegal arms smuggling by Russian groups, which also armed themselves from that source. Although the Vilnius Brigade, run by a Georgian, was the most powerful group in Lithuania until 1995, indigenous groups generally have dominated organized crime from the year of independence.[207] In the late 1990s, Lithuanian organized crime followed the pattern of that in Estonia and Latvia, moving into quasi-legitimate ventures in business and finance while maintaining a strong interest in profitable trafficking operations. The alleged financing of hotels in Vilnius by cocaine deals with Columbian dealers is an example of the recent blending of illegal and legal activities.[208]

Lithuanian criminal groups move narcotics into Western Europe from domestic laboratories and from Central and South America, and Lithuania is a transit point on a number of other routes. Poppy straw moves through Lithuania from Central Asia to Latvia and Kaliningrad. Heroin from Afghanistan crosses the Russian and Ukrainian borders on its way to Scandinavia. South and Central American cocaine arrives in Lithuania via Germany and the Netherlands. Amphetamines are produced domestically and also are imported from Poland and the Netherlands. Marijuana arrives from a number of foreign points.[209] The volume of such imports has been increasing since 1995. Some narcotics traffickers also collaborate with stolen vehicle smugglers, using the same routes and at times concealing drugs within the vehicles.[210]

Money laundering, a financial tool of the groups involved in a variety of crimes, also has appeared in Lithuania. Although Lithuania began efforts to improve money laundering legislation in the 1990s, an assessment by the European Union in late 2001 found that those

---

[207] Patricia Rawlinson.
[208] Patricia Rawlinson.
[209] U.S. Department of State, *International Narcotics Control Strategy Report 2001*.
[210] Patricia Rawlinson.

efforts had only succeeded in part.[211] In 2002 new amendments were passed to the basic money laundering law of 1997.[212]

Trafficking in human beings, which was a major problem in Lithuania in the mid-1990s, decreased sharply with the introduction of stricter border procedures in the late 1990s; the European Union has praised the efficacy of legislation on visas, border controls, and immigration.[213] However, the salaries of border guards, which remain very low, still make such individuals vulnerable to bribes, especially if and when a wave of emigration occurs abroad. In mid-2002, one incident of attempted smuggling of radioactive materials occurred in Lithuania. One kilogram of cesium-137 was seized after having been brought into Lithuania from an undisclosed country in the former Soviet Union. The potential buyer was identified as a German with likely connections to organized crime. Lithuanian authorities discovered several similar smuggling efforts in the mid-1990s.[214]

Belarus

The state of the national economy has been an important factor in promoting organized crime in Belarus. Because Belarus has not passed through the rigors of conversion from a communist to a market economy (government policy has maintained state control of most production resources), privatization has not been a significant source of corruption. However, the overall poverty of the economy has stimulated various types of domestic criminal activity and cooperation with transnational groups. The standard of living has declined significantly since Belarus emerged from the collapse of the Soviet Union in 1991; in 2000 that standard was estimated to be four to five times lower than that of the Russian Federation.[215] Although accurate unemployment figures are not available, it is known that the economy has contracted rather than expanded in recent years.

---

[211] European Union, "Activities of the European Union, Summaries of Legislation," 1 February 2002. <http://europa.eu.int>
[212] Lithuania, Ministry of the Interior, Financial Crime Investigative Service, "Money Laundering Prevention: Legal Acts." <http://www.fntt.lt/eng/mlp>
[213] "Lithuania."
[214] Roman Kupchinsky, "Cesium Sale Thwarted in Lithuania," *RFE/RL Crime and Corruption Watch*, 2, no. 22 (6 June 2002). <http://www.rferl.org/corruptionwatch/2002>
[215] Larissa G. Titarenko, "The Walls That Have Yet to Fall: Belarus as a Mirror of CIS Transition," *Demokratizatsiya*, 8, no. 2 (Spring 2000): 232-33.

Belarus is an important country of origin and transit of women and children for sexual exploitation to Russia, Ukraine, Lithuania, Germany, Israel, Poland, the Czech Republic, Turkey, Cyprus, Greece, Hungary, and Yugoslavia. Russian mafia groups have been especially active in trafficking Belarusian women.[216] Although the criminal code of 2001 criminalizes trafficking and sexual exploitation, the Belarusian judiciary has prosecuted few cases under that law. Law enforcement agencies receive no specific training in trafficking, and corruption has blocked criminal investigations. Border controls do not effectively prevent trafficking into neighboring countries, and cultural biases reduce the chances of a female victim receiving a fair hearing.[217]

Belarus is susceptible to Russian organized crime activities because of its geographical position adjacent to northwestern Russia (an area where criminal activity is concentrated), because bilateral agreements with Russia call for lax border security, and because of domestic institutional failure. In 1998 Chechen organized crime groups appeared in Belarus as large numbers of refugees arrived from Chechnya, many of them illegally. Those groups have been implicated in east-to-west narcotics trafficking through Belarus. In rivalries between Chechen and Slavic crime groups within Belarus, the Chechens have had the advantage because of greater ethnic cohesion. Chechens who arrived in Belarus after the 1996 armistice between the Republic of Chechnya and Russia tended away from "ordinary" crime such as narcotics trafficking and toward businesses with legal fronts. Chechens have been involved in laundering profits from illegal activities in Belarus and sending the money to Chechnya or to European banks.[218]

Since the mid-1990s, close ties with Russia have made Belarus a major exporter of illegal arms, although Belarus has almost no domestic arms industry. Large amounts of those exports are believed to have reached forbidden customers such as Iraq, Iran, the Pakistani armed forces in Kashmir, and terrorist bases in Sudan. Experts believe that Belarus exhausted its supply of Soviet-era military supplies in 1997, after which time it has used more modern weapons from Russia to maintain its arms export activity. Illegal export deals apparently proliferate because they have the approval of the Belarusian government. For the Russian arms industry, Belarus is a

---

[216] International League for Human Rights, "Belarus Update," 2, no. 42 (October 2001). <http://www.ilhr.org>
[217] U.S. Department of State, *Trafficking in Persons Report 2002*.
[218] Sergey Anisko, "Belarusian Chechens Display Patriotism: Local Power Departments Claim That Chechen Mafiya Sends Half the Money It Earns to the Homeland," *Segodnya* [Moscow], 12 January 1998, 7 (FBIS Document FTS19980113001126).

convenient and willing intermediary for products to reach wealthy but "politically incorrect" customers.[219]

Official corruption has been an ongoing problem in Belarus. A 1999 European Study on Values identified Belarusians as the Europeans most tolerant of corruption.[220] Although the lack of market reforms has minimized privatization-related economic corruption, bribery of government officials is a regular occurrence. The agencies most often bribed are the customs service, border patrol, road and tax inspectorates, and providers of official documents and licenses.[221]

The Caucasus Republics

Because of its geographic position between the major narcotics producing region of the Golden Crescent (Afghanistan and Pakistan) and the major narcotics markets in Russia and Europe, the Caucasus region has become an important narcotics corridor. Georgia's location on the southern border of the Russian Federation's insurgent Republic of Chechnya-Ichkeria has made Georgia's northern territory a base for Chechen rebel forces, estimates of whose size have varied widely. An additional factor is the weakness of post-Soviet law enforcement agencies in Armenia, Azerbaijan, and Georgia. Armenia, slightly to the southwest of the main narcotics routes, has had the least exposure to narcotics traffic. However, Azerbaijan's southern neighbor, Iran, has established an effective anti-trafficking regime that has pushed narcotics routes northward into Azerbaijan, where corruption has invited such activity. Georgia, which is experiencing a collapse of law enforcement, the Chechen civil war on its northern border, an alarming rate of official corruption, and effective loss of control of large sectors of its national territory to separatist movements, has provided traffickers the most favorable conditions of the three countries. Armenian and Azerbaijani officials have warned that narcotics activity will increase significantly in their countries if effective interdiction measures are not taken.

---

[219] Natalya Khmelik, "Military Bookends," *Sovershenno Sekretno* [Moscow], 1 August 2002 (FBIS Document CEP20020813000393).

[220] "Government Publishes Report on Widespread Corruption in Slovakia," *TASR* [Bratislava], 8 September 2002 (FBIS Document EUP20020908000132).

[221] International League for Human Rights, "Belarus Update."

Armenia

The U.S. Department of State has identified Armenia as a source country for the trafficking of women for sexual exploitation to Germany, Greece, Russia, Turkey, and the United Arab Emirates. Armenia has no specific law against such trafficking and, according to the Department of State report, "is not making significant efforts" to eliminate trafficking.[222] Despite the country's location along the traditional narcotics route from Asia to Europe and poor funding for anti-narcotics enforcement personnel, narcotics trafficking through Armenia has been minimized by the closure of borders with Azerbaijan and Turkey as a result of the Nagorno-Karabakh conflict. Most of the drugs that enter the country come instead through Georgia.[223]

A 2002 public opinion poll sponsored by the Organization for Security and Cooperation in Europe (OSCE) showed that more than 90 percent of Armenians believe that corruption is a serious problem, and that most people identify the government as the main source. Poor law enforcement and insufficient legislation and regulations were the proximate causes most frequently cited.[224] In 2002 the Armenian Center for National and International Studies noted that the current culture of government service in Armenia places a higher priority on personal gain than on public service, and that Armenia's civic culture does not encourage public criticism of unethical conduct.[225] Regional expert Richard Giragosian finds a source of corruption in the political environment, noting of President Robert Kocharian, "… his [Kocharian's] reliance on the backing of the country's oligarchs has hindered any real crackdown on corruption, a long-overdue move essential to Armenia's stability and security."[226] Bribery of officials is a common device used to circumvent Armenia's complex bureaucracy in routine matters such as licensing and pensions.[227]

---

[222] "U.S. Department of State's Human-Trafficking Report," *RFE/RL Crime and Corruption Watch*, 2, no. 23 (14 June 2002). <http://www.rferl.org/corruptionwatch>

[223] Avet Demurian, "Armenia Escapes Drugs Epidemic," Institute for War and Peace Reporting, *Caucasus Reporting Service*, no. 130 (23 May 2002). <http://www.iwpr.net>

[224] "OSCE Assists in Public Opinion Survey on Corruption in Armenia," OSCE press release, 4 October 2002. <http://www.osce.org>

[225] Armenian Center for National and International Studies, "ACNIS Roundtable on Anti-Corruption Strategies," 27 September 2002. <http://www.acnis.am>

[226] Richard Giragosian, "A Troubling Trend in Armenia," *RFE/RL Newsline*, 7, no. 3 (7 January 2003).

[227] "Armenian Anticorruption Drive Creates Doubt," *RFE/RL Crime and Corruption Watch*, 2, no. 30 (30 August 2002).

Azerbaijan

Narcotics trafficking has been a controversial topic between Armenia and Azerbaijan, whose struggle for control of the Armenian enclave of Nagorno-Karabakh remains unsettled. Azerbaijan, which has suffered significant increases in narcotics traffic and domestic addiction in recent years, has accused Armenia of fostering traffic into Azerbaijan from Iran via the 90-mile section of the Azerbaijan-Iran border that Armenia occupies.[228] In any case, the long struggle over Nagorno-Karabakh has impeded law enforcement over a wide area of Azerbaijan. The conflict also has created hundreds of thousands of refugees, mainly Azeris. Such groups are easy targets for human trafficking, and the diaspora groups that they form provide shelter for transnational criminal activity.

Azerbaijan has significant institutional weaknesses that promote transnational crime. Transparency International's 2002 Corruption Perceptions Index placed Azerbaijan 95th out of 102 countries surveyed for public perceptions of government and business corruption.[229] The organization's 1999 survey had placed Azerbaijan fourth-worst. According to a 2002 study, 59 percent of foreign investors feel that bribes are necessary to sidestep Azerbaijan's complex legal system.[230]

According to the International Organization for Migration (IOM), Azerbaijan does not have sufficient legislation to combat trafficking, and the institutional capacity for detection and prevention of trafficking is insufficient.[231] According to a 2002 IOM study, trafficking in persons (especially women) is facilitated by poverty, unemployment and gender inequality in Azerbaijan.[232] Most women smuggled from Azerbaijan have gone to Turkey and the United Arab Emirates.[233]

---

[228] R. Nadiroglu, "Bin Laden's Ties to Armenians Are Much More Extensive than It Appears," Internet report of *Zerkalo* [Baku], 6 December 2001 (FBIS Document CEP20011206000417).

[229] Transparency International.

[230] A. Rasidoglu, "Corruption Has Taken on a Menacing Character," *Zerkalo* [Baku], 22 June 2002 (FBIS Document CEP20020710000409).

[231] International Organization for Migration, "Azerbaijan: Trafficking in Women," IOM Press Briefing Notes, 15 March 2002. <http://www.iom.int>

[232] International Organization for Migration, "Azerbaijan: New Study on Human Trafficking," IOM Press Briefing, 4 October 2002. <http://www.iom.int>

[233] "Azerbaijani Women Mainly Trafficked to Turkey, United Arab Emirates," Trend News Agency [Baku] report, 14 June 2002 (FBIS Document CEP20020614000274).

Georgia

In 2000 Georgian legal expert Georgi Glonti wrote, "The drug business is very widespread in Georgia today....Ethnic groups from Abkhazia, South Ossetia, Chechnya, Azerbaijan, and people from other CIS countries as well as Turkey are involved in the drug business. Considering Georgia's location, many countries are using it as a corridor, especially the regions with weak government control."[234] According to a report in April 2002, the value of drugs trafficked in Georgia has reached $US1 billion per year, a sharp increase from previous years.[235] In 2002, by its own admission, the government of Georgia had not been able to deal effectively with such growth. An important center of narcotics activity has been the Pankisi Gorge, a remote area along Georgia's northern border with Russia. Competition for the region's brisk narcotics trade increased with the arrival of Chechen rebels under the command of Ruslan Gelayev, who by 2002 reportedly had used contacts with Georgian authorities to take over the trade from local drug barons.[236] Gelayev's enterprise appears to have enjoyed at least passive cooperation from Georgian authorities, who have been only an intermittent presence in the Pankisi region.

The complexity of controlling trafficking from Georgia into Russia is increased by conditions on the Russian side of the border. Although Russia has augmented border personnel in selected portions of its Caucasus border, most of the border remains porous because the ongoing impoverishment of Russia's military forces and the destructive effect of the Chechnya conflict on military morale make the bribes of drug traffickers an irresistible temptation.

Georgia also has been beset by corruption, some of which the republic inherited from the Soviet era. On that subject, Gia Nodia, head of the Caucasian Institute for Peace, Democracy, and Development, has said: "...in this country corruption is the norm. Corruption is the foundation on which public management and economic relations are built."[237] In 2000, a presidential report described illegal lobbying groups in all three branches of government and

---

[234] Georgi Glonti, "Problems Associated with Organized Crime in Georgia," report for the Institute of Legal Reform [Tbilisi], 2000.

[235] *Moscow Interfax* report from Tbilisi, 22 April 2002 (FBIS Document CEP2002042000161).

[236] Timofey Borisov, "Has Gelayev Got His Eye on the Chechen Leadership? But Before That, He Tried Out the Route to Ichkeria via Dagestan," *Rossiyskaya Gazeta* [Moscow], 15 May 2002 (FBIS Document CEP20020515000283).

[237] Jean-Christophe Peuch, "Georgia: Corruption Seen as the 'Norm,'" Radio Free Europe/Radio Liberty report, 10 May 2001. <http://www.rferl.org>

"'criminal overlapping interests' in the public and private sectors." The report depicted massive corruption in a pyramid that included all levels of public and private endeavor, with huge sums of money changing hands at the top level. Many of President Eduard Shevardnadze's friends allegedly have profited from corruption at that level. Despite universal recognition of the problem, the national government has done very little to control corruption in Georgia.[238]

The Central Asian Republics

This large, sparsely populated region of the former Soviet Union has provided favorable conditions for terrorist bases and intense narcotics trafficking. Those activities, which in some cases are conducted by the same organizations, have been facilitated by the poor border control that is a legacy of Soviet rule. Especially in the Fergana Valley, which is by far Central Asia's most densely populated region, the complexities of Soviet-established national boundaries make border control extremely difficult for states with limited financial and human resources. Only one of the five—Uzbekistan—has successfully implemented strong border controls, mainly as a protection against terrorist incursions of the Islamic Movement of Uzbekistan (IMU) such as occurred in Uzbekistan in 1999 and 2000. Uzbekistan undertook such measures in part as a response to the poor border controls exercised by all of its neighbor states.[239] Because the IMU has been an important narcotics trafficking agency in the region, effective border and visa controls also have reduced Uzbekistan's flow of narcotics. However, poor controls and official corruption in Kyrgyzstan and Tajikistan have had the effect of pushing the IMU and narcotics trafficking in general from Uzbekistan into those countries. Uzbekistan has accused its neighbors of harboring IMU groups and threatening Uzbekistan's well being by failing to reinforce mutual borders.

The IMU was a major regional terrorist and narcotics-trafficking presence until it sustained major losses in the Afghan conflict of late 2001. Although the IMU's size and capabilities have been the subject of speculation since that time, in 2002 intelligence reports

---

[238] Zaza Namoradze, Goka Gabashvili, and George Papuashvili, "Georgia Appeals to Public to Help Fight Corruption," *Open Society News*, Spring 2001. <http://www.soros.org/open_society_news>
[239] Zamira Eshanova, "Central Asia: Border Issues an 80-Year-Old Headache for Region," *Turkistan Newsletter*, 20 October 2002.

indicated significant resumption of its recruiting activity in the Fergana Valley.[240] Such activity would again take advantage of poor border controls and international border disputes in the Fergana region, especially in Kyrgyzstan and Tajikistan, for narcotics trafficking and possible terrorist attacks. The poverty-stricken condition of the populations of those countries has eased recruitment and establishment of cells for the IMU and Hizb-ut-Tahrir, a larger but less violent radical Islamic group in the region. According to reports in 2003, at least some parts of the disparate Hizb-ut-Tahrir organization were rejecting non-violent tactics in response to severe repression by the regime of Uzbekistan's President Islam Karimov.[241]

Experts believe that in recent years trafficking in human beings has increased significantly throughout Central Asia. Although no statistics are available and Central Asian governments have recognized the problem only recently, the IOM estimates that several thousand women from the five former Soviet republics of Central Asia have been sold into the sex trade by transnational traffickers. Because Central Asian cultures reject women suspected of prostitution, victims often are not able to return home. Although all five countries have laws against human trafficking, sophisticated transnational groups have been able to stymie local law enforcement authorities.[242]

Kazakhstan

Although Kazakhstan has not been a base for Central Asian terrorists, it has been a major transit country for narcotics trafficking from Afghanistan to Russia and thence into Western Europe. The northern Kazakh cities of Pavlodar and Kustanay, close to the Russian border, are the most frequent transit points into Russia. Russian customs authorities have identified the Kazakhstan-Russia border as the source of 80 percent of the heroin, 70 percent of the opium, and 60 percent of the marijuana reaching Russia.[243] Such transnational trafficking is promoted by pervasive corruption in Kazakhstan's poorly paid law enforcement agencies. Police often

---

[240] "Banned Islamic Movement Still a 'Real Threat' to Uzbek Security—Kazakh Paper," *BBC Monitoring Central Asia Unit*; based on report in *Karavan* [Almaty], 1 March 2002; and Artie McConnell, "Islamic Radicals Regroup in Central Asia, 15 May 2002, online report of *Eurasia Insight*. <http://eurasianet.org>
[241] For example, see Peter Baker, "Renewed Militancy Seen in Uzbekistan," *Washington Post*, 27 September 2003.
[242] "Central Asia: Governments Slowly Changing Approach to Human Trafficking," *Eurasianet* report, 6 July 2003. <http://www.eurasianet.org/departments/rights/articles/eav070603.shtm>
[243] "Major Busts Made by Hungarians, Russians, Romanians," *RFE/RL Crime and Corruption Watch*, 2, no. 35 (4 October 2002). <http://www.rfe.rl.org/corruptionwatch>

demand bribes of narcotics dealers who have been apprehended; dealers who identify wealthy colleagues to the police receive a share of the bribe. Upon payment, the dealer and his drugs are released. Because such practices were well established even in the Soviet era, Kazakhstan society shows strong cynicism toward law enforcement.[244] The highest echelons of the Kazakh government may have shown a poor example. In mid-2002, close relatives and associates of President Nursultan Nazarbayev were implicated in an international scheme to launder money received from foreign companies to promote business in Kazakhstan. The participants allegedly used a Swiss bank account for this purpose.[245]

Kazakhstan, which was a nuclear weapons site in the Soviet era, also may have been involved in the theft and smuggling of osmium-187, a radioactive substance that is not used in making nuclear weapons. In the last three years, several reports have named Kazakhstan as the source of smuggled osmium-187, possibly en route to terrorist organizations or Iraq. In December 2001, Moscow authorities arrested a group of Chechens from Kazakhstan, who had osmium-187 in their possession.[246] Such reports indicate that Kazakhstan has exercised lax security for sensitive materials and porous border controls. As of mid-2002, Kazakhstan still was negotiating with the United States about removing the weapons-grade nuclear material remaining in the country.[247]

Kyrgyzstan

Among the five Central Asian republics of the former Soviet Union, Kyrgyzstan has the poorest resource base and the weakest overall economy. In 1999 the country nearly went bankrupt because of a loss of foreign currency.[248] Kyrgyzstan has become a major narcotics transit country because its weak economy cannot support competent military and border guard units. The political system still is dominated and fragmented by a regional clan system, which in the first decade of independence persistently threatened to divide the country into two parts, and

---

[244] Daur Dosybiev, "Kazakhstan: Police Corruption Worsens," Institute for War and Peace Reporting, *Report on Central Asia,* no. 128 (5 July 2002). <http://www.iwpr.net>

[245] Viktor Antichenko, "The State: It Is I and My Daughter," *Novaya Gazeta* [Moscow], 17 June 2002 (FBIS Document CEP20020620000337).

[246] Dmitriy Starostin, "Osmium Worries the FSB," *Vremya Novostey* [Moscow], 27 September 2002. <http://www.nti.org>

[247] Nuclear Threat Initiative, "Kazakhstan Overview," February 2002. <http://www.nti.org>

[248] Steven Blank, "Kyrgyzstan: Strategic Pivot," *Central Asia/Caucasus Analyst,* 18 December 2002. <http://www.cacianalyst.org>

poverty makes younger Kyrgyz very vulnerable to a life of crime, Islamic radicalism, or both. Bribes to high government officials have bought protection for trafficking routes from neighboring Tajikistan,[249] and criminal organizations have taken advantage of chronic unrest in the Fergana Valley, a resource-rich, ethnically fragmented region that Kyrgyzstan shares with Tajikistan and Uzbekistan.

Trafficking volume along the Tajikistan-Kyrgyzstan routes also has increased because of interdiction in alternative transit countries such as Iran and Uzbekistan. The city of Osh, strategically located on the Uzbekistan border in the Fergana Valley, has become a hub of narcotics movement. The capital city of Kyrgyzstan, Bishkek, also has experienced rapid growth in narcotics trafficking, partly because it lies near the border of Kazakhstan, the next "stop" on the narcotics highway from Afghanistan to Russia. As of 2001, Bishkek's drug control department had a staff of only 19 to patrol a city of nearly 1 million. In recent years, optimal growing conditions have made domestic marijuana a profitable cash crop for villagers in the Issyk-Kul (northeastern) and Osh regions.[250]

Kyrgyzstan increasingly has been a source country for human trafficking. The International Organization for Migration estimated that 4,000 women had been trafficked abroad in 1999. This is a large number, considering Kyrgyzstan's small population, although Kyrgyz courts found only four people guilty of such trafficking in 2000. The most frequent destinations for illegally trafficked Kyrgyz women have been brothels in Germany, Russia, Turkey, and the United Arab Emirates.[251] Human trafficking, which is promoted by widespread poverty, has followed the same routes as narcotics trafficking through Kyrgyzstan.

According to Prime Minister Kurmanbek Bakiyev, economic crime in Kyrgyzstan also has been growing rapidly in recent years. This condition is promoted by widespread corruption in financial and monetary institutions, whose transition to a free market economy has not been backed by a comprehensive legal system, effective law enforcement, or protection of the right to own property. Under these conditions, Bakiyev estimated that in the year 2000 economic crimes

---

[249] Tamara Makarenko, "Crime, Terror and the Central Asian Drug Trade," *Harvard Asia Quarterly*, Summer 2002. <http://www.cornellcaspian.com/briefs/25_0207CA_Drugs.pdf>
[250] Sashka Shpakova, "A War Against Drug Trafficking in Kyrgyzstan," *Central Asia/Caucasus Analyst*, 25 April 2001. <http://www.cacianalyst.org>
[251] Global March Against Child Labour, "Worst Forms of Child Labour Data: Kyrgyzstan." <http://www.globalmarch.org>

inflicted damage amounting to 10 percent of the national budget.[252] In December 2002, a report by the International Crisis Group noted the growing role of Kyrgyzstan's police in suppressing opposition on behalf of the Akayev government.[253] As in Uzbekistan, such perversion of police authority has a result similar to that caused by conventional police corruption. Under such circumstances, especially when police personnel and resources are very limited at best, the detection and apprehension of criminals and terrorists is determined by factors unrelated to the public good or national security.

Tajikistan

The central government of Tajikistan has full control over only a small part of the country, around the capital city of Dushanbe. Particularly in the mountainous eastern and northwestern sectors of the country, smuggling routes and encampments of the terrorist IMU have met only sporadic resistance from Tajik authorities.[254] Although experts credit Tajikistan's border forces with substantial improvement in recent years, smuggling statistics have not decreased proportionately. Under the best of circumstances, control of borders and inland territory is extremely difficult because of mountainous terrain.

Five years after the end of an extremely destructive civil war, Tajikistan remains one of the poorest of the former Soviet states; its political fabric still is based on regional clans and warlords, many of whom profit from smuggling operations and owe only nominal fealty to the central government. Poor economic prospects and low salaries make citizens and government officials susceptible to bribes and direct participation in criminal activity. In a 2002 report, the International Crisis Group described Tajikistan's police and other state security agencies as having changed since the Soviet era only to the extent that since 1991 organized crime has gained greater influence over those agencies. The report describes growing illegal political and economic roles for the police, who reportedly have taken over some sectors of the national

---

[252] "Crime Rate in Kyrgyzstan Impedes Socio-Economic Reforms," *Pravda.ru* report, 21 August 2001. <http://english.pravda.ru/cis/2001>

[253] Zamira Eshanova, "Central Asia: Report Says Police Have Improved Little since Soviet Era," *Eurasia Insight*, 18 December 2002. <http://www.eurasianet.org>

[254] Vladimir Davlatov, "Rakhmonov Warns of Afghan Terror Threat," Institute for War and Peace Reporting, *Report on Central Asia,* no. 127 (28 June 2002). <http://www.iwpr.net>

economy and play a large role in narcotics trafficking. Organized crime and terrorism also are promoted by corruption at very high levels of government.[255]

Because of its chaotic law enforcement situation and its location directly north of a primary heroin-producing region of Afghanistan, Tajikistan has become the primary route for smuggling narcotics northward and westward to markets in Russia and Western Europe.[256] Traffickers of various nationalities reportedly ensure their survival by bribing high government officials.[257] In the first months of 2003, a resurgence of heroin production in Afghanistan doubled the volume of confiscations by Tajik border forces. Although part of that increase is attributable to improvements in interdiction practices, the Tajik Drug Control Agency requested international assistance to deal with the problem.[258] Aside from providing funds to bribe officials, domestic profits from the narcotics trade (estimated at US$200 million for 2001) also have stimulated a large-scale money-laundering system in Tajikistan, which has had no effective laws against such practices.[259]

Turkmenistan

Although Turkmenistan has remained on the periphery of reports about organized crime activity in the former Soviet Union, in 2002 transnational criminal activity in that country increased significantly. Turkmenistan occupies a central geographical position between primary heroin producer Afghanistan and key narcotics trafficking routes west of the Caspian Sea. Intelligence sources have documented the involvement of major Turkmen clans in various types of smuggling. Although Turkmenistan is a dictatorship, political power still is based on the loyalty of major clans; government indulgence of money-making activities of those groups is an effective method of buying such support. Evidence indicates that the government of President Saparmyrat Niyazov permits trafficking operations at the country's main airport at Ashgabat, and that major narcotics routes transit Turkmenistan before crossing the Caspian Sea to the

---

[255] Eshanova.
[256] U.S. Department of State, *International Narcotics Control Strategy Report 2001.*
[257] Makarenko, "Crime, Terror and the Central Asian Drug Trade."
[258] Mark Berniker, "Tajikistan Strives for Growth amid Risk and Poverty, *Eurasianet* report, 11 June 2003. <http://www.eurasianet.org>
[259] "Arrest Illegal Capital but Grant No Amnesty," *Asia-Plus* [Dushanbe], 18 April 2002 (FBIS Document CEP20020427000054).

Azerbaijani port of Sumgait.[260] Because law enforcement officials are poorly paid but exert substantial authority, they are susceptible to corruption and are known to solicit bribes even for routine traffic stops. The general public's distrust of the police discourages cooperation.[261]

Uzbekistan

Uzbekistan is mainly a transit country for narcotics; little domestic production is known. Although Uzbekistan has taken strong interdiction action in recent years, administration of its anti-narcotics program has been fragmented among three separate agencies: the Ministry of Internal Affairs, the National Security Service, and the State Customs Committee. The National Center for Drug Control, which nominally coordinates and separates the activities of those agencies, has not done so effectively. In addition, none of the three agencies specializes in narcotics interdiction, and they all face an acute shortage of resources. Corruption and bribery, which are a general problem in Uzbekistan's law enforcement agencies, have affected narcotics operations in some cases.[262]

A 2002 report by the International Crisis Group identified police brutality as a chronic problem in Uzbekistan. Says the report, "….the situation is so bad that it is vital that the government does something about changing the culture of police brutality within Uzbekistan."[263] The government of Uzbekistan routinely has used the police to detain and torture a variety of individuals deemed dangerous to the state on the pretext of criminal activity. This practice undermines public trust and the genuine crime-fighting authority of police agencies.

Moldova

Moldova is one of the poorest countries in Europe. Its economy has not responded successfully to the economic reforms of the 1990s, leaving a substantial part of the population in worse economic condition than it was when Moldova was a Soviet republic. The country's gross national product has shrunk by 60 percent since 1991, prompting extensive emigration. In the

---

[260] Personal communication from Tamara Makarenko, 7 October 2002.
[261] U.S. Department of State, *International Narcotics Control Strategy Report 2001.*
[262] U.S. Department of State, *International Narcotics Control Strategy Report 2001.*
[263] Eshanova, "Central Asia: Report Says Police Have Improved Little since Soviet Era."

same period, organized crime groups and official corruption grew rapidly when the Soviet collapse made public assets available to well-placed officials and existing mafia groups.

Corruption has remained endemic throughout the post-Soviet period; in 2002 Transparency International rated Moldova number 93 out of 102 countries evaluated in the organization's Corruption Perceptions Index.[264] Comparison with the number 64 ranking (out of 91) that Moldova received in 2001 indicates that corruption has increased substantially, in spite of the establishment of a Department to Combat Organized Crime and Corruption in the Ministry of the Internal Affairs. Police and prison officials reportedly are the most corrupt categories.[265]

The independence movement of Moldova's Transnistria region has fragmented law enforcement and created a zone of unrestricted smuggling in that region. According to international journalist Peter Landesman, "….there might be no place on earth that better represents the overlapping interests of governments, organized-crime syndicates and arms traffickers…."[266] Because Transnistria adjoins Ukraine and has poor customs controls, the province is a weak link in the country's anti-trafficking efforts. The large amounts of arms and munitions that remain in the region after its long post-Soviet occupation by Russia's 14th Army are attractive targets for arms dealers.[267] In 2002 the Ministry of Defense of Moldova was implicated with criminal organizations in a scheme to use smuggled oil to purchase arms in Transnistria, then sell the arms to Chechen rebels. According to a newspaper report, in this arrangement "….a criminal trade union was practically created under the umbrella of the top authorities. It includes gangsters on the one hand and high dignitaries on the other hand."[268]

Economic weakness has combined with weak law enforcement to make Moldova a primary country of origin for trafficking in women, many of whom see no hope of gainful employment in their home country. By 2000, such trafficking had become linked with trafficking in illegal arms and narcotics. At that time, trafficking in women was estimated to be one of the most profitable forms of organized crime in Moldova. According to the British Helsinki Human Rights Group, 60 percent of women active in the European sex trade are from Moldova. From

---

[264] Transparency International 2002.

[265] "Human Rights Group Says Corruption, Abuse of Power Still High," reported in *Basapress* [Chisinau], 21 May 2002 (FBIS Document CEP20020521000255).

[266] Peter Landesman, "Arms and the Man," *New York Times Magazine*, 17 August 2003, 55.

[267] Boris Volkhonsky, "Moldovan President Offers Dniester Region Compromise but Europe Pushes Him Toward Tough Stance," *Kommersant* [Moscow], 6 February 2002 (FBIS Document CEP20020206000176).

[268] "Paper Accuses Communist Authorities of Protecting Oil, Arms Smugglers," reported in *Tara* [Chisinau], 13 June 2002 (FBIS Document CEP20020617000276).

Moldova, women usually enter a trafficking network in Romania, where they are "sold" to traffickers who move them through Serbia to Bosnia, Kosovo, Albania, Greece, or Italy. (Relatively few Moldovan women go to countries in Western Europe, aside from Italy.) Along this route, women often come under the control of several trafficking groups.[269]

The market for Moldovan women in the Kosovo region, which is controlled by Albanian crime groups, has grown substantially since the 1999 occupation of that province by NATO and United Nations forces stimulated the demand for prostitutes.[270] In "competition" with Ukraine, Europe's other major source of women for the sex trade, Moldovan traffickers have the advantage of cooperation with their counterparts in neighboring Romania, based on their common language. A second advantage is Moldova's relative proximity to growing markets for the sex trade in the Balkans. There also seems to be a social base for the trade: in many cases, parents in Moldova have been willing to virtually sell their daughters to traffickers or pimps. Despite the prevalence of such trafficking, Moldova's police have little capability to respond. In 2001 the vice squad of Chisinau, the capital, consisted of seven men with no cars or special equipment.[271] A shortage of human organs for transplant operations in Europe and Israel also has promoted illegal trafficking in organs, which traffickers purchase for cash from poverty-stricken Moldovans.[272]

Narcotics sales within Moldova have been limited by economic conditions. However, narcotics seizures indicate some international traffic through the country. Moldovan traffickers are known to be closely connected with dealers in other East European countries. Domestic enforcement of narcotics trafficking is limited by a lack of government support funds.[273]

Russia

Terrorist activity in Russia has been connected with the ongoing independence movement of one of the federation's republics, Chechnya-Ichkeria, which began in 1992 and has included two periods of armed hostilities, 1994-96 and 1999 to the present. Despite cease-fires and

---

[269] British Helsinki Human Rights Group, "Sex Slaves: Trafficking in Human Beings from Moldova to Italy," 2001 report. <http://www.bhhrg.org>
[270] British Helsinki Human Rights Group.
[271] British Helsinki Human Rights Group.
[272] Peter Baker, "In Struggling Moldova, Desperation Drives Decisions," *Washington Post*, November 7, 2002, A14.
[273] U.S. Department of State, Bureau of International Narcotics and Law Enforcement Affairs.

diplomatic negotiations, factions of the Chechen freedom movement continued kidnappings and attacks on Chechen and neighboring territory throughout the 1990s and into the following decade. In October 2002, Moscow suffered the occupation of a concert hall and the taking of several hundred hostages by Chechen insurgents. The government attributed earlier detonations in apartment buildings in Moscow and elsewhere to Chechen rebels, although the allegations never received independent confirmation. In their second war against Russia, which began in 1999, Chechen insurgents have had an unknown degree of support from al Qaeda, which supplied the cause one major military leader, the Jordanian-Saudi mercenary known as Khattab.

As the largest of the countries emerging from the collapse of the Soviet empire in 1991, as well as the heart of that empire's economic existence, Russia suffered from many conditions promoting organized crime during its first post-Soviet decade. In 2000, Russian domestic policy expert Sally Stoecker described the domestic situation thus:

> In the wake of globalization and the weakening of the state, criminal organizations have assumed the roles that the state previously played and…have asserted their own form of authoritarianism. Not only do these criminal organizations exploit the chaos and high unemployment trends in Russia, they actively intimidate the populace in a manner not unlike the coercive KGB-informants and operatives of the Soviet era. Criminal organizations have penetrated the financial structures and political circles and block efforts to foster the growth of civil society in Russia. At the present time, Russia appears not only to be penetrated, but also ruled by corrupt officials and financial oligarchs and involved in crime and corruption at all levels of society.[274]

Pervasive crime within Russia also has engendered participation in transnational crime. Said regional crime expert Louise Shelley in 2003:

> Post-Soviet organized criminals are now major actors in international organized crime. They have acquired the distinction because of the diversity of their activities, the global reach of their operations, their links with other organized crime groups, and the sheer volume of their activity. Their involvement in weapons trade internationally and in massive money laundering has made them threats to national security on a regional and international level.[275]

---

[274] Sally Stoecker, "The Rise in Human Trafficking and the Role of Organized Crime," *Demokratizatsiya*, 8, no. 1 (Winter 2000): 130.
[275] Louise I. Shelley, "Crime and Corruption: Enduring Problems of Post-Soviet Development," *Demokratizatsiya*, 11, no. 1 (Winter 2003): 113.

The roots of such a condition extend back into and prior to the Soviet period. Soviet rule reshaped a long history of corrupt bureaucracy into its present form, in which specific groups of well-placed people benefit from links with government officials. Although Russia has experienced an economic upturn since Stoecker's words were written, the fundamental conditions have remained essentially unchanged. In the 1990s, criminal organizations took advantage of the availability of large state industrial enterprises to gain strong connections in critical industries such as aluminum and oil. Such a presence has assured those organizations of ongoing political leverage.[276]

Russia's organized criminal organizations evolved in the 1990s after the "thieves in law," as the founders of the Soviet-era black markets were called, adapted successfully to the post-Soviet collapse of law enforcement in Russia. The thieves in law have been traditional, tightly organized groups with territorial definition, although they are not based on ethnic or family structures as are equivalent groups in Italy and Albania.[277] In the late 1990s, such groups gradually were replaced by a younger generation referred to as the "authorities," whose legitimate outer surfaces are more compatible with the new tone of globalization. An important domestic condition for the growth of such groups is the inefficiency of Russian courts in arbitrating legitimate financial disputes. Instead of waiting for a court decision, many Russian businesses have turned to "security firms" controlled by organized crime.[278]

The new groups have given a more fragmented and pragmatic quality to organized crime, although territorial battles still occur. According to one estimate, between 1992 and 2002 the number of criminal groups in Russia tripled to 12,000. The "authorities" are much more willing to further their interests by establishing cooperative agreements with other domestic or foreign criminal organizations, and they move comfortably between the criminal world and the world of legitimate business.[279] This policy has reduced territorial battles with equivalent groups in Eastern Europe and other republics of the former Soviet Union while establishing international contacts that diversify Russian activity.

---

[276] Henry Meyer, "Russian Mafia Extends Tentacles Across the Globe," Agence France Press report, 15 August 2002.

[277] James O. Finckenauer and Yuri A. Voronin, *The Threat of Russian Organized Crime* (Washington, D.C.: U.S. Department of Justice, 2001), 4.

[278] Finckenauer and Voronin, 22.

[279] "The End of the Vory?" *Jane's Intelligence Review*, 1 March 2002; and Walter Zalisko, "Russian Organized Crime: The Foundation for Trafficking." <http://www.monmouth.com>

High levels of corruption in both civil and military sectors of Russia's government have caused serious concern about the security of the country's still formidable array of nuclear weapons and materials. Authorities have uncovered many incidents of conventional arms and technology sales by high military officials. The Russian military has been a fertile recruiting ground for organized crime groups requiring individuals familiar with weapons and security procedures.[280]

Nuclear security remains primarily the responsibility of a military force in which onerous duty conditions and low pay have constantly increased fragmentation, corruption, and incompetence. Antiquated security procedures complicate effective monitoring at nuclear storage facilities. Most known incidents of theft of nuclear materials have involved Russian security personnel.[281] In 1998 Department of State official Robert Gallucci described the threat posed by such a situation thus: "Russian mobsters would find a ready market for any stolen radioactive materials in Iraq, Iran and Libya, all of which are shopping for nuclear weapon components and maintain ties to terrorist groups."[282] In mid-2002, Russia's Federal Security Service reported increasingly frequent attempts by criminals to sell nuclear and chemical weapons components in Russia and in other countries of the former Soviet Union.[283] In October 2002, authorities in East Siberia stopped the alleged smuggling of 27 tons of enriched uranium out of Russia.[284]

Several areas of Russia have become centers of organized crime activity. Among the most heavily affected are St. Petersburg in the northwest, Yekaterinburg and Sverdlovsk in the Urals, and several population centers of the Far East. Because of the proximity of Western Europe and the existence of trafficking routes before 1991, Russia's northwest saw a heavy concentration of criminal groups in the early post-Soviet years, and St. Petersburg became known as Russia's "crime capital." The government of Vladimir Putin, who is a native of St. Petersburg, has attempted to reduce the role of the city as a hub of trafficking and violent crime.

---

[280] Todd H. Nelson, "Russian Realities: Nuclear Weapons, Bureaucratic Maneuvers, and Organized Crime," *Demokratizatsiya*, 8, no. 1 (Winter 2000): 146-47.
[281] Nelson, 148.
[282] Mark Johnson, "Nukes and the Russian Mob," *Journal of Commerce*, 13 (March 1998), 6, quoted in Todd H. Nelson, "Russian Realities: Nuclear Weapons, Bureaucratic Maneuvers, and Organized Crime," *Demokratizatsiya*, 8, no. 1 (Winter 2000): 147.
[283] Dmitriy Staroshin, "Osmium Worries FSB," Internet version of report from *Vremya Novostey* [Moscow], 27 September 2002 (FBIS Document CEP20020927000315).
[284] "Russian Customs Officials Seize over 27 Tonnes of Enriched Uranium," TVS [Moscow] report, 8 October 2002.

In recent years, organized crime has grown especially fast in the Far East of Russia, in large part because that region is politically and geographically remote from the center of national authority in Moscow. The increasing presence of Chinese and Japanese immigrants also has established connections between organized crime groups in the Orient and Russian groups in the Far East. In recent years, various combinations of Russian and Oriental gangs have opened a wide variety of trafficking and smuggling operations through the porous controls of eastern cities such as Vladivostok and Kharbarovsk. Fish, narcotics, stolen cars, and prostitutes are among the most lucrative categories. Organized crime groups have gained a strong foothold in municipal law enforcement and judicial agencies, stymieing the investigations of federal authorities.[285]

The industrial cities of the Urals also are a region of intense criminal activity. In the late 1990s, new groups in the Urals who engaged in economic types of crime merged with more traditional groups who still held significant power in the region. The resulting groups, included in what is called the Uralmash network, focus on global investment, the export of strategic raw materials (occasionally including radioactive materials) and arms, and buying real estate for money-laundering purposes. Uralmash also is firmly entrenched in legitimate business as co-owner of the Urals Commodity and Raw Materials Exchange and an estimated 140 commercial enterprises, including banking and financial institutions. Two major rival groups hold territory in the Sverdlovsk-Yekaterinburg area. In partnership with Western groups engaged in economic crime, Uralmash now has connections in Belgium, Cyprus, Hungary, the Netherlands, and the United Arab Emirates.[286]

Russia's border guard force and migration authorities, like its military, are vulnerable to corruption because of extremely low pay and poor working conditions. A number of regional offices of the Federal Migration Service (FMS), which controls the passage of migrants into Russia, have shown the effects of recent budget reductions. In 2001, the service's average monthly salary was US$36. Bribery and other misuse of authority have arisen in many such offices. Such behavior has been encouraged by the most recent Criminal Code of the Russian Federation (1996), which abolished imprisonment as a penalty for taking bribes.[287] Nikolay

---

[285] Yana Aminyeva and Viktoria Chernysheva, "Organized Crime in the Far East: Press Survey for the Maritime Province, January 2000," *Organized Crime and Corruption Watch*, Summer 2000, 28-30.

[286] Finckenauer and Voronin, 14-15.

[287] Fyodor Sinitsyn, "Corruption in the Federal Migration Service of Russia," *Organized Crime and Corruption Watch*, 3, no. 1 (Spring/Summer 2001): 15-19.

Kovalev, chairman of the State Duma Commission for Combating Corruption, offered a cultural explanation for the prevalence of bribe-taking by Russian authorities: "… in Russia in almost all cases there is no extortion, for there is no need for it: people voluntarily offer bribes. Therefore, on the one hand society complains, but on the other hand it provokes corruption and does not want to fight it. It is both an ailment of our society and its diagnosis."[288]

Among smuggling operations involving Russian cooperation with international criminal groups, compact discs and women are two of the fastest-growing categories. In mid-2002 United States authorities identified "massive CD pirating," some of which allegedly takes place in plants owned by Russia's military-industrial complex. Another plant allegedly participating in CD piracy was owned in 2002 by a company whose director, Oleg Gordyiko, at the same time also headed the Russian Chamber of Commerce's commission on intellectual property rights.[289] Under the control of organized crime groups, Russia also has become an important country of origin for the trafficking of women for sexual exploitation to Western Europe, the Middle East, and North America. Russia has no law specifically criminalizing trafficking; recruitment for prostitution is not a felony, and the early age of legal consent (14) makes prosecution difficult. Russia has prosecuted very few individuals for trafficking in persons.[290]

The incidence of currency and credit-card counterfeiting in Russia has increased sharply in recent years. In 2002 authorities reported a 50 percent increase in the counterfeiting of large-denomination United States and Russian currency; no counterfeit European currency (euros) had been identified as of August 2002. Chechen militants have been identified as primary distributors. Prosecution of alleged counterfeiters is difficult because Russia's law requires identification of counterfeit currency in circulation prior to an arrest.[291]

Ukraine

In 1998 regional crime expert Louise Shelley wrote, "The most pernicious element of the crime phenomenon in Ukraine is the criminal-political axis, the alliance among former Party

---

[288] Quoted in "'Overindulgence in Bribery,'" *RFE/RL Crime and Corruption Watch*, 2, no. 27 (July 25, 2002). <http://www.rferl.org/corruptionwatch/2002>
[289] "…And U.S. Ambassador in Moscow Calls for End to CD Piracy," *RFE/RL Newsline*, 1 August 2002. <http://www.rferl.org/newsline/2002/08/1-RUS/rus-010802.asp>
[290] U.S. Department of State, *Trafficking in Persons Report 2002*.
[291] "Russian Counterfeiting on the Rise," *RFE/RL Crime and Corruption Watch*, 2, no. 28 (8 August 2002). <http://www.rferl.org/corruptionwatch>

elite, members of the law enforcement and security apparatuses, and gangs of organized criminals. Much crime in Ukraine combines government officials' access to information or goods with the use or threat of force by organized criminals." More recent sources indicate that in 2002 these conditions still shape fundamentally the nature of criminal activity in Ukraine. In 2003 Jonathon Winer, a former deputy assistant secretary of state for international law enforcement, summarized the situation in Ukraine: "There's concentrated power, resources in very few hands, no oversight, no separate functioning judiciary, a huge porous border, huge inherited military facilities, lots of airstrips, a bunch of old planes. Ukraine is the epicenter for global badness….It's a one-stop shopping infrastructure for anyone who wants to buy anything."[292]

According to 1997 figures from the Ministry of Interior, only 3 percent of the criminal groups in Ukraine had international connections at that time. However, those groups, called *soobshchestva* (sg. *soobshchestvo*), have a broad base that includes former communist party officials, members of law enforcement and security agencies, and organized criminals. Such groups infiltrate legitimate industries and enterprises, and they stay ahead of law enforcement agencies by methodically updating their technological capabilities. They also cultivate relationships with the international criminal community. Although individual groups often specialize in a single criminal activity, as a whole the *soobshchestva* cover a wide variety of smuggling activities, vehicle theft, counterfeiting, money laundering, and the sex trade. Their international activities have been identified in nearly all countries of Western and Eastern Europe, the United States, Canada, and some republics of the former Soviet Union, with links to the indigenous organized crime groups in most of those countries.[293]

In the post-Soviet era, arms trafficking groups have taken advantage of two circumstances: the large and varied stock of military equipment left in Ukraine when Soviet forces withdrew and the disappearance of controlling military authority that resulted from the Soviet Union's collapse. In the 1990s, an estimated one-third of that stock was stolen and re-sold abroad. Arms originating in Ukraine have appeared in international conflict areas such as Angola, Bosnia, Liberia, Peru, Rwanda, Sierra Leone, and Sri Lanka. Some of Ukraine's legal

---

[292] Landesman, 31.
[293] Tamara Makarenko, "Ukrainian Mafia Moves into the International Crime Arena," *Jane's Intelligence Review*, 1 February, 2002. <http://web.osis.com>

arms exports to Pakistan are believed to have reached the Taliban in Afghanistan. Such a volume could not have been achieved without active participation by the national customs and security services and other government agencies. In 2001 a former mayor of the port city of Odessa said, "The [Ukrainian] arms business is totally criminalized. Here you will find the business interests of a number of institutions coming together."[294]

In October 2002, a United States and British fact-finding team reported on the possible sale of a radar aircraft detection system to Iraq and on the status of the Ukrainian arms export system in general. The poor cooperation that the team received from the Ukrainian arms manufacturing and marketing system led to the conclusion that "illegal arms transfers, particularly with the complicity of third parties, remain a credible possibility."[295]

Large-scale narcotics trafficking is a relatively new activity of the *soobshchestva*. Its development coincided with the expansion of the "Northern Route" that carries narcotics from Afghanistan through Central Asia and the Caucasus to Russia and Western Europe. Ukrainian groups have used their ties with Russian and Central Asian groups to make Ukraine a major transit country from east to west. In turn, the increased domestic demand for narcotics has promoted the growth of local groups catering to individual customers.

Smuggling of persons—both for the sex trade and for illegal immigration–also is a major activity with international implications. The declining economic conditions of the 1990s made Ukraine a major supplier of women for an international sex trade that extended from the Mediterranean to the Far East. Traffickers have delivered as many as 500,000 Ukrainian women to the sex industries of Greece, the Netherlands, and Turkey. In September 2001, Ukraine for the first time criminalized human trafficking, pornography, and sexual exploitation. The government also has formed anti-trafficking units at the national and regional level.[296] However, shortages of resources and ongoing corruption may block effective interdiction.

The smuggling of migrants by Ukrainian groups has depended on links with organized crime in China, Pakistan, Russia, and Sri Lanka. International authorities believe that Ukraine is a transit area for this form of smuggling as well. According to an unconfirmed report, as many as

---

[294] Makarenko, "Ukrainian Mafia Moves into the International Crime Arena."
[295] Australia, Ministry for Defence, "Report of the Experts Team Visit to Ukraine," 28 November 2002.
[296] "U.S. Department of State's Human-Trafficking Report," *RFE/RL Crime and Corruption Watch*, 2, no. 23. <http://www.rferl.org/corruptionwatch>

200 al Qaeda fighters may have been moved from Afghanistan to Ukraine by Pakistani smugglers who had ties in Ukraine.[297]

The unregulated commercial conditions of the 1990s also permitted Ukrainian criminal groups to penetrate the national financial infrastructure. Direct control of banks has provided the means for large-scale money laundering and the information necessary to engage in extortion rackets. In addition to banks, casinos, hotels, and exchange bureaus have become sites for regular money-laundering operations. Meanwhile, penetration of legal businesses has cemented the link of criminal and business groups and expanded the foundation of illegal financial operations. According to Ukrainian security authorities, organized crime has penetrated financial and credit systems, production markets, the energy industry, and the agro-industrial business. For these reasons, Ukraine has gained an international reputation as a hospitable location to launder illegal funds. In 2001 an international investigation requested that the Ukrainian National Bank close 20 accounts suspected of having terrorist connections. This request has met resistance because Ukrainian authorities fear the commercial repercussions of such a breach of bank secrecy.[298]

Like other countries of the former Soviet Union, during the past decade Ukraine has responded to international pressure with a variety of laws, decrees, committees, and resolutions dedicated to reducing corruption and organized crime. However, organizations such as the national government's Coordinating Committee to Struggle Against Corruption and Organized Crime (in operation since 1993) have been used mainly against small-scale offenders and political dissidents. Such organizations also have been the subject of political rivalries: in 1999 Parliament eliminated the Coordinating Committee's National Bureau of Investigation, and the Ministry of Internal Affairs and the Security Service have anticorruption agencies similar to the Coordinating Committee.[299]

An important factor in this lack of success is the continued existence of a very large shadow economy, where commercial and financial activities are beyond government monitoring. Many government officials have second jobs in the shadow economy, where their incomes are protected from taxation. Frequent changes of legislation, high taxes, and a complex bureaucracy

---

[297] Makarenko, "Ukrainian Mafia Moves into International Crime Arena."
[298] Makarenko.
[299] Taras Kuzio, "Ukraine's Virtual Struggle Against Corruption and Organized Crime," *RFE/RL Crime and Corruption Watch*, 2, no. 31 (6 September 2002). <http://www.rferl.org/corruptionwatch>

of inspection agencies are additional factors inhibiting effective shrinkage of the shadow economy.[300]

Privatization of state enterprises is another commercial condition that has promoted the criminal-political elite to which Louise Shelley referred. In the privatization process, former Soviet officials used their ongoing ties to post-Soviet governments to gain powerful economic resources. This elite continues to exert power by its control of the media and businesses in combination with access to government funds. Such a structure creates an axis of government officials, pro-government businessmen, and political parties, in which officials overlook corrupt and illegal practices by the other two segments in return for political support.[301]

The Former Yugoslavia

The nations that emerged from the collapse of the Socialist Federal Republic of Yugoslavia (SFRY) in 1992 have been plagued with crime-promoting conditions that have existed in the region since it was part of the Ottoman Empire. Bosnia-Herzegovina, Croatia, Macedonia, and the former Yugoslav Republic, now known as Serbia and Montenegro, all have societies based on family and clan ties that have resisted the rule of law. Says Balkan expert Christopher Corpora, "….a history of authoritarian regimes in the Balkans had led to tight informal networks at the grassroots level, some of which had turned to crime, hindering the growth of civil society."[302] In this context, organized crime groups have gained protection for a wide variety of criminal activities by establishing connections with state security and intelligence agencies, forming autonomous power centers that are immune to prosecution and are able to control local politicians and manipulate the media.[303]

The region also has been deprived of peaceful development by a long history of ethnic struggle. The most recent chapter of that struggle, in the 1990s, combined with geopolitical developments elsewhere in Eurasia to promote especially strong growth of organized criminal and terrorist activity and pervasive corruption. Because of its small, homogenous population and

---

[300] Kuzio.

[301] Kuzio.

[302] Nir Rosen, "Mafia Fuels Balkans Turmoil," Institute for War and Peace Reporting, *Balkan Crisis Report*, no. 333 (26 April 2002). <http://www.iwpr.net>

[303] Michael Dziedzic, Laura Rozen, and Phil Williams, "Lawless Rule Versus Rule of Law in the Balkans," *United States Institute of Peace Special Report*, no. 97 (December 2002), 1.

uniquely close ties with Western Europe, Slovenia is the only former republic of the SFRY not to be a major launch site for transnational criminal operations.

Bosnia and Herzegovina

Ethnic fragmentation among three groups—the Christian Croats and Serbs and the Bosnian Muslims—has played a major role in promoting criminal activity in this former republic of the SFRY. Historically, that fragmentation has been intensified by the prevalence of informal local power structures that have resisted central governance. The most recent manifestation of ethnic conflict, a war between the Serbian Bosnians on one side and the Croatian and Muslim Bosnians on the other, created new opportunities for criminal organizations and left structural problems that have survived the armistice of 1995. During the war the three nationalist parties, which "formed the nucleus of Bosnia's criminalized power structures,"[304] funded their political and military activities by smuggling and illegal financial transactions. The war profiteering activities of officials often crossed ethnic lines, and gray and black markets supplanted legitimate economic enterprises. The structures that permitted such activity have not changed substantially since 1995. The black market has in fact expanded since the end of the war, Bosnia continues to play a vital role in the highly profitable Balkans Route of narcotics trafficking, and the three ethnic parties continue to divert profits from state enterprises in the areas they control. According to a 2002 report, "Corruption continues to be endemic in the wake of the armed conflict. The impact of official connivance in, protection for, and even direction of smuggling and other forms of tax evasion is enormous."[305]

In the fall of 2002, an arms export scandal exposed a weakness in Bosnia and Herzegovina's arms export controls. The aircraft components firm Orao, which is owned by the state in the Serbian Republic of Bosnia-Herzegovina, acknowledged delivery of spare parts for fighter aircraft to Iraq, in violation of international sanctions on that country. Two or more other Bosnian Serb companies also may have been involved in the transaction, which was overseen by the Belgrade-based import-export firm Yugoimport and allegedly brokered by Serbian radical nationalist leader Vojislav Šešelj. Bosnia-Herzegovina's unique two-part state, which combines Serbian and Croatian-Muslim entities and has a rotating presidency, creates a division of

---

[304] Dziedzic, Rozen, and Williams, 6.
[305] Dziedzic, Rozen, and Williams, 6.

authority. In the Orao case, a Bosnian Serb arms company cooperated with a Serbian trading company, assumedly with the knowledge of the government of Bosnia's Serbian Republic. (The president of the Serbian Republic, Mirko Šarović, is a former executive in the Orao company.) In the wake of the Orao scandal, the government of Bosnia-Herzegovina suspended all arms exports until authority for such exports could be transferred from the two constituent republics to the central government.[306]

The breakdown of central authority and border controls also has acted to promote trafficking in women, for which Bosnia is mainly a destination country. Other important factors in this form of crime are geographic location near primary source countries Romania, Moldova, and Ukraine, which account for 95 percent of women in this status, and the absence of laws under which the operators of sex establishments can be prosecuted. The trafficking route usually leads through Hungary or Serbia. Local police are a major clientele group for the sex trade in which these women work; according to one survey, another 10 percent of the women work for "international clients," meaning civilian and military personnel in peacekeeping and diplomatic roles. Bribery and the falsification of documents are normal parts of the trafficking operation, in which a woman may be bought and sold several times along the route.[307] Border police often are instrumental in bringing women across the border between Yugoslavia and Bosnia.[308] The "Arizona" market, in rural Bosnia near the Croatian and Serbian borders, is one of Europe's largest black markets for women and a wide variety of smuggled commodities, including compact discs.[309] According to one 2002 report, traffickers routinely use Bosnia-Herzegovina's 432 "mostly unmanned" crossing points along the extensive mountainous border with Croatia.[310]

Corruption has weakened border controls and promoted trafficking. Because the economy has not improved substantially since the end of fighting in 1995, many Bosnians see appointments to official positions as opportunities to gain a profitable income through bribes.[311] The customs service of the Serbian Republic of Bosnia-Herzegovina suffered a major scandal in

---

[306] "Bosnia Suspends Military Exports," VOA News report, 29 October 2002. <http://www.voanews.com>

[307] Fredric Larsson, "Trafficking in Women to Bosnia and Herzegovina," *Trafficking in Migrants*, Autumn 2000.

[308] Andrea Gerlin, "Sex Trafficking Is Flourishing in Balkans," *Philadelphia Inquirer*, 15 April 2002. <http://www.philly.com/mld/inquirer>

[309] Michael Voss, "'Slave Trade' Thrives in Bosnia: High Unemployment Makes Women Easy Prey," University of Rhode Island Trafficking in Women from Ukraine Research Project, 8 March 2001. <http://www.uri.edu/artsci/wms/hughes/ukraine/slavebosnia>

[310] Ian Burrell, "Sex, Drugs, and Illegal Immigrants: Sarajevo's Export Trade to Britain," *The Independent* [London], 21 January 2002. <http://www.independent.co.uk>

[311] Burrell.

mid-2002 when 27 customs officers admitted having extracted an estimated US$15 million in bribes from customers. Customs service chief Groan Popover, who also is a senior member of the Serbian Democratic Party, was suspected of having masterminded the extortion scheme, which allegedly was supervised by his appointee as chief of the anti-smuggling department of the customs service.[312] This breakdown seemingly is another result of the autonomy of Bosnia's two republics from federal authority.

Croatia

In recent years, criminal groups in Croatia have been increasingly active. Based on substantial evidence, they have been implicated in a variety of domestic and foreign activities, including racketeering, narcotics trafficking, extortion, and international arms smuggling. However, numerous recent press reports indicate that Croatian authorities have not pursued such groups consistently or completely. The inconclusive results of domestic investigations of arms smuggling organizations, most notably the Opal Metals Plant, have been met with media accusations of official corruption. Well-publicized exchanges of narcotics and arms, managed by Croatian organized crime groups, have received limited responses from Croatian authorities. According to a 2001 newspaper report, arms smuggling has been protected by officials in Croatia's ministries of defense and internal affairs, the customs service, the intelligence services, and one of Croatia's main political parties, the Croatian Democratic Union (HDZ). Under such protection, says the report, "Croatia has become one of the larger distributors of arms and explosives for the European criminal and political underworld."[313]

Domestic crime activities also have not been prosecuted fully. Although two major, Zagreb-based organizations were known to dominate organized crime in Croatia in the late 1990s, in 2001-02 the Croatian state has recognized and prosecuted major figures of only one. The second, a narcotics-trafficking and racketeering group that Veto Slink ran before his assassination in 2001, has escaped prosecution. One explanation is that the state used

---

[312] Dragan Jerinić, "Bosnia: Serb Minister Resigns over Customs Scandal," Institute for War and Peace Reporting, *Balkan Crisis Report*, no. 343 (14 June 2002). <http://www.iwpr.net>

[313] Jasna Babić, "MORH [Defense Ministry] Protects Arms Dealers Who Smuggle Weapons to ETA and IRA," *Nacional* [Zagreb], 24 July 2001 (FBIS Document EUP20010724000372).

information from the Slink group in prosecuting the other group; the other explanation is that that group has bought protection from influential government authorities.[314]

Hrvoje Petrač, often characterized as the most powerful figure in the Croatian underworld, is connected with criminal groups elsewhere in the Balkans, but his link with the two domestic groups was not known as of September 2002. Although substantial evidence exists of Petra's criminal activities, the state never has sought to prosecute him.[315]

Croatia is an important transit country along the Balkan Route connecting Turkey with Western Europe. At present Croatia does not have the resources to adequately patrol its land borders or the extensive islands and inlets of its Adriatic seacoast, which is adjacent to the crime-ridden Albanian coast. The end of armed conflict in the former Yugoslavia has restored a large part of the pre-1992 trafficking along the Balkan Route.[316] Narcotics traffickers have sought to exploit Croatia's financial system to launder their profits. The system is handicapped in resisting such exploitation because it is widely dispersed and mainly cash-based. Bureaus of currency exchange and the real estate sector have been particularly vulnerable. Although money-laundering legislation was passed in 1997, as of 2000 no convictions had been achieved under those laws.[317]

The incidence of human trafficking through Zagreb has increased since international agencies put stronger border and customs procedures into effect in neighboring Bosnia-Herzegovina, which had been the "weak point" of the region for the smuggling of persons. Because neighboring Yugoslavia has no visa requirement for Arab and Chinese citizens, the successful reduction of trafficking through Bosnia has diverted many illegal migrants to Belgrade, from whence many move through Zagreb before entering Western Europe.[318]

---

[314] "Croatian Press Speculates on Underworld Groups' Ties to Establishment," FBIS Report, 24 September 2002 (FBIS DocumentEUP20020923000505).

[315] "Croatian Press Speculates on Underworld Groups' Ties to Establishment."

[316] U.S. Department of State, Bureau for International Narcotics and Law Enforcement Affairs, *International Narcotics Control Strategy Report 2003*.

[317] Organisation for Economic Cooperation and Development, Financial Action Task Force on Money Laundering, "Croatia." <http://www1.oecd.org/fatf/Ctry-orgpages/ectry-hr_en.htm>

[318] Hassan Haidar Diab, "Panic in Slovenia Due to Possible Release of Josip Lončarić," *Večernji List* [Zagreb], 21 November 2001 (FBIS Document EUP20011121000202).

Kosovo

Kosovo, economically the poorest region of the Federated Socialist Republic of Yugoslavia that disintegrated in 1991-92, has been a hotbed of crime and the raison-d'etre of several regional terrorist organizations. In the last decade, organized crime has become what East European security expert Neil Barnett characterizes as "the mainstay of the Yugoslav province's [Kosovo's] economy." Ongoing economic deprivation has combined with a strong but frustrated nationalist movement (including the goal to incorporate Kosovo and northern Macedonia into a "Greater Albania") and the involvement of Serbia in a series of regional conflicts, to make law enforcement impossible.[319] In addition, the Yugoslav government of Slobodan Milošević, faced with international economic sanctions from 1992 through 2000, ignored or encouraged the activities of organized crime groups whose smuggling supported the national economy.

The intense nationalism of the Kosovo liberation movement combined with severe repression by the Milošević regime to reinforce the collective identity of Kosovars, strengthening the unity of criminal groups.[320] Kosovar society's view of law enforcement as only a tool of repression has inhibited crime reduction measures.[321] These factors have made organized crime, particularly narcotics trafficking, an integral part of the volatile political situation in Kosovo.[322]

The United Nations and NATO forces that occupied Kosovo in 1999 were slow to take action against organized crime. Their reluctance to face this problem had two reasons: the establishment of political order and borders was the top priority, and the Western forces feared alienating local Albanian officials by assuming law enforcement functions. The view of many local Albanians and Kosovars that Western forces lack the authority to reinforce borders promotes the movement of illegal goods through the region. Typical of this phenomenon was the negative reaction of Kosovars and Albanians to the Belgrade-Skopje agreement of February 2001, which attempted to re-establish a firm border between Serbia (including Kosovo) and Macedonia. The terms of the agreement brought widespread opposition among the ethnic Albanian populations of Kosovo, Macedonia, and Serbia proper, prolonging the lawless status of

---

[319] Neil Barnett, "The Criminal Threat to Stability in the Balkans," *Jane's Intelligence Review*, 1 April 2002.
[320] Barnett.
[321] Ralf Mutschke, "Links Between Organized Crime and 'Traditional' Terrorist Groups," testimony to U.S. House of Representatives, Judiciary Committee, Subcommittee on Crime, 13 December 2000. <http://www.russianlaw.org/Mutschke>
[322] Barnett quotes a Kosovo police official on this subject: "Discussing Albanian politics without considering narcotics trafficking is like discussing Saudi politics without considering oil."

the region. According to Barnett, the political influence wielded by powerful heroin-trading groups is likely to delay stability in the region.[323] International authorities also are hampered by requirements of Yugoslav law, which remains in force because of Kosovo's ongoing international status as a province of Yugoslavia. Yugoslav law prohibits the use of devices such as sting operations, paid informants, and electronic surveillance. Albanian translators, on whom authorities must rely for communication with the populace, often pass police intelligence to criminals.[324]

The activities of a series of Albanian insurgent groups also have served the interests of organized crime in Kosovo. The Kosovo Liberation Army and its smaller successor groups, the National Liberation Army and the Albanian National Army, pursued guerrilla and terrorist activities for the liberation of Kosovo from Serbia and for the liberation of Macedonia's Albanian population from the Slavic majority in Macedonia. Smuggling and other criminal activities have flourished in regions held by rebel groups. The KLA and its successor groups are widely assumed to have gained substantial support from active participation in the smuggling of people and narcotics, which often have been exchanged for arms. Rebel areas also reportedly have supported production of amphetamines and the smuggling of cigarettes and weapons.[325]

The most significant criminal activity in Kosovo is the trans-shipment of heroin from Turkey into Western Europe, along the so-called "Balkan route." Heroin shipments move from Turkey through Bulgaria and Macedonia, then pass over the porous border between Macedonia and Kosovo before continuing either into southern Serbia and Hungary or into Albania. NATO forces have not been successful in blocking routes across the difficult terrain of the Macedonia-Kosovo border. Passage from Kosovo into Albania has been eased by especially poor security at Peč, on the Kosovo side. An important transit point in Kosovo is Podujevo, where rich and influential Kosovars support the trade. The so-called Italian Route, which passes through Kosovo and Albania before crossing the Adriatic Sea into Italy, has been established by closely related clans in Kosovo and Albania, each of which has its own specifically defined territory.[326] Fuel

---

[323] Barnett.
[324] "Law Enforcement in Kosovo," *Jane's Intelligence Review*, 1 April 2002.
[325] Barnett.
[326] Barnett.

smuggling also is a profitable form of crime, especially in the security zone between Kosovo and Montenegro.[327]

Macedonia

Lying between Bulgaria and Kosovo, Macedonia falls naturally on the narcotics transit line of the Balkan Route. Macedonia's location immediately south of the Federal Republic of Yugoslavia, which has been the subject of international trade sanctions since 1992, also has made it a natural path for smuggling activity in a variety of otherwise legal commodities. Although Macedonia has not suffered armed conflict at the level of its neighbors Bosnia-Herzegovina and Kosovo, internal ethnic conflict and the conflict between neighboring Serbia and Kosovo have removed some regions of Macedonia from effective law enforcement over a long period.

Especially important in this regard has been the city of Tetovo in northern Macedonia, which has been the site of fighting between Albanian insurgents and Macedonian forces, as well as between different groups of Albanian insurgents. Although the Macedonian government nominally controls Tetovo, local police have not cooperated in stopping likely smugglers as they pass through the city.[328] The government's border policy has been pragmatic. Macedonia has signed a bilateral agreement with Bulgaria, the one neighbor with which it has stable relations, but has relied on stopgap measures on the more problematic borders with Albania, Serbia, Greece, and Kosovo.

The U.S. Department of State does not characterize Macedonia as a major narcotics transit country, although regional instability caused trafficking to increase markedly in 2001. Nevertheless, the report notes, "The political will does not exist within the government to address seriously drug trafficking and its effects…, and needed legislation is likely to languish for at least another year."[329] Macedonia has several clan-based domestic narcotics networks, which specialize in transit links with and resale to organizations outside the country. Narcotics activity is centered in the western part of Macedonia, although transit lines extend to all

---

[327] "Kosovo: Fuel Smugglers Flourishing," Institute for War and Peace Reporting report, 28 February 2002. <http://www.iwpr.net>
[328] Barnett.
[329] U.S. Department of State, Bureau for International Narcotics and Law Enforcement Affairs.

regions.[330] The cities of Kumanovo and Skopje, which lie on a weapons smuggling route, have been documented as points where Kosovar insurgent groups exchange narcotics for weapons.[331]

The U.S. Department of State has identified Macedonia as both a destination and a transit country for the trafficking of women and children originating in Ukraine, Moldova, Romania, and Bulgaria and destined for Albania, Kosovo, and Italy. However, in 2002 Macedonia passed a new law against trafficking and associated activities, the judiciary has effectively prosecuted cases against traffickers, and government programs provide assistance to victims.[332]

Macedonia's role as a smuggling corridor and the recent decade of regional turbulence have made the country a likely target for money laundering and other types of financial crime. In 2001 the Ministry of Finance reported that about 1,000 financial crimes are committed per year, including fraud and forgeries related to privatization in the public sector, tax evasion, and money laundering. Money laundering is associated with trafficking in arms, alcohol, cigarettes, coffee, narcotics, and stolen cars; tax evasion; fraud; and corruption. According to the ministry, the main weak point promoting such activity is the Macedonian financial system's inability to monitor cash transactions, nonresidential bank accounts, and the privatization process. In August 2001, Macedonia passed a new law against money laundering, designed to comply with West European standards. The law established a Directorate for Money Laundering Protection.[333]

Criminal organizations operating in Macedonia have benefited from government corruption. An August 2002 report by the International Crisis Group described dishonest practices at the highest level of the government. Said the report, "In effect, the state has come to function in important respects as a 'racket,' and the racketeers thrive in a culture of impunity. It [corruption] is also a cross-community shared enterprise, and collusion between ethnic leaders serves to heighten tensions." Transparency International has estimated that corruption has deprived the state of 250 million euros (about US$250 million) in revenues. Irregularities have

---

[330] "Macedonia Has the Largest Transit of Drugs for the Albanian Narco Mafia," *Reality Macedonia* report, 6 November 2001. <http://www.realitymacedonia.org.mk>
[331] "Macedonian Government Confirms Ethnic Albanians Buying Arms from Drug Funds," *Nova Makedonija* [Skopje], 20 February, 2002.
[332] U.S. Department of State, *Trafficking in Persons Report*, June 2002.
[333] Darko Arsov, "Money Laundering: The Most Sophisticated Form of Organized Crime," *Ministry of Finance Bulletin* [Skopje], December 2001. <http://www.finance.gov.mk/gb/bulletins>

been found in the privatization of state enterprises, and customs officials have been implicated in freight transport and tobacco-smuggling schemes.[334]

Serbia and Montenegro

In the past 20 years, the states of Serbia and Montenegro, which since June 2003 have been the constituent parts of a loose federation formerly known as the Yugoslav Republic, have suffered especially from criminal activity because of political and international conditions. Although those conditions have improved markedly since 2000, reform has not yet disrupted many of the corrupt power relationships formed under the regime of Slobodan Milošević (1989-2000). That government has been characterized as a "kleptocracy."[335] According to former Belgrade police chief Marko Niković, the democratic coalition that gained power after Milošević accepted the support of the same criminal elements that had supported the previous regime, thus perpetuating the power base of those groups.[336]

In the 1990s, the international position of the Milošević regime contributed to criminal activity. At that time, trafficking of goods became more profitable in Yugoslavia when international sanctions cut the country's normal supply lines. The government and trafficking groups shared profits on fuel, consumer goods, cigarettes, electronic equipment, agricultural goods, and spare parts. State authorities worked with criminal groups to strip assets from state-owned enterprises, manipulate the national monetary system, and smuggle arms. Although the Yugoslav Republic[337] has made some reforms in the institutions that promoted organized crime since the ouster of the Milošević government in October 2000, in late 2002 Serbian criminologist Dobrivoje Radovanović reported that the infrastructure of criminal organizations, which was promoted intentionally by government authorities in the 1990s, remained intact:

> "… it is true that the police have been largely responsible for the existence of organized crime in our country since 1992. The State Security [Service] to be precise. They invited prominent underworld bosses to be their associates in the battle for the Serbian national interests in Bosnia, Croatia, and other parts. The secret police was through them involved in the plundering, war crimes, and war profiteering. They enabled every prominent

---

[334] Ana Petruseva, "Macedonia: Threats Follow Corruption Report," Institute for War and Peace Reporting report, 21 August 2002. <http://www.iwpr.net>

[335] Dziedic, Rozen, and Williams, 4.

[336] Michael Dobbs, "Pivotal Alliance Frayed Before Serb's Death," *Washington Post*, 14 March 2003, A18.

[337] This report treats one province of the Yugoslav Republic, Kosovo, in a separate section because of its unique circumstances.

criminal to have a DB [Security Service] identity card. A consequence of that was the overlapping of the secret police, the underworld, and the police."[338]

Although Radovanović found substantially more transparency in government operations than he did in the Milošević era, two years after the end of that era he still reported a substantial connection between Serbia's political underworld and its criminal underworld.[339] Confirming that view, a 2002 report of the United States Institute of Peace characterizes the State Security Service and the Military Security Service, which are Yugoslavia's two major intelligence agencies, as "virtually autonomous entities."[340] A 2002 regional corruption report found significant increases in corruption rates in Montenegro, the smaller of the states of Yugoslavia, between 2001 and 2002.[341]

According to Radovanović, Serbia is home to Albanian, Chinese, and Russian organized crime groups, although a "Serbian mafia" per se does not exist. Chinese groups have used Serbia as a staging area for illegal immigrants to move into the West, and Russians groups have used Serbia for both recruiting and transit of women for their prostitution industry. Serbia is a major transit country for women trafficked from the eastern source countries Moldova, Romania, and Ukraine to Bosnia-Herzegovina and points west. Some progress has been made against trafficking in recent years, however. The present government of Yugoslavia has eliminated black markets in cigarettes, oil, and precious metals, which attracted substantial foreign criminal activity in the 1990s.[342]

In the fall of 2002, the Yugoslav Republic was accused of government-sanctioned exports of illegal arms to two critical areas of the world, Iraq and West Africa. The nature of the transactions indicates knowledge by at least some officials in Yugoslavia's Ministry of Defense, and a major import-export firm has been directly implicated in the transaction with Iraq. International press reports also have accused Serbia's Yugoimport trading firm of having cooperated with the Orao defense plant in Bijeljina, Bosnia, and two other Bosnia arms companies in shipping fighter aircraft engines and air defense equipment to Iraq via Syria.

---

[338] B. Ristić, "Whose Arm Runs Serbia?" *Glas Javnosti* [Belgrade], 3 November 2002 (FBIS Document EUP20021104000406).
[339] Ristić.
[340] Dziedzic, Rozen, and Williams, 5.
[341] Southeast European Legal Development Initiative.
[342] Ristić.

Allegedly, ultranationalist Serbian Radical Party leader Vojislav Šešelj received a large profit from his role as mediator of the export deals with Iraq.[343]

In the West Africa case, six arms shipments were sent by the Serbian firm Timex, nominally on behalf of the Serbian military, via the Serbian shipping company Jitterbug.. The nominal recipient was the Ministry of Defense of Nigeria, but the actual destination was Liberia. In this case, Yugoslav authorities made two mistakes: they accepted false documentation from arms brokers stating that the shipment was destined for Nigeria, and they ignored a moratorium on small arms shipments to West African states, including Nigeria.[344]

The circumstances of the two arms export cases indicate weak arms export controls and official corruption. Although Yugoslavia is not rated as a major source of military supplies, United Nations authorities have urged the Republic of Yugoslavia to tighten arms-export procedures to reduce Yugoslavia's participation in chronic arms trafficking from Eastern Europe to trouble spots in Africa.[345]

Conclusion

In the past decade, the activities of criminal groups have found fertile ground in most of the countries of Central and Eastern Europe, and a substantial amount of terrorist activity has occurred in parts of the former Soviet Union and the former Yugoslavia. Such success has resulted from two sets of factors. First, the overall globalization and increased versatility and sophistication of criminal organizations (and, to a lesser extent, terrorist groups) have improved their ability to take advantage of weak customs systems, poorly guarded borders, corrupt officials, poverty-stricken national economies, and well-established shadow economies. Second, geopolitical and domestic conditions have provided such groups an increasing range of such favorable circumstances. Intense poverty in countries such as Moldova and Belarus creates a supply of women for transnational traffickers, and social mores prevent those women from returning to a normal life. The collapse of a major empire (the Soviet Union) has left large, poorly guarded arsenals of weapons in countries desperately needing money. This situation is

---

[343] Michael Wrase and Waltraud Kaserer, "Belgrade Smuggled Weapons to Iraq," *Welt am Sonntag* [Hamburg], 27 October 2002 (FBIS Document EUP20021027000097).
[344] Robert McMahon, "Yugoslavia: Arms Expert Traces Belgium-to-Liberia Arms Trafficking, Radio Free Europe/Radio Liberty report, 11 January 2002. <http://rfc/rl.org>
[345] "Yugoslav Arms-Export Scandal Grows," *RFE/RL Newsline*, 6, no. 207, pt. II (1 November 2002).

most alarming in Russia, where remnants of the Soviet Union's nuclear stockpile remain under very dubious control.

The collapse of the Yugoslav federation, which led to an escalated version of earlier ethnic strife in the region, has combined with the authoritarian ambitions of some leaders to destroy the rule of law in the western Balkans and created a platform for all forms of trafficking on the doorstep of Western Europe. The stress of the drastic economic transition that began in the former Yugoslav federation in the 1990s has left most governments unable to pay civilian officials or security officers enough to prevent widespread official corruption and the illegal sale of state property.

In many cases, in this region the corruption, trafficking routes, and shadow economies of the 1990s already were well-established under authoritarian regimes of the old Soviet system. In discussing these nations as hospitable to transnational crime, the role of such traditions cannot be over-emphasized. Even given substantially better economic incentives, in the countries most insulated from the incentives of participation in Western institutions (most of the Caucasus and the Central Asian republics), overcoming intrinsic attitudes toward the rule of law and economic behavior may simply require a passing of generations.

SOUTH ASIA

Introduction

South Asia is characterized by a disproportionately large number of intra- and inter-state conflicts having varying levels of intensity. These conflicts create a permanent degree of instability in the region that tends to attract and create organized criminal groups as well as insurgents with both internal and external agendas. Under these conditions, severely limited government resources face numerous battle fronts: illegal trafficking, separatist insurgencies, poverty, population explosions, an AIDS epidemic, and porous borders that states do not have the resources or will to police adequately.

Each of the countries of South Asia is a major producer, exporter, or transit area for narcotics. Many actors, including growers, traffickers, and government officials, have a stake in perpetuating this situation. In South Asia, politicians have frequently used violence and coercion as a means to attain political victory: votes often are won at gunpoint. This practice creates a nexus between politicians and criminals, as the latter supply guns and manpower to "sway" voter opinion.

South Asia has appeared prominently in international terrorism reports as well. Since the end of the Cold War, this part of the world has shown a strong linkage between terrorist and criminal activity. The relationships among parties who cause and benefit from South Asia's instability are extremely complex. Tribal, ethnic, sectarian, and economically motivated violence is so prevalent and intermixed that no single cause or motive can be identified. One factor in this complexity is the ambiguous distinction between terrorism and national liberation movements, which are very different labels applied to groups such as the Sri Lankan Tamil Tigers of Elam (LTTE) by different sides in Sri Lanka's chronic unrest. Nonetheless, certain identifiable trends and conditions in individual countries and across the region make South Asia ripe for organized criminal and insurgent activity, both inter- and intra-state.

A number of terrorist and criminal groups in the region have integrated themselves in the legal economies of more than one country. For example, the United Liberation Front of Assam, an insurgent group based in India's northeastern territory, owns legitimate businesses, including travel agencies, public relations companies, hotels, medical clinics, motor instruction schools, and shops in Bangladesh and Bhutan.[346] The D-Company of Dawood Ibrahim, one of India's most powerful criminals, is essential to Pakistan's economy. Ibrahim reportedly is highly influential in Pakistan's stock market, has invested billions in real estate, and has given financial assistance to the Central Bank during a financial crisis.[347]

Another regional problem is the interconnection of violent groups with government officials. Legitimate political parties often represent insurgent groups in government. For example, in Pakistan the leader of the banned Sipah-e-Sahaba Pakistan Party (SSP) won a seat from central Punjab province while in detention, and the Muthida Qaumi Movement, which is said to receive funds through both organized crime and the Indian government, also functions as a political party.[348]

---

[346] "United Liberation Front of Assam (ULFA)," *Jane's World Insurgency and Terrorism,* 7 March 2003.
[347] Nick Meo, "All Eyes on India's Most Wanted," *Sunday Herald* [Glasgow], 27 January 2002. <http://www.sundayherald.com/print21831>
[348] "South Asia, Internal Affairs," *Jane's Sentinel Security Assessment,* 15 May 2003.

Bangladesh

Bangladesh has suffered from the widespread organized crime and linkages to regional terror, criminal, and political groups prevalent in South Asia. Terrorism has been much less of a problem in Bangladesh than wide-ranging violence and lawlessness. Those conditions are fed by an arms market located at Cox's Bazar on the Bay of Bengal in the country's far southeast corner. Lawless and violent conditions in the northeast territory of India, which borders Bangladesh on the east, help to explain the location of this smuggling center. The ready availability of arms in turn contributes to Bangladesh's attractiveness to foreign terror groups and transnational smugglers. Much of the responsibility for this hospitable environment can be placed on the government and its legacy.

Role of Government

Newspaper accounts accuse political leaders in Bangladesh of fostering terrorism and crime to win the political upper hand and/or grow rich.[349] This situation is partially the legacy of years of military dictatorship, but it persists because of the ruling civil-military oligarchy's use of "thugs and goons" against political opponents.[350] Armed conflicts between supporters of the major political parties are a common occurrence in the countryside.[351]

According to one scholar, violence was an essential part of Bangladesh's coming into being and identity. The violence is carried over into the students' political groups, which traditionally play an important role in supporting political parties and have served as arenas for proxy wars by politicians. Student wings of parties now have their own armed cadres, supplied by underground arms dealers.[352] The only force available to counter this perpetual state of "human insecurity" is an ill trained and underpaid police force that is highly susceptible to bribes and often is directly involved in the arms trade.[353] In 2002 Transparency International named

---

[349] Dia Ganguly, "Justice and Force in Bangladesh," *World Press Review*, 12 December, 2002. www.worldpress.org/Asia/861.cfm.

[350] Neila Hussain, "Proliferation of Arms and Politics in South Asia: The Case of Bangladesh," Regional Centre for Strategic Studies [Colombo], *Policy Studies*, 7 (May 1999). <www.rcss.org/policy.html>

[351] "Daily Details Bangladesh as Transit Point for Arms Smuggling," *Dainik Janakantha* [Dacca], 16 July 2000 (FBIS Document SAP20000722000010).

[352] Hussain

[353] Ganguly

Bangladesh the most corrupt nation in the world for the second year in a row.[354] Even when corrupt officials are prosecuted, they generally receive no more than a reprimand.[355]

Student politics and terrorism have been strongly associated in Bangladesh. With the rise of the Jamiat e-Islami, the Islamic party, this association is becoming stronger. Militant Islamic groups such as the Harakat ul-Jihad ul-Islami, reportedly supported by al Qaeda, have grown bolder since the Jamaat e-Islami gained two cabinet positions and became the third largest holder of parliamentary seats in the elections of October 2001. In recent years, the militant youth wing of that party, dominated by students of madrassas, private Islamic schools, has increased in influence.[356] Because public schooling is unavailable to most students in Bangladesh and the madrassas attract funding from Saudi Arabia, those schools have grown rapidly in the last ten years.[357] Religiously motivated violence, particularly against the Hindu minority, has increased since the 2001 election, indicating at least a degree of political sanction.[358]

Arms Availability and Insurgent Alliances

Bangladesh's cycle of violence is perpetuated by the ready availability of arms from international smugglers operating at Cox's Bazar and Bandarban, a second arms trafficking point in the far southeast. That region also is home to insurgent groups and refugees from the conflict in Burma such as the Rohingya Solidarity Organization (RSO). Consignments of firearms enter Bangladesh through 30 unauthorized border points in addition to the international seaport of Chittagong and Cox's Bazar.[359] Smugglers receive arms from Cambodia via Thailand on high-speed fishing boats; directly from the Burmese military; indirectly from Burmese insurgent groups selling weapons stolen from the military; by theft or purchase from the Bangladeshi

---

[354] Transparency International, *Corruption Perceptions Index 2002.*
<http://www.transparency.org/cpi/2002/cpi2002.en.htm>
[355] U.S. Department of State, Bureau for International Narcotics and Law Enforcement Affairs, *International Narcotics Control Strategy Report 2002.* <http://www.state.gov/g/inl/rls/nrcrpt/2002/html>
[356] "United Liberation Front of Assam (ULFA)," *Jane's World Insurgency and Terrorism* [London], 16 (7 March 2003).
[357]Bertil Lintner, "A Cocoon of Terror," *Far Eastern Economic Review,* 4 April 2002.
[358] Rob Fanney, "Bangladesh: Harakat-ul-Jihad-ul-Islami," *Jane's World Insurgency and Terrorism*, 14 November 2002.
[359] "Daily Details Bangladesh as Transit Point for Arms Smuggling."

Rifles, a paramilitary group; and from private arms dealers on the Thai-Cambodia border, a transit point for illicit arms sales since the 1980s.[360]

Arms reportedly reach a variety of regional terror groups as well, including the Tamil Tigers of Tamil Eelam (LTTE) in Sri Lanka, rebel groups in India's northeast territory, Burmese insurgents, and domestic political groups.[361] The far southeast also is considered a stronghold of the Jamaat-e-Islami and its youth wing, as well as more extreme groups. Islamic fundamentalism appears to be on the rise in Bangladesh, equaling other domestic political movements in its use of violent means.

According to unconfirmed reports, training camps in Bandarban and Cox's Bazar have sent fighters to insurgent conflicts in Kashmir, Chechnya, and Afghanistan. Other reports describe fleeing members of the Taliban and al Qaeda having received shelter in southeastern Bangladesh in January 2002.[362] Indian intelligence has claimed that Pakistan's Interservice Intelligence Agency (ISI) has established outposts in India's West Bengal state, which adjoins Bangladesh's lawless corner, with the help of extremists from Bangladesh. Several legal arms factories in West Bengal may have facilitated such a move. Arms traffickers are known to have expropriated explosives, ammunition, and arms from those plants for the illegal arms trade.[363]

India

Several conditions make India potentially hospitable to transnational organized crime and terror groups. India is flanked by the leading producers and exporters of illicit heroin and is itself the largest producer of licit opium and illicit methaqualone in the world. The regional drug trade, over land, air and sea routes, is extremely profitable for groups willing to take risks, and pervasive poverty makes risk-taking worthwhile for a large percentage of the population. India's many internal separatist movements create a permanent state of instability and violence.

India has five less than ideal neighbors: Pakistan which is a long-time adversary in an enduring struggle over the northeastern state of Kashmir; Bhutan, Burma, and Nepal, which continue to battle their own insurgencies with inadequate resources backed by largely ineffectual state structures; and Bangladesh, which faces insurgencies similar to those in India's northeast

---

[360] Fanney.
[361] "Daily Details Bangladesh as Transit Point for Arms Smuggling."
[362] Fanney.
[363] "Daily Details Bangladesh as Transit Point for Arms Smuggling."

territory and is essentially the continent's arms bazaar.[364] The porous borders among such neighbors offer numerous opportunities for cooperation among groups willing to achieve similar short-term illegal goals, often with the assistance of corrupt politicians on both sides of a border. India's legal system is too slow and unwieldy to deter criminal behavior effectively.

Destabilizing Factors

According to regional experts, India suffers from at least five protracted internal wars, not including the Kashmir conflict, and approximately 100 domestic insurgent/terrorist groups are active.[365] The northeast region is host to several separatist ethnic groups that employ terrorist tactics and have forward bases in Bangladesh and Bhutan, revealing the transnational character of the conflicts in this area. Many of these same groups cooperate with each other or with other insurgent groups across India and the region, for the sake of expediency. Some of the groups allegedly receive support from Pakistan's ISI as well. Another destabilizing factor, extreme poverty, feeds perceptions of disparity and is coupled with coincidental ethnic, religious or tribal cleavages.

Regional Insurgencies and Conflicts

India's northeast region is connected to the rest of India through a very narrow corridor that is surrounded by territory belonging to Bhutan and Bangladesh. This geographical factor complicates India's efforts at control and exposes the region to transnational insurgency and criminal activity. Pakistan's ISI reportedly provides bases, weapons, and training to insurgents in the region, for example, and Bangladeshi law enforcement personnel engage in smuggling across their border into the region. Because of this situation, insurgents are able to establish bases in adjoining territory of Bhutan and Burma, over which those countries have little control.

---

[364] "The Arms Race in Bangladesh: Issues and Challenges," *The Daily Star* [Dacca], 29 July 2001.
<http://www.dailystarnews.com/law/200107/05/right.htm>
[365] Derived from listing at *South Asia Terrorism Portal*.
<http://www.satp.org/satporgtp/countries/india/terroristoutfits/index.html>

Smuggling and illegal migration are rampant in the region.[366] India has been fighting rebels in two states of the northeast region, Nagaland and Assam, since 1955 and 1990, respectively.[367]

Each of the region's seven Indian states is characterized by lawlessness, under-performing and corrupt institutions, and separatist conflicts that blur the distinction between insurgency and crime. According to one estimate, the United Liberation Front of Assam (ULFA) earned US $22 million from extortion in 2001. The ULFA also demonstrates another trend in the region: the growing cooperation among groups and the permeability of borders. At the end of the 1980s, the ULFA joined the Indo-Burmese Revolutionary Front (IBRF), which also includes the National Socialist Council of Nagaland, the Kuki National Front of Manipur Province, and the Chin National Front (a Burmese insurgent group fighting the government in Yangon). The United National Liberation Front (UNLF), based in Manipur, conducted activities on behalf of the ULFA in 2002. It also has alliances with groups in Burma that arrange weapons for the group, as does the ISI, by facilitating links with the LTTE in Sri Lanka and the Harkat-ul-Jihad-ul-Islami in Bangladesh. Bangladeshi and Burmese groups reportedly have crossed the border into India to escape reprisals after conducting raids in their respective countries. [368]

The nexus between crime and insurgency in the northeast region is growing as many of the insurgent groups engage in smuggling, extortion, and kidnapping. The drug trade is part of this nexus as well, crossing the border in both directions and leaving in its wake a narcotics addiction epidemic and a sharp increase in HIV/AIDS cases. The ULFA reportedly supplements its criminal activities with profits from legitimate businesses and front companies in Bangladesh and Bhutan. Such a strategy marks the passage of such groups into a kind of self-sustaining legitimacy.[369]

Conflicts in the states of Kashmir and Punjab have been active for more than ten years. Although Kashmir is an international conflict and Punjab domestic, both require long-term military presences. India has been in intermittent conflict with Pakistan over the disposition of

---

[366] Christopher Jasparro, "Transnational Pressures Destabilize India's Northeast," *Jane's Intelligence Review,* 12 November 2002.
[367] P. Sahadevan, "Coping with Disorder: Strategies to End Internal Wars in South Asia," Regional Centre for Strategic Studies [Colombo], *Policy Studies*, 17 (November 2000). <www.rcss.org/policy.html>
[368] "United Liberation Front of Assam (ULFA)."
[369] "United Liberation Front of Assam (ULFA)."

Kashmir since 1989. The conflict diverts 700,000 of India's combined army and paramilitary forces, leaving scant security to deal with other threats or groups that exist.[370]

Organized Crime

In some ways, organized crime in India is typical of the region. It is facilitated and spread by extreme levels of corruption and government inefficiency. It is used by politicians to coerce voters or to intimidate opponents. The opposite also is true; criminals enter politics to gain a different kind of legitimacy—and often are successful. There are also reports of collusion between entire ruling parties and certain organized crime groups, whose fortunes change as ruling parties change.[371]

Organized crime in India has an unusual transnational character and involves a variety of players. Transnational crime does not flow in the typical direction; its major figures are Indian, but they live abroad. The major figures—Dawood Ibrahim, Chota Rajan, Fazlur Rahman, Babloo Srivastav, and Farjan Malik—all operate from foreign bases, most often Dubai. The location of Ibrahim, who is the undisputed crime boss of Mumbai (Bombay), is unknown. Some sources claim that he is under the protection of Pakistani intelligence in Karachi.[372]

Ibrahim's notoriety is due less to his success as a crime boss than to his role in a 1993 terrorist bomb attack in Mumbai in which hundreds were killed. That attack purportedly was in retaliation for the destruction of a mosque and the slaughter of hundreds of Muslims by Hindu fundamentalists.[373] Another Dubai-based gangster, Farjan Malik, claimed responsibility for the January 2002 bombing of the American Cultural Center in Calcutta. Indian sources claim that both Farjan and Ibrahim are agents for Pakistan's ISI. Dawood and six other members of his gang are on a list of "20 most wanted terrorists" whose extradition India has demanded from Pakistan.[374]

---

[370] Ahmed Rashid and Joanna Slater, "Threats and Consequences," *Far Eastern Economic Review*, 6 June 2002.
[371] Molly Charles, "The Growth and Activities of Organised Crime in Bombay," *UNESCO*, 2001 Oxford, England; Charles, "The Drug Scene in India," presentation at Drug Abuse: A Symposium on Social Processes, Narcotics and the State," Mumbai, August 2001. <http://www.india-seminar.com/2001/504/504%20molly%20charles.htm>
[372] Meo.
[373] Meo.
[374] Muzamil Jaleel, "India's Demands," *The Observer*, 13 January 2002. www.observer.co.uk/international/story/0,6903,632110,00.html

Further highlighting the coalescing of groups and motives throughout the region is the case of another gang boss, Ashwin Naik, who is based in New Delhi. In 2000 investigators learned that Naik had been cooperating with the Sri Lankan LTTE in narcotics trafficking and extortion rackets in Mumbai.[375] According to Indian intelligence, during his election campaign in Uttar Pradesh state gangster Chhota Shakeel was implicated in an assassination attempt on Union Home Minister L. K. Advani in 2002, as were the ISI, Al-Furkan (formerly Jaish-e-Mohammed) and assorted "underworld people"[376] Ali Khan, a "Pakistani druglord," sent consignments of heroin across Pakistan's border with the Indian state of Rajasthan, from where it entered an LTTE-controlled network culminating in Sri Lanka.[377]

Because of its location, India always has been a key transit country for narcotics moving from Pakistan and Afghanistan and from the Golden Triangle to Europe. According to Molly Charles of the National Addiction Research Centre in Mumbai, in India's early days organized crime groups took advantage of restrictive national tariff and foreign exchange policies to establish profitable channels of illegal trafficking in numerous items, including narcotics. Although trade liberalization eventually removed the profit motive for the first wave of narcotics traffickers, their network still was in place in the early 1980s when new groups began developing a heroin market in India. Like other forms of trafficking, narcotics smuggling has profited from ongoing corruption in political parties and government bureaucracy.[378] Domestic heroin production benefits from India's international status as the world's largest legal grower of opium poppies for the pharmaceuticals industry; experts estimate that 10 to 30 percent of the legal opium crop is diverted to the manufacture of illegal heroin. In 2000 India produced 1,300 tons of opium gum.[379]

India is a major transition country in two narcotics routes that link Pakistan with Sri Lanka. The first moves heroin and hashish from Pakistan to Mumbai, where they are packed and sent by boat to the ports of Tuticorin or Rameswaram in Tamil Nadu state at the southern tip of

---

[375] "… But What about Remote-Control Operations?" *The Times of India* [Mumbai], 27 March 2000.
[376] "Advani's Security Beefed Up," *The Times of India* [Mumbai], 13 February 2002.
<http://timesofindia.indiatimes.com/cms.dll/xml/uncomp/articleshow?msid=882143>
[377] Nurupama Subramanian, "Delhi-Chennai-Colombo-Narcotics Racket Flourishes," *Indian Express* [Mumbai], 2 November, 1999. <www.indianexpress.comie/daily/19991102/ige02045.html>
[378] Molly Charles, "The Drug Scene in India," presentation at "Drug Abuse: A Symposium on Social Processes, Narcotics and the State," Mumbai, August 2001. <http://www.india-seminar.com/2001/504/504%20molly%20charles.htm>
[379] U.S. Drug Enforcement Administration, "India Country Brief," May 2002.
<http://www.usdoj.gov/dea/pubs/intel/02022/02022p.html>

India. The second route moves the same drugs from Pakistan to Delhi via Jaisalmer and Bearmer in Rajasthan, whence they are sent overland to Tamil Nadu. Both routes then bring the drugs from Tamil Nadu to Colombo or Jaffna in Sri Lanka.[380] Narcotics couriers move heroin via commercial airlines, mainly from Mumbai and New Delhi, to more distant international points.

India's large pharmaceuticals industry is the world's largest producer of illegal mandrax (the commercial name of the depressant drug methaqualone, whose legal use as a sedative ended in the 1980s). That substance has contributed substantially to addiction and drug-related crime in South Africa, which is a major consumer of that substance. Mumbai is the main Indian transit point for mandrax that is smuggled into South Africa.[381] In 2000 and 2001, Indian authorities confiscated shipments of more than one ton of mandrax each in Hyderabad and Mumbai, respectively. India's chemical industry also legally produces large amounts of chemicals such as acetic anhydryde and ephedrine that are precursors for the manufacture of amphetamines and other types of illegal drugs. As of 2002, the Narcotics Control Bureau, India's primary drug enforcement agency, monitored the distribution of some but not all of those chemicals.[382]

Organized criminal activities in India also include a thriving gems and semi-precious stones trade with both South Africa and Belgium. In trafficking transactions involving India, gold and diamonds frequently are an exchange medium for transnational money laundering. Diamonds also are used to disguise shipments of heroin because the value and weight of the two commodities are similar.[383] Other criminal activities include smuggling of luxury items; extortion; professional killings; money laundering through the hawala network; and trafficking in small arms, narcotics, and humans.[384]

As India develops into an important regional financial center, proceeds from criminal activities such as trafficking arms, gems, narcotics, and migrants increasingly are laundered in the country's financial institutions. Funds for terrorist groups also pass through India's system. India also licenses offshore banking units, which are not monitored strictly. Much of India's illegal money transfer is part of the international *hawala* system, which is impossible to control effectively because it depends heavily (although not exclusively) on barter and credit. Gold and

[380] "LTTE's Drug Trafficking Links," *Daily Reports from Reality of Sri Lanka*, 15 March 2000. <www.realityofsrilanka.com/d153Mar00.htm>
[381] "Mandrax," *Electronic Doctor* [South Africa]. <http://www.edoc.co.za/drughelp/mandrax>
[382] U.S. Drug Enforcement Administration.
[383] Charles.
[384] Neeraj Kumar, "Organized Crime," *PoliceSpeak*, November 1999. <www.india-seminar.com/1999/483.htm>

diamonds are the most frequently exchanged commodities in this system. India passed a comprehensive bill criminalizing money laundering only in January 2003; the new financial investigative unit required by the bill has not yet gone into service.[385]

Corruption

Although India has official policies against organized criminal activity, corruption at all levels of the government, from border officials to law enforcement agencies to politicians, makes them wholly ineffective. In fact, corruption is so endemic that crematorium workers demand bribes to ensure enough wood is used to burn the dead.[386] Of the 68 precincts in Mumbai, eight are regularly auctioned off to the officers with the highest bid. Their popularity is due to their locations near brothels, airports, and the homes of major criminals where bribery will make these officers rich over a term that lasts at least three years.[387]

Corruption has been especially dangerous in the northeast region, where the ability to control international borders is especially important. In some cases, government personnel assigned to this region collect their pay without ever taking their post or continue to collect after having abandoned the post. Corruption among law enforcement personnel in the northeast is so serious that army units burn narcotics confiscated at border crossings to avoid handing the drugs over to superiors who would resell them.[388]

The involvement of politicians at the national level with organized criminal groups is indicated by the rise and fall of these groups with changes in the political leadership. The Congress Party, for example, backed the Varadharajan criminal group, which had a strong Tamil membership in Mumbai. With the rise of the anti-Tamil Shiv Sena Party in Mumbai in the mid-1990s, the Varadharajan group lost its strong position and other groups prospered in its place.[389]

---

[385] U.S. Department of State, Bureau for International Narcotics and Law Enforcement Affairs, *International Narcotics Control Strategy Report 2003*. (Washington, D.C.: 2003), XII-183-84.
[386] "India 2002-2003," *Jane's World Armies*, 8 April 2002.
[387] Charles, "The Growth and Activities of Organised Crime in Bombay."
[388] Jasparro.
[389] Charles, "The Growth and Activities of Organised Crime in Bombay."

Government-Sanctioned Sectarian Violence

Political parties and elements of the national government are known to have supported violent actions against certain groups in India. The Hindu nationalist ruling party, the Bharatiya Janata Party or BJP, has taken actions against Muslims in the provinces of Gujarat and Kashmir that have the effect of promoting and condoning sectarian violence. If the BJP remains in power, like-minded transnational groups might begin operating with impunity. The government of India currently employs a force of former militants and criminals, the so-called "Special Operations Group," to fight its war in Kashmir. The force has been better known for extortion from innocent villagers than for combating militants. Indian government officials also have been implicated in the murder of a popular anti-India Kashmiri leader, Abdul Ghani Lone, in May 2002.[390]

India's prosecution of military actions also has come into question. According to the 2001 Human Rights Watch World Report, India's security forces and unofficial paramilitary forces in the Kashmiri conflict have been guilty of "extra-judicial executions, "disappearances," "deaths in custody, torture, and rape," and the government has not investigated these charges.[391]

The Indian government has tried to pressure its neighbors and keep them weak through the proxy use of militants. Examples of this practice are support for insurgencies such as the LTTE in Sri Lanka and the Chittagong Hill rebels in Bangladesh. In such cases, India's neighbors have followed suit when they have had the capability to exploit the presence of insurgencies in India. A newer trend in India is support by the Hindu nationalist government for domestically rooted sectarian terror against Muslim and other targets.[392] In the case of deadly riots against Muslim communities in Gujarat Province in June 2002, human rights groups contended that much of the violence was planned carefully in advance and carried out with state approval and orchestration.[393]

Nepal

Nepal's porous borders and proximity to unstable neighbors recently has made that country a growing transit point for illegal trafficking. Trafficking in people for the sex trade is a

---

[390] Rashid and Slater.
[391] Human Rights Watch, "World Report 2001." http://www.hrw.org/wr2k1/
[392] "South Asia," *Jane's Sentinel Security Assessment:*, 3 September 2002.
[393] Human Rights Watch, "World Report 2003." <http://www.hrw.org/wr2k3>

chronic problem. According to one estimate, 12,000 Nepalese girls and women are trafficked into the sex trade in India annually.[394] In the words of one report, "Brothels in the big cities of India and Pakistan are overflowing with women and girls from villages in Nepal and Bangladesh."[395] The major factors in this situation are the acute poverty that afflicts many regions of Nepal, a patriarchal society in which women have subservient status, the caste system, and the virtual lack of border controls between Nepal and India. A concentration of busy market towns on both sides of the Nepal-India border provides transnational agents and brokers an anonymous atmosphere and easy access to transportation.[396] A 2001 report identified eight primary trafficking routes from Nepal into India. The final destination may be a brothel, a circus, or a factory.[397] As of late 2002, the government of Nepal had taken no effective action against the trafficking problem.[398]

Narcotics trafficking is an emerging problem in Nepal. Heroin is smuggled across Nepal's open border with India and through Tribhuvan International Airport at Katmandu. Nepal lacks adequate security measures to control transit along borders or at the airport. Recent arrests of Nepalese couriers may indicate that Nepal's role is increasing in trafficking to points in South and East Asia.[399]

Pakistan

In Pakistan, as elsewhere in the region, the line between political and criminal violence is becoming obscured. As in Bangladesh, this situation is partly a result of the ready availability of arms and the presence of armed party activists who also are engaged in criminal activities. In some cases, such groups also have links to terrorist organizations. Pakistan's distinctiveness in this area comes from the well-known and significant role of its intelligence services in backing certain terrorist organizations and in furthering the army's political goals. Combined with a

---

[394] Debra Armentrout, "Child Trafficking Continues to Threaten Young Women in India," Digital Freedom Network report, 15 November 2002. <http://www.dfn.org/news/india/trafficked.htm>

[395] Saurabh Bhattacharya, "Sex Workers See Freedom in Rules and Regulations," Inter Press Service report, 15 December 1997. <http://www.oneworld.org/ips2/dec/india3.html>

[396] Armentrout.

[397] International Labour Organization, "Nepal: Trafficking in Girls with Special Reference to Prostitution: A Rapid Assessment," November 2001. <http://www.ilo.org/public/english/standards/ipec/simpoc/nepal/ra/trafficking.pdf>

[398] Armentrout.

[399] U.S. Department of State, Bureau for International Narcotics and Law Enforcement Affairs, *International Narcotics Control Strategy Report 2003,* VII-18, 19.

corrupt and ill-trained police force, these conditions make Pakistan a particularly popular and willing host for non-indigenous and indigenous criminal and terrorist groups.

Terrorism and Destabilization Movements

Having fought three wars with India in the past 50 years, and being constantly on the verge of a fourth over the issue of independence for India's state of Kashmir, Pakistan views its national security as inversely proportionate to India's strength. Thus, Pakistan's military and intelligence agencies, notably the ISI, focus on destabilizing or otherwise occupying India through various means. In Kashmir this has meant supplying and training armed groups involved in Kashmir's nationalist struggle.[400] Militant groups trained and armed by the ISI and often based in Pakistan have assumed increasing roles in the Kashmir region. Such groups are composed mainly of non-Kashmiris and include individuals with ties to the Afghan wars and al Qaeda.[401] Because repatriation of such groups is a domestic security risk for Pakistan, duty in the Kashmir campaign serves as a convenient alternative.[402]

Beginning in the 1990s, Pakistan has been a key home base for several Islamic extremist groups, which have enjoyed substantial support among sectors of the population. Such groups benefit from Pakistan's tribal social structure, which affords substantial regional autonomy and impedes law enforcement by central authorities. The groups also reportedly have benefited from the protection of the ISI, which earlier had been deeply involved in the sale of drugs to support the mujahideen in Afghanistan,[403] and from the military, which cultivated the groups as a bulwark against India.[404]

After September 11, the Musharraf government yielded to pressure from the United States by beginning repression of several major extremist groups believed to have direct or indirect connections with al Qaeda. Those groups included the designated terrorist groups Lashkar-e-Tayyaba and Jaish-e-Mohammed and the Jamiat Ulema-l-Islami Islamic religious group, one faction of which is aligned with Jaish-e-Mohammed.. The central goal of all three

---

[400] Maseeh Rahman, "Facing into a Storm," *Far Eastern Economic Review*, 11 October 2001.
[401] Muzamil Jaleel, "Kashmiris Tell Militants to Go," *The Observer*, 13 January 2002.
[402] "Pakistan," *Jane's World Armies*, 12 (17 June 2002).
[403] Suba Chandran, "Drug Trafficking and the Security of the State: Case Study of Pakistan," Institute for Defence Studies and Analyses [New Delhi] report, 1997. <http://www.idsa-india.org/an-sep8-7.html>
[404] Regional expert Ahmed Rashid, cited in John Lancaster, "Reshaping Pakistan along Religious Lines," *Washington Post*, 20 June 2003, A1.

groups is the liberation of Kashmir from rule by India, and all three have been linked to al Qaeda.[405] The government also began restriction of the curricula of the madrassas (Islamic religious schools). Especially in northwestern Pakistan, madrassas taught exclusively an extremist version of Islam, to the exclusion of other subjects. A number of terrorist activists allegedly had emerged from this system.[406] Because of the ISI's earlier links with terrorist organizations,[407] however, the commitment of the Pakistani government to ridding the country of terrorist organizations has remained unclear. In mid-2003, a coalition of six radical Islamist parties constituted the main opposition party to Musharraf's military government and fully controlled Pakistan's Northwest Province, which borders Afghanistan. The cultural and political influence of fundamentalist groups reportedly was increasing in other parts of Pakistan as well.[408]

The ISI has been accused of cooperating with non-indigenous terror groups to destabilize India and other neighboring countries. Recent reports claim that the ISI has supported the use of Nepal as a base for insurgent attacks in the strategic Shiliguri corridor, which links India's northeast territory with the rest of India.[409]

Evidence indicates that gunmen of the Pakistan-based Harakat ul-Mujahidin Islamic militant group were involved in the American Cultural Center attack in Calcutta in January 2002. The Harakat, which reportedly receives substantial funding from Saudi Arabia,[410] also has been accused of links to the radical groups in Kashmir, including the Lashkar-e-Tayyiba and Jesh-e-Mohammedi, as well as to al Qaeda. The Harakat also may have maintained a presence in Afghanistan before October 2001.[411] In June 2003, regional expert Ahmed Rashid reported that most of the senior leaders of the Taliban had found refuge in Pakistan and were reconstituting the

---

[405] "Lashkar-e-Toiba," BBC News report, 25 November 2002.
<htttp://news.bbc.co.uk/2/hi/south_asia/2510613.stm>; and U.S. Department of State, "Jaish-e-Mohammed (JEM) (Army of Mohammed)," *Patterns of Global Terrorism 2001*, cited in *Naval Postgraduate School Terrorist Group Profiles, 2002*. <http://library.nps.navy.mil/home/tgp/jem.htm>
[406] U.S. Department of State, *Patterns of Global Terrorism 2001*.
<http:www.state.gov/s/ct/rls/pgtrpt/2001/html/10237.htm>
[407] See, for example, Michel Chossudovsky, "The Role of Pakistan's Military Intelligence (ISI) in the September 11 Attacks." <http://globalresearch.ca/articles/CHO111A.html>
[408] Lancaster.
[409] Jasparro.
[410] "South Asia, Internal Affairs," *Jane's Sentinel Security Assessment*, 15 May, 2003.
[411] "United Liberation Front of Assam (ULFA)."

Islamic fundamentalist movement that United States forces pushed out of Afghanistan in 2001 and 2002.[412]

Trafficking Activities

Pakistan plays an important role in regional arms trafficking. In the 1980s, the country was a major conduit of arms from the United States to the mujahideen insurgents fighting the Soviet Union in neighboring Afghanistan. According to one estimate, 70 percent of the total arms in the conduit were diverted from their intended destination by Pakistan's ISI, which controlled distribution from Pakistan into Afghanistan. Many of those weapons and supplies have remained in Pakistan, supporting an abundant, diversified market that has been centered around the city of Peshawar. In recent years, that market has supplied several of the insurgent groups of South and Southeast Asia, including the Abu Sayyaf and Moro Islamic Liberation Front in the Philippines.[413] This source also has armed Islamic extremist groups within Pakistan and in the disputed territory of Kashmir.[414]

Pakistan also has played a primary role in the narcotics trade of its region, as a producer, a transit country, and a final destination. In the 1970s and 1980s, Pakistan became a center of narcotics trafficking because of several factors. Events in Iran and Afghanistan pushed narcotics trafficking from those countries eastward into Pakistan. Narcotics earnings also proved an effective way for Pakistan to support the mujahideen insurgent groups in Afghanistan against the Soviet Union occupation that began in 1979. In the same period, Pakistani narcotics trafficking clans gained substantial political power by establishing ties with parties and government and army officials, thus protecting the narcotics trade.[415] As vigorous government campaigns virtually eliminated domestic poppy cultivation in Pakistan by 2001,[416] the easy availability of heroin from Afghanistan sharply increased addiction rates in Pakistan, maintaining the country's place along the South Asian trafficking routes. Pakistan's poor drug treatment program has

---

[412] Ahmed Rashid, "America's War on Terror Goes Awry in Pakistan, *Yale Global*, 4 June 2003.
[413] Peter Chalk, "Light Arms Trading in SE Asia," *Jane's Intelligence Review*, 1 March 2001.
<http://www.rand.org/hot/op-eds/030101JIR.html>
[414] International Action Network on Small Arms, "Pakistan Begins Major Campaign to Seize Illegal Weapons," 30 May 2001. <http://www.iansa.org/news/2001/may_01/pak_beg.htm>
[415] Chandran.
[416] U.S. Department of State, *International Narcotics Control Strategy Report 2002*.

allowed this driver to increase domestic demand in recent years.[417] The Anti-Narcotics Force, Pakistan's chief narcotics law enforcement agency, suffers from low personnel and funding levels, although the agency's performance improved in 2002.[418]

Thus Pakistan remains an important transit country for Afghan opiates and hashish. Heroin and opium enter across the Northwest Frontier and Baluchistan provinces. Some of these drugs supply the local market, and others go on to India via Lahore, Pakistani ports, or Iran.[419] Pakistani organized crime plays an important role in financing and organizing opium production in Pakistan. Actors involved in the drug trade include the ISI, politicians, and criminals. Among major drug traffickers indicted in 2002 were two politicians, one of whom was re-elected despite pending drug trafficking charges.[420]

The events of September 11 prompted the U.S. Department of State to initiate the Pakistan Border Security Project to aid Pakistan in controlling its mountainous, notoriously porous, 1,450-mile border with Afghanistan, across which narcotics, arms, and terrorist fighters (including perhaps Osama bin Laden) have passed virtually without control. Based on that program, in 2002 the government of Pakistan began a large-scale border security program, the results of which are not yet clear.[421]

Sri Lanka

In Sri Lanka, terror and organized crime share largely the same source, the Tamil Tigers of Tamil Eelam (LTTE). The LTTE, which has a distinctly transnational dimension, is rated as one of the deadliest terror groups in the world. The LTTE finances its insurgency through various forms of organized criminal activity, mostly drug and immigrant smuggling. Because of its geographic position and easy accessibility by sea and air, Sri Lanka is a convenient transit route for drugs moving to Europe from the Golden Crescent and the Golden Triangle. The LTTE is heavily involved in both this trade and human smuggling, using the group's own networks of Tamils throughout Europe. Large sections of Sri Lanka are actually under the control of the

---

[417] Nadeem Iqbal, "Drug Abuse Grows on Bumper Poppy Crop in Afghanistan," Inter Press Service report, 15 January 2003. <http://www.aegis.com/news/ips/2003/IP030107.htm>
[418] U.S. Department of State, *International Narcotics Control Strategy Report 2003.*
[419] "South Asia, Internal Affairs."
[420] U.S. Department of State, *International Narcotics Control Strategy Report 2002.*
[421] U.S. Department of State, *International Narcotics Control Strategy Report 2002.*

LTTE, severely limiting the government's ability to control crime. Law enforcement resources are stretched thin by the government's campaign against the LTTE insurgency.

Liberation Tigers of Tamil Eelam (LTTE)

Although a ceasefire was declared in Sri Lanka's civil war in December 2001, in 2002 the U.S. Department of State reported that the LTTE had not yet renounced its use of terror.[422] Of the estimated 65,000 people who have died in the civil war that has raged intermittently since 1983, most were victims of the LTTE. Known for a cadre of suicide bombers called the Black Tigers, the LTTE claimed responsibility for the assassinations of former Indian prime minister Rajiv Ghandi in 1991 and Sri Lankan President Ranasinghe Premadasa in 1993. The LTTE reportedly purchases weapons, raises funds, and propagandizes overtly. Its front organizations support LTTE by lobbying foreign governments and the United Nations.[423]

The LTTE, which is fighting for creation of an independent Tamil state in northern and eastern Sri Lanka, uses its control of the strategically vital Jaffna Peninsula to take a percentage of all goods smuggled into the country. In addition, the LTTE extorts money and property from citizens in the areas it controls. The group has begun supplementing its military power with technological weapons; in 2000 the LTTE became the first militant group known to engage in cyber warfare when it paralyzed Sri Lankan government websites worldwide and broadcast its own political messages over the Internet.[424]

Organized Crime Activity

Much of Sri Lanka's growing narcotics traffic from South Asia is controlled by the LTTE. Sri Lanka's 1,100 miles of coastline cannot be adequately patrolled because Sri Lanka has no coast guard and its naval forces are heavily involved in intercepting arms deliveries to the LTTE.[425] In June 2000, authorities made a record seizure of 38 kilograms of heroin from a vessel

---

[422] U.S. Department of State, *Patterns of Global Terrorism 2002.*
<http://www.usis.usemb.se/terror/terror/rpt2002/index.html>
[423] U.S. Department of State, *Patterns of Global Terrorism 2001.*
[424] Nirmal Ghosh, "LTTE's Global Shadow Economy Behind Violence," *The Straits Times*, 24 May 2000.
[425] U.S. Department of State, *International Narcotics Control Strategy Report 2002.*

sailing from India to Sri Lanka.[426] Officials believe that much of the hundreds of pounds of heroin seized in southern India each year is bound for Sri Lanka. Large consignments of cannabis and heroin from Pakistan are believed to reach Sri Lanka for shipment through Colombo International Airport and Sri Lankan seaports to destinations outside the region[427]

Sri Lanka's narcotics trafficking is characterized by the cooperation of various national groups and by official corruption. A Delhi-based gangster, Ashwin Naik, was implicated in drug and extortion rackets with the LTTE before his arrest in 2000. According to a 1999 report, similar connections involved Pakistan. Tamils involved in the India-Sri Lanka drug trade were not only associates of Naik but also of Ali Khan, a "Pakistani drug lord" who sent consignments of heroin across Pakistan's border with the Indian state of Rajasthan, from where it entered the Tamil network at Delhi.[428] Two narcotics routes are known to link India, Pakistan, and Sri Lanka. The first moves narcotics from Pakistan to Mumbai, where they are packed and sent by boat to the ports of Tuticorin or Rameshwaram in Tamil Nadu state at the southern tip of India. The second route moves drugs from Pakistan to Delhi via Jaisalmer and Bearmer in Rajasthan, whence they are sent overland to Tamil Nadu. Both routes bring the drugs in Tamil Nadu to Colombo or Jaffna in Sri Lanka.[429]

SOUTHEAST ASIA

The Southeast Asian nations of Indonesia, Malaysia, the Philippines, and Thailand have provided valuable services for international terrorist groups and organized crime groups. These countries have functioned as safe havens, training grounds, meeting places, money-laundering centers, and centers for trafficking in arms, humans, and narcotics. The area is ripe for this kind of activity because of its large populations of Muslim minorities (excepting predominantly Muslim Indonesia), poor banking transparency, weak border controls, and geographic proximity to the Golden Triangle, a region that includes parts of western Burma, northwestern Thailand, and China's Yunnan Province and is the origin of most of the region's drug supply. Slow

---

[426] U.S. Department of State, Bureau for International Narcotics and Law Enforcement Affairs. *International Narcotics Control Strategy Report 2001.*
[427] Asian Harm Reduction Network, "Revisiting The Hidden Epidemic: A Situation Assessment of Drug Use in Asia in the Context of HIV/AIDS." <http://www.ahrn.net/rapidassessment.pdf>
[428] Subramanian.
[429] Ghosh.

economic development and governmental instability add to the mix, as do the bustling tourist markets and lax visa laws that lead to relatively unimpeded transnational movement. In Indonesia, Malaysia, and the Philippines, discontented Muslim groups provide a friendly environment for terrorist activity. Government and corruption, which manifests itself in various ways in the region, plays a role in promoting criminal activity in all the Southeast Asian countries discussed in this report. Another Southeast Asian nation, Singapore, does not provide the same hospitable environment and hence is thought to have become a target, rather than a haven, for terrorist organizations.[430]

Indonesia

Terrorist Activity

In the past decade, Indonesia has been a significant target of terrorist acts and the base for terrorist groups. A major factor in this situation has been the laxness of the Indonesian government in controlling indigenous and foreign terrorist groups, which have found adequate shelter in the country's Muslim population. Constituting about 87 percent of Indonesia's 212 million people, Indonesia's is the largest Muslim population in any country of the world.[431] Continued Muslim dissatisfaction over political rule and consistently unstable government contribute directly to the ease with which Islamic terrorist organizations are capable of permeating Indonesia's borders. Indonesia's primary problems have been maintaining internal stability and control in the face of separatist movements and direct challenges to its military authority by local militias.

On October 12, 2002, a terrorist bombing in Bali prompted the Indonesian government to arrest Abu Bakar Bashir, leader of the radical Islamic Jemaah Islamiya (JI) group. The arrest was implicit recognition that the country had pursued a dangerous and unwise policy by turning a blind eye to radical organizations.[432] After the overthrow of President Suharto in May 1998, JI

---

[430] "Organized Crime Moves into Migrant Trafficking," *Trafficking in Migrants Quarterly Bulletin* [Geneva], no. 11 (June 1996).
[431] Population Resource Center web site. Last viewed December 13, 2002.
<http://www.prcdc.org/summaries/indonesia/indonesia.html>
[432] John McBeth, "What if He Isn't Guilty?" *Far Eastern Economic Review*, 165, no.44 (7 November 2002): 17.

leaders had taken advantage of lax anti-terrorist policies by Suharto's successors to re-establish regional operations in Java and the island of Sulawesi, north of Java.[433]

After the Bali bombing, the Indonesian government identified the increased intervention of militant international organizations in Indonesian domestic politics as a major threat to national security.[434] Leaders of the government, which "realized that it lacked the legal basis to deal with terrorism," issued an emergency anti-terrorism decree immediately after the bombing, pending passage of permanent legislation.[435] As of December 2002, evidence in the Bali case pointed either to direct involvement of al Qaeda operatives in setting the bomb, or to al Qaeda direction of JI terrorists who set the bomb.[436] JI's operations chief, Riduan Isamuddin (also known as Hambali), reportedly is an elite member of al Qaeda, with responsibility for recruiting in Indonesia and arranging Indonesian recruit training in the Philippines and Afghanistan.[437] In June 2003, a senior member of JI testified that al Qaeda had planned a series of church bombings that were carried out in Indonesia by JI at Christmas 2000. This was the first direct acknowledgment of ties between JI and al Qaeda.[438]

In addition to its two operational divisions in Indonesia, the loosely structured JI has established two other territorial divisions: one in peninsular Malaysia and Singapore, the other in Australia and Papua New Guinea.[439] In recent years, Indonesian cells have been involved in a war against Christians in Sulawesi and the Moluccas Islands and in attacks on Christian civilians in several other locations within Indonesia.[440]

Contributing Factors

Analysts cite a lack of political will as the primary reason for the proliferation and strength of al Qaeda and other terrorist groups in Indonesia. Prior to the Bali bombing,

---

[433] "Indonesia Backgrounder: How the Jemaah Islamiya Terrorist Network Operates," *ICG Asia Report*, no. 43 (11 December 2002). <http://www.crisisweb.org>
[434] Paul Burton, "Behind the Bali Bombing," *Jane's Sentinel Online*, 16 October 2002. <http://www.janes.com>
[435] Rudy Madanir and Christine Tjandraningsih, "Indonesia Issues Terror Decree, Arrests Muslim Leader," *Kyodo* [Tokyo], 19 October 2002 (FBIS Document JPP20021019000087).
[436] Ellen Nakashima, "Jailed Indonesian Suspect Details Links to Bombings," *Washington Post*, 9 November 2002, A15.
[437] McBeth, 19.
[438] Alan Sipress, "Bin Laden Named in Asian Terror Plots," *Washington Post*, 27 June 2003, A24.
[439] "Indonesia Backgrounder: How the Jemaah Islamiyah Terrorist Network Operates."
[440] Jean-Claude Pomonti, "The Terrorist Network Covers All of Southeast Asia," *Le Monde* [Paris], 20 December 2002 (FBIS Document EUP20021220000074).

Indonesian officials had been unwilling to crack down on either domestic or international Islamic terrorist organizations. The Indonesian government also has lacked the professionalism and resources necessary to effectively eliminate such a threat. The Indonesian military and police do not have the technological tools and training to detect and track down insurgent groups.[441] Military morale and ethics are also damaged by chronically low wages. According to a 2002 government report, even senior enlisted personnel earn only about US$100 per month.[442] In addition, Indonesia's civilian government has not been able to curb corruption and the sale of arms and explosives by the army.[443] The International Crisis Group has reported possible links between Indonesian military intelligence groups and the JI and recommended that anti-terrorist measures be enforced by the police rather than the military.

Indonesia's policy of suppression of dissident groups has limited much of the development of domestic threat. However, The Free Aceh Movement (Gerakin Aceh Merdeka, GAM), based near a key international shipping lane on the western end of Sumatra, is a domestic insurgent organization that has committed some terrorist acts in the name of regional autonomy. Located in Indonesia's most profoundly Muslim province, the GAM has survived since its establishment in the 1970s, despite several years of occupation and harsh counter-insurgency operations by Indonesia's military.[444] Although the GAM has not presented a threat to Indonesia's national security or engaged in significant transnational activity, its continued presence suggests that Indonesia lacks an effective policy for dealing with dissident groups. In mid-2002, Indonesian authorities identified an extensive arms-trafficking network within the military that was selling arms to the GAM.[445] The GAM also has purchased arms from transnational traffickers based in Thailand.[446] In December 2002, the GAM, which reportedly

---

[441] John McBeth, "Weak Link in the Anti-terror Chain," *Far Eastern Economic Review*, 165, no. 42 (4 October 2002): 15.

[442] "The Military's Social Safety Net," *Laksamana* [Jakarta], 27 June 2002 (FBIS Document SEP20020702).

[443] "Bali Bombing: Rift Emerges Within Jemaah Islamiyah," *ICG News Media Release*, 11 December 2002. <http://www.intl-crisis-group.org>

[444] Colin Robinson, "In the Spotlight: Indonesia's Free Aceh Movement," Center for Defense Information Terrorism Project Report, 10 May 2002. <http://www.cdi.org/terrorism>

[445] Wenseslaus Manggut, Edy Budiyarso, and Chandra, "Angry Indonesian Army Chief: Death for Soldiers Stealing, Selling Weapons," *Tempo* [Jakarta], 25 August 2002 (FBIS Document SEP20020905000036).

[446] Suthep Chaiviwan, "Gun Running: Transit to Terror," *Bangkok Post* [Bangkok], 14 July 2002 (FBIS Document SEP20020714000011).

has strongly opposed the JI in Sumatra, signed a peace agreement with the government of Indonesia.[447]

Complicating governance by Indonesia's civilian leaders is the strength of the state's regional military forces. After the removal of Suharto, the Indonesian military was forced to enlist the help of local militias to maintain control of the country and quell separatist factions. Since that time, the militias have built up formidable pockets of regional authority that challenge state control. Fearing that such organizations could become fully free of civilian control and realign themselves with non-indigenous terrorist forces such as al Qaeda, the Indonesian military has called for these militias to disband.[448] One such militia is the Laskar Jihad, which reportedly has received training from al Qaeda and other international terrorist organizations in Afghanistan.

Transnational Crime

Although insurgent terrorist groups are the primary concern in Indonesia, recent growth in drug trafficking also poses a threat. Bali, for example, has seen increasing drug activity. The island's growing tourist economy and the increased number of flights moving in and out of the island have contributed significantly to this drug culture. In addition, corruption among civilian military officials has afforded protection to traffickers. In the 1990s, arrests for narcotics trafficking increased regularly in Bali, but most incidents involved recreational drug use by tourists.[449] In 2002 authorities also identified large numbers of marijuana smugglers based in Aceh, which is Indonesia's primary marijuana-growing region. Reportedly, those smugglers are connected with a transnational narcotics network whose overseas point is Malaysia.[450]

In 2002 Indonesia's National Narcotics Agency reported that Indonesia has become the world's third-largest producer of ecstasy. Most ecstasy is exported (Indonesian ecstasy has been

---

[447] "Bali Bombing: Rift Emerges Within Jemaah Islamiyah."
[448] "Indonesia: Bali Bombing Forcing Military to Address Militia Dilemma," *Strategic Forecasting*, 8 November 2002. <http://www.stratfor.biz>
[449] "Officer Describes Bali as Drug Transit Point," *Jakarta Suara Pembaruan,* 2 March 1997 (FBIS Document FTS19970303000479).
[450] "Marijuana Trafficking Involves International Syndicates," *Medan Analisa* [Banda Aceh], 1 May 2002 (FBIS Document SEP20020501000096).

found in the United States for example), but Indonesia also has a growing domestic market for the substance. Tangerang, west of Jakarta, has been identified as a production center.[451]

Malaysia

Malaysia, like Indonesia, faces political unrest within its Muslim population. Although Malaysia shows little evidence of the same degree of illicit drug trafficking or money laundering that is present in Thailand and the Philippines, international authorities place Malaysia high on the list of countries to monitor for international terrorist activities and human trafficking. It is significant, too, that President Mahathir Mohamad faces political opposition from the Pan-Malaysia Islamic Party, an organization that has established links to extremist Islamic groups inside Malaysia that are sympathetic to the activities of al Qaeda.[452]

Terrorist Activity

Reports indicate that Malaysian businessman Yazid Sufaat, who was captured by United States forces in Afghanistan, had worked with Muslim terrorist organizations such as al Qaeda prior to the September 11th attack on the United States. Sufaat's company, Infocus Tech, was directly involved in exchanging information with al Qaeda operative Zakarias Moussaoui. Previous to his work in Infocus, Sufaat was a captain in the Malaysian army and a member of the extremist group JI, which is known to be sympathetic to various terrorist groups.[453] JI's relationship with al Qaeda has been established throughout Asia in connection with cases such as the Bali bombing in Indonesia.

Terrorist groups are able to easily meet and organize in Malaysia because Malaysia's loose visa regulations for all domestic and foreign Muslims provide easy passage for Muslim terrorists.[454] In addition, the Malaysian capital, Kuala Lumpur, is a technologically advanced city with all the amenities needed for high-speed global communication and the secure banking transactions required for international data and money transfer.

---

[451] Radio Australia broadcast, 16 April 2002 (FBIS Document SEP20020416000090).
[452] Dan Murphy, "US Pushes Southeast Asian States on Islamic Radicals," *Christian Science Monitor*, 93, no. 223 (12 October 2001): 7.
[453] Daniel Klaidman, "A Good Place to Lie Low," *Newsweek*, 139, no. 5 (February 2002): 34.
[454] Klaidman.

Transnational Crime

In August 2001, Malaysia passed an anti-money laundering act.[455] Although no reports indicate that Malaysia has a particular problem with money laundering, the existence of a strong sex trade and the activities of international terrorist groups within its borders are at least preliminary conditions for significant money laundering activity.

Malaysia's lax visa laws also promote human trafficking. Currently, Malaysia serves as a receiving country for women trafficked from most other Southeast Asian countries.[456] Because trafficking in humans for the sex trade and for illegal immigration is lucrative, international organized crime organizations have become deeply involved in Malaysia's global trafficking rings.[457] Although little evidence indicates the physical presence of non-indigenous organized crime rings within Malaysia, domestic crime groups cooperate in transporting immigrants to these groups internationally. Malaysian criminals also cooperate with international organized crime groups in countries such as the Philippines and Vietnam in the recruiting and abduction of women destined for Malaysia's illicit sex trade.[458] Although prostitution is illegal in Malaysia, corrupt members of the Mahathir government reportedly have been complicit in supporting the industry.[459]

Philippines

The Philippines hosts a variety of international organized crime and terrorist groups not unlike those found in other Southeast Asian countries. Among the foremost problems are human trafficking, money laundering, narcotics, and the presence of four domestic radical separatist groups, at least one of which has links to al Qaeda. With the exception of groups engaged in human trafficking and corrupt political officials, illegal activities in the Philippines appear to have the single purpose of supporting the Muslim separatist movements and Osama bin Laden's terrorist network.

---

[455] Mary Swire, "New Malaysian Money Laundering Act Now in Force," *Tax-News* [Hong Kong], 28 August 2001. <www.tax-news.com>

[456] "A Human Rights Report on Trafficking of Persons, Especially Women and Children," *The Protection Project*, March 2002, 341.

[457] Rina Jimenez-David, "Sex Abuse and Sex Trafficking in Malaysia," *Asia Intelligence Wire: Financial Times*, 5 September 2002.

[458] "A Human Rights Report on Trafficking."

[459] Jimenez-David.

Terrorist Activity

The Philippines has been an ideal hideout and training ground for terrorist insurgents from al Qaeda and JI because of its rugged terrain and multiplicity of uncontrolled islands.[460] Furthermore, the Philippine legal system is not geared to enforcing international law or protecting against transnational crime. Loopholes in that system frustrate the efforts of Philippine police to prosecute non-indigenous insurgent groups.[461]

The four radical separatist groups are Abu Sayyaf, the Communist New People's Army, the Moro Islamic Liberation Front (MILF), and the Moro National Liberation Front (MNLF). The first three have been linked to terrorist acts. The MNLF is considered the most moderate of the four. Abu Sayyaf is based in the jungles of the southern islands of the Philippines, the Communist New People's Army in the center of the country. Although experts believe that geographical and ideological differences preclude lasting alliances, all three are known to have cooperated with one of the others in specific terrorist attacks. Filipino authorities attributed an assault on a Philippine Army headquarters in November 2001 to the MILF and Abu Sayyaf. Most recently, a terrorist attack in Zamboanga del Norte was described as a coordinated effort between the MILF and Abu Sayyaf. Explosions in Davao City in March and April 2003 have been called a combined attack by the Communist New People's Army and Abu Sayyaf.[462]

Al Qaeda established a presence in the Philippines in 1987, when leader Osama bin Laden's brother-in-law Jamal Khalifa established a business front, called Benevolence International, to funnel money to insurgent groups.[463] Reportedly, Khalifa assisted in the founding of the Abu Sayyaf, a terrorist gang known especially for kidnapping tourists and politicians for ransom. The Philippines has been, and may continue to be, a major training ground for al Qaeda operatives and a haven for refugees from the Russian invasion of Afghanistan. Abu Sayyaf leader and founder Abdurajak Jalanjani was trained by Osama bin Laden in Afghanistan. Ramzi Yousef, who masterminded an attack on the World Trade Center in

---

[460] Ricardo Tiuseco Pamintuan, "Country Paper on Effective Methods to Combat Transnational Organized Crime in Criminal Justice Processes," *UNAFEI Resource Material Series 58* [Tokyo], December 2001. <www.unafei.co.jp>
[461] Pamintuan, 184.
[462] "Philippines: Rebel Alliance or Aid Ploy?" Stratfor report, 8 May 2003.
[463] Jean-Claude Pomonti, "Al-Qa'ida's Invisible Presence in Southeast Asia," *Le Monde* [Paris], 1 November 2001, 12 (FBIS Document EUP20011112000434).

1993, is known to have trained al Qaeda and Abu Sayyaf members in the creation and use of explosives while hiding out in the Philippines.[464] Although most reports indicate that by 2002 Abu Sayyaf had become nothing more than a gang of kidnappers, a recent report by domestic financial investigators stated that a portion of the kidnapping ransoms obtained by the Abu Sayyaf is being laundered in Manila and being redistributed to al Qaeda.[465] In addition, reports from the Moro National Liberation Front indicate that local al Qaeda operatives continue to train members of Abu Sayyaf.[466]

Transnational Crime

Although Islamic extremist groups are able to launder money through the hawala system,[467] the lack of transparency in the Philippines financial system also permits money laundering through the national banking system. In October 2002, responding to the loophole, the government adopted an anti-money laundering law designed to reduce this source of funding for terrorist and international organized crime organizations. The new law was adopted after a special joint meeting of fifteen European Union (EU) member states released an ultimatum demanding that the Philippines and several other countries reduce the flow of "dirty money" through their banks. Possible sanctions would include restricting EU banks from opening branches in the Philippines.[468] The new law requires banks to open the accounts of suspected launderers for investigation.[469]

Some of the illegal funds flowing through the Philippines stem from the sale of narcotics. The drug trade in the Philippines is mainly limited to methamphetamines known as *shabu*, and "ice." The Philippines is at the end point of an international narcotics ring that traffics most of its illicit drugs from China and Hong Kong for domestic use rather than for transport to other

---

[464] Alan Dawson, "Al-Qaeda Links Run Deep," *Bangkok Post* [Thailand], 29 May 2002 (FBIS Document SEP2002529000048).

[465] Dawson.

[466] Dawson.

[467] Patrick M. Jost, "The Hawala Alternative Remittance System and Its Role in Money Laundering," Interpol report, January 2000. <http://www.interpol.int/Public/FinancialCrime/MoneyLaundering/hawala/default.asp>

[468] "EU to Target Philippines, Nauru in Money-Laundering Crackdown," Agence France Presse [Paris], 12 October 2001 (FBIS Document EUP20011012000252).

[469] Aurea Calica, "Analysts say Philippines' Anti-money Laundering Law 'Lacks Teeth,' *The Philippine Star* [Philippines], 1 October 2002 (FBIS Document SP20011001000034).

countries.[470] Chinese drug traffickers (generally members of the mainland Chinese gangs 14K and Big Circle) sell shabu to native Filipino dealers out of Manila.[471]

The predominance of Chinese nationals in Philippine drug trafficking has led the Philippine and Chinese governments to initiate a cooperative effort to stem all organized crime activities, including human trafficking, terrorism, money laundering, and narcotics trafficking.[472] In late 2001, reports of corruption raised suspicion that Senator Panfilo Lacson and the Philippine Department of Justice had links to Chinese and Hong Kong organized crime syndicates trafficking drugs in the Philippines. Although it is not clear to what degree the corruption exists, Colonel Victor Corpus, chief of the Intelligence Service of the Armed Forces of the Philippines (ISAFP), has reported that Lacson maintains bank accounts in the United States, Canada, and Hong Kong estimated to value over US$1 billion.[473] Corpus has found proof that senators, including Lacson, have had dealings with Chinese drug lord Kim Wong and other Chinese Triad members.[474]

Trafficking in humans is also widespread in the Philippines. Organized crime syndicates from Malaysia and China have been successful in transporting women from their countries to destinations in the West via the Philippines, and Filipino women to customers in the international sex trade. In September 2001, immigration officials captured Chinese national Chung Chee Hui, a suspected leader of a smuggling ring that utilized false documents and passports to export Chinese women to other countries.[475] The trafficking, however, is not limited only to the sex trade. A human trafficking operation exposed in France utilized the valid passports and working visas of Filipinos living in Europe in a process that enables Filipino men and women to enter Western countries.[476]

---

[470] Mustafa Abdullah, "Analysis of Current Situation on Illicit Drug Trafficking," *UNAFEI Resource Material Series* [Tokyo], 58 (December 2001). <http://www.unafei.co.jp>

[471] Mercedes Rullan, "Five 'Big Circle' Members Arrested, P116-M Shabu Recovered," *Manila Kabayan* [Philippines], 23 December 2001 (FBIS Document SEP20011223000011).

[472] Perseus Echeminada, "Lina: RP-China Anti-Crime Cooperation in the Works," *The Philippine Star* [Manila], 25 December 2001 (FBIS Document SEP20011225000035).

[473] Maritess N. Reyes, "Philippines on Its Way to Becoming a Narco-state," *Intersect Magazine,* 27 November 2001. <http://www.cyberdyaryo.com/features/f2001_1127_03.htm>

[474] Amando Doronila, "The Senate—the Nation's Laundry Machine," *Philippine Daily Inquirer* [Manila], 24 August 2001 (FBIS Document SEP20010824000031).

[475] "Chinese National of Human Smuggling Syndicate Nabbed in Cebu," *Philippine Star* [Manila], 4 September 2001 (FBIS Document SEP20010904000063).

[476] "Human Trafficking Syndicates' Scheme in Smuggling Filipinos to Europe Uncovered," *Philippine Daily Inquirer* [Manila], 27 June 2002 (FBIS Document SEP20020627000090).

Contributing Factors

The proliferation of trafficking in humans is the result of both economic and social problems. Poor living conditions and the lure of better lives overseas contribute to the "push" factor of human trafficking, creating a steady pool of candidates for export. Researchers have also identified social reasons for participation. A 2001 Belgian study on the trafficking of women from the Philippines reported factors such as the patriarchal social system and the status conferred by society on families with members working overseas as two of the major contributors to human trafficking. Moreover, the nation's loose emigration laws and the low cost of employing such emigrants in Western countries are also large factors.[477] The Sri Lanka-based Tamil Tigers terrorist organization, which has come to see human trafficking as a source of income comparable in profitability to narcotics, has been active in transporting undocumented Sri Lankans into the Philippines. Such individuals later become wards of the state or move on to other countries as refugees.[478] The funds received from these activities are laundered and then funneled back to Sri Lanka to aid in the secessionist movement.[479]

Issues of governance have helped to maintain the illicit Philippine economy. Not only is the Philippine government lax in its enforcement of the law, but the language of existing laws is not easily applicable to conditions created by transnational organized crime and terrorist threats. The Philippine government has been linked with corruption and may lack the political will to apply obscure legal procedures when political patronage is commonplace. Also, the governing system lacks an appropriate prosecutorial agency to investigate and try the offenses of transnational criminal groups and terrorists. Finally, at the lowest level of law enforcement, the system does not provide appropriate training for officers investigating instances of such activity.[480]

---

[477] Brice De Ruyver and Koen Van Heddegem, "Human Trafficking Between Belgium and the Philippines," *Tijdschrift voor Criminologie* [Amsterdam], 10 January 2001 (FBIS Document EUP20020823000403).
[478] Rey Arquiza, "Tamil Guerrillas in Philippines Engage in Raising Funds for War in Sri Lanka," *The Philippine Star* [Manila], 16 August 2000 (FBIS Document SEP20000816000040).
[479] Arquiza.
[480] Pamintuan, 183.

Thailand

Geographical location in the Golden Triangle (the tri-border region renowned for illicit drug production) and on Burma's eastern border makes Thailand a prime narcotics trafficking route for heroin and methamphetamines. Thailand also is a center for trafficking in humans, money laundering, arms smuggling, and document forgery. Thailand is technologically advanced enough to provide the communications and transportation infrastructures that increasingly are a requirement for the transnational activities of terrorist and transnational organized crime groups. In addition, long-established, widespread corruption among Thai government officials and the police eases greatly the operating conditions of crime syndicates and terrorist organizations.

Transnational Crime

Most of Thailand's criminal activities are conducted in conjunction with its illicit drug trade, which in turn spurs money laundering and arms trafficking.[481] In 1984 a crackdown on heroin trafficking routes throughout the country made Thailand less hospitable to heroin. However, since that time methamphetamines have continued to stream across the Burma border, via more obscure routes into Bangkok, in the form of an "ant army" of large numbers of traffickers each carrying small amounts of narcotics.[482] Sources indicate that Thailand is currently Asia's largest consumer of amphetamines. Its most popular domestic drug is a cheap street drug referred to as *yaabaa* (mad pill) previously known as *yaamaa* (horse pill).[483] Although *yaabaa* is manufactured mainly by domestic organizations or separatist groups from Burma, evidence shows that international organized crime groups from China increasingly are involved in the transport and sale of amphetamines to the Thai narcotics industry. The most prominent of these syndicates are the Chinese triads known as 14K and the Wa family, who utilize Bangkok as a commercial and trafficking base.[484] Although the bulk of the *yaabaa* that

---

[481] Pasuk Phongpaichit, *Guns, Girls, Gambling, Ganja: Thailand's Illegal Economy and Public Policy* (Bangkok: Silkworm Books, 1998), 248-49.

[482] Pierre-Arnaud Chouvy, "New Drug Trafficking Routes," *Jane's Intelligence Review*, 1 July 2002.

[483] Pierre-Arnaud Chouvy, "Drugs and War Destabilize Thai-Burma Border Region," *Jane's Intelligence Review*, 1 April, 2002.

[484] King-O Laohong, "Foreign Mafias Take Over Rachada Road Areas as Place to Launder Money and Carry Out White Slavery and Narcotics Trafficking, " *Bangkok Krungthemp Thurakit* [Bangkok], 4 November 2001 (FBIS Document SEP20011105000049).

comes into Thailand originates in Burma, Chinese drug syndicates are also reportedly responsible for the actual sale of drugs on the streets of Bangkok.[485]

A large part of Thailand's narcotics industry is wrapped in a centuries-old conflict with Burma. Starting in the 16th century and continuing through the 1999 seizure of the Burmese consulate in Bangkok, cooperation between the two countries has been virtually non-existent.[486] The lack of cooperation has resulted in only limited success in stemming the flow of methamphetamines manufactured in Burma into Thailand. Compounding the issue is the fact that internal conflict between the current ruling party and Burma's pro-democracy ethnic minorities consistently spills into Thai territories. Since both the parties manufacture methamphetamine for the Thai drug trade to raise funds for the purchase of arms, both forces (the current ruling junta and the insurgents) stand to gain little by fully participating in a crackdown on the illicit drug trade through Thailand.[487]

Reports also indicate that the Thai government also may covertly support the sale of narcotics and arms to select insurgent groups in Burma. At the very least, the junta ruling Burma has alleged that the Thai government turns a blind eye to arms and narcotics smuggling conducted by pro-democratic forces such as the Shan (an ethnic group whose activities are based near the Thai border) in an indirect attempt to overturn political authority in Burma.[488] Conversely, Thai and U.S. officials have accused the ruling junta of the same activities in Thailand utilizing the United Wa State Army (USWA). USWA is a militant Burmese group that occupies the area near the Thai border, and is currently supported by the junta to combat pro-democratic minorities residing in Burma.[489] More recently, Thailand has responded to the increase in trafficking by strengthening its anti-narcotics unit and establishing anti-trafficking posts along the border, and has begun working with the current leadership of Burma to curtail illegal activities.[490] As of December 2002, the two sides were at least superficially working together to reduce the amount of drugs trafficked from Burma into Thailand.[491] However, a

---

[485] Chouvy, "New Drug Trafficking Routes."
[486] Roger Mitton, "Myanmar-Thailand Relations: Still Lousy After All These Years," *Asiaweek*, 19 October 1999. <http://www.asiaweek.com/asiaweek/intelligence/9910/19/>
[487] Shawn Crispin, "Drug Tide Strains Ties," *Far Eastern Economic Review*, 162, no. 36 (September 9, 1999): 25.
[488] Phongpaichit.
[489] Chouvy, "Drugs and War Destabilise Thai-Burma Border Region."
[490] Phongpaichit, 37.
[491] "Burma, Thailand Draw Up Joint Plan to Fight Drugs," Agence France-Presse [Paris], 14 December 2002. <http://www.clarinews.net>

history of ill will and openly hostile rhetoric between the two parties does not bode well for successful cooperation. Even with the best of governmental intentions, the porosity of the borders and the multitude of established trafficking routes through Thailand combine with the political instability of neighbors such as Burma to stymie efforts to eliminate the drug trade.

As a regional air transportation hub, Bangkok also functions as a transit base for the smuggling of arms and illegal immigrants. The Liberation Tigers of Tamil Eelam (LTTE) utilizes the city as a transit point en route to Sri Lanka.[492] The LTTE continues to procure arms from arsenals abandoned after Cambodia's civil war and via Cambodia from sources in the Chinese military. Although Cambodia's lack of a strong police force and judicial system makes that country ideal for arms trafficking, Thailand is the lynchpin of the LTTE network. It serves as such because of its proximity to Sri Lanka, the Bay of Bengal, Burma, and Cambodia; its strong communications infrastructure; and the ease with which one can cross its borders.[493] According to sources, bribery of border officials is standard procedure.[494]

Arms trafficked through Thailand reach customers in several countries. According to a 2002 Bangkok newspaper report, "Most of the rebel groups in foreign countries, both near and far from Thailand, who are engaged in armed insurgencies against their governments, continue to order second hand supplies and war weapons from gunrunners along the borders of Thailand."[495] Among the buyers are groups in Bangladesh (the Chittagong Hill and Chakma groups), Indonesia (the GAM), northeastern India, the Andaman Islands, and at least four insurgent groups in the Philippines. Some arms arrive in Thailand by sea from the Chinese plants Norinco and Poly Technology. Land routes cross into Thailand from Cambodia and Laos, and sea routes cross the Gulf of Thailand from the Cambodia-Thailand border to points in southern Burma. As of mid-2002, Thailand's Counter-Terrorism Operations Center was unable to foresee what paths arms shipments would follow. In recent years, some of Thailand's arms trafficking groups have expanded or shifted entirely into narcotics trafficking.[496]

---

[492] "Special Report—Case Study: The Liberation Tigers of Tamil Eelam," *Jane's Intelligence Review,"* 1 October 2001. <http://www.janes.com>
[493] Anthony Davis, "Tamil Tigers Continue Procurement," *Jane's Intelligence Review*, 1 May 2002. <http:\\www.janes.com>
[494] Suthep Chaiviwan, "Gun Running: Transit to Terror," *Bangkok Post* [Bangkok], 14 July 2002 (FBIS Document SEP20020714000011).
[495] Chaiviwan.
[496] Chaiviwan.

The trafficking of women and illegal aliens into and through Thailand also is a high-profit industry that has attracted transnational and domestic organized crime networks. Organizations such as the Japanese Yakuza have an established presence in Bangkok, through which they obtain women for Japan's sex and entertainment trade.[497] After international attention led to a crackdown on Thailand's Japanese-run sex tours in the 1980's, Yakuza groups began bringing prostitutes, mainly from Southeast Asian nations, to Japan to continue business. The women are smuggled out of Thailand using fake passports produced in Thailand or by bribing local police.[498] Lax visa laws make it easy for organized crime organizations such as the Yakuza to traffic women into Japan with forged documents.[499]

Several foreign gangs are known to be involved in the smuggling of illegal immigrants. The Chinese "Piglet Gang" and the South Asian "Baby Goat Gangs" (mainly from Bangladesh, Pakistan, and Iran) use Thailand's wealth of false and stolen passports to transport immigrants from their home countries to wealthier countries such as the United States and Canada. Similarly, the Chinese Wang Kao Niu Gang smuggles Chinese women from locations in China to Bangkok to work as prostitutes.[500] In similar cases, loose visa regulations and fake passports permit illegal aliens to transport people from the Middle East to Western countries by utilizing fake Indian and Bangladeshi documents.[501]

International organized crime syndicates operating from Bangkok long have utilized Thailand's banks and shops to launder profits from narcotics, the sale and transport of humans to prostitution rings, and trafficking in illegal immigrants. Thailand's cities offer criminals and terrorists varying opportunities to launder funds from illicit activities. Those engaged in money laundering can simply carry large amounts of cash with them as they travel and deposit their money in local banks that maintain discretion in business matters. Front companies and wire transfers also offer protection for laundering operations.[502]

---

[497] Melanie Orhant, "Human Trafficking: Gangs Make Thailand a Regional Hub: Yakuza Operating," *Stop Traffic News*, 22 September 2000. <http://www.friends-partners.org>

[498] Kinsey Alden Dinan, "Trafficking in Women from Thailand to Japan," *Harvard Asia Quarterly*, 6, no. 3 (Summer 2002). < http://www.fas.harvard.edu/~asiactr/haq/200203/index.htm>

[499] Melanie Orhant, "Abused Thai Women 'Trafficked' to Japan Need Help," *Stop Traffic News*, 24 September 2000. <http://www.friends-partners.org>

[500] Laohong.

[501] Chaiyakorn Bai-ngern, "Thai Police Investigate Three Alien-Smuggling Gangs," *The Nation* [Bangkok], 9 June 1999 (FBIS Document FTS19990608002032).

[502] Pisan Mookjang, "Current Situation and Countermeasures Against Money Laundering in Thailand," *UNAFEI Resource Material Series 58* [Tokyo], December 2001. <www.unafei.co.jp>

As of mid-2002, Thailand's Criminal Procedure Code and money-laundering law contained serious flaws that prevented effective action against terrorist organizations. As the law stands, terrorism is not a criminal offense, and the national Anti-Money Laundering Office does not have the authority to investigate or block the transfer of funds to finance terrorism.[503] Although the national parliament has discussed improvements, the enactment of meaningful reforms has proved politically complex.

Terrorist Activities

Reports confirm that prominent Islamic terrorist networks also utilize Bangkok as a center for false documents and passports.[504] As an increasingly cosmopolitan city, Bangkok offers both the level of technology required for document falsification and an abundance of authentic passports that can be altered to suit the needs of terrorist networks.[505] One report indicates that false documents are usually transported to Pakistan where they are distributed to Islamic terrorist groups and individuals to facilitate global travel. The reports also indicate that these passports generate money that is funneled into those same organizations. According to the Bangkok police, the groups involved in the purchase and distribution of such passports include al Qaeda and Hizballah.[506]

Singapore

Despite the arrest of 15 purported terrorists in December of 2001, some of which had been trained by al Qaeda in Afghanistan, Singapore generally has not exhibited conditions hospitable to transnational organized crime or terrorist groups. JI and al Qaeda cells in Singapore are believed to have targeted Singapore for attack rather than utilizing it as a safe haven or for financial gain.[507] Singapore's intelligence agencies are well equipped with sophisticated technological machinery and well-trained officers to counter the international

---

[503] Surath Jinakul and Songpol Kaopatumtip, "Towards a Terror-Free Thailand," *Bangkok Post* [Bangkok], 2 June 2002 (FBIS Document SEP20020602000027).
[504] "Malaysian Police Say Islamic Militants 'May Be Hiding on Thai Soil," *The Nation,* 22 September 2001 (FBIS Document SET20010922000003).
[505] "Thailand Source of Fake Passports," *Bangkok Post,* 21 June 2002. <http://scoop.bangkokpost.com>
[506] "Thailand Source of Fake Passports."
[507] Rohan Gunaranta, "The Singapore Connection," *Jane's Intelligence Review,* 1 March 2002. <www.janes.com>

threat. Singapore authorities disclosed that intelligence operatives had been observing the cells for a long period and knew of their al Qaeda links.

Singapore operates against organized crime networks almost as efficiently as against terrorist groups. To prevent the development of crime networks, the government engages in what it calls preventative detainment of secret society leaders. Although this practice is questionable in terms of human rights, the results contrast strongly with the political and social instability of neighboring states.[508] Singapore maintains tight control over its borders and controls its public through strict laws and regulations. The low drug addiction rate in Singapore is attributed directly to the mandatory death penalty for drug traffickers.[509]

WESTERN EUROPE AND TURKEY

Introduction: Conditions in Western Europe

As a region, Western Europe has adopted sophisticated multinational law enforcement systems that provide a distinct advantage in dealing with transnational criminal organizations and terrorist groups. Nevertheless, Western Europe's geographic location, its approach to transnational law enforcement, and its advanced infrastructure have continued to make it an attractive base for transnational crime and terrorist groups. Within the region, specific countries have exhibited conditions favoring particular types of illegal activity. For example, Belgium and the Netherlands, which have extremely active seaports and relatively lax cargo inspection procedures, have provided opportunities for the trafficking of narcotics, gems, and arms. Spain, whose geographic location makes it a "gateway" to Europe from the Atlantic Ocean and whose ethnic composition gives it a natural connection with Latin American traffickers, has acted as a major transit country for narcotics from South America. And the banking systems of Cyprus and Monaco are favorable for transnational money laundering activities. Before addressing conditions in specific countries, the following paragraphs discuss regional conditions favorable to transnational crime and/or terrorism.

Although there is a growing convergence between terrorist and conventional criminal groups, authorities in Western Europe have treated the activities of the two types of group quite

---

[508] "Singapore: Internal Affairs," *Jane's Sentinel Security Assessment Southeast Asia*, 8 July 2002. <www.janes.com>
[509] "Singapore: Internal Affairs."

differently. The activities of organized crime groups (extortion, money laundering, counterfeiting, smuggling, racketeering, and trafficking in arms, narcotics, and people) have been prosecutable offenses that in most cases have carried high penalties. On the other hand, the activities of non-indigenous terror groups in Western Europe more commonly comprise fund-raising, recruiting, planning, and the dissemination of propaganda. The emphasis on personal liberties by democratic governments in Western Europe has provided leeway for such activities.

In many cases, the profits of operating a criminal organization in Western Europe outweigh the difficulties. By comparison with essentially ungoverned areas such as Somalia and parts of Central Asia, law enforcement poses a substantial obstacle in Western Europe. However, Western Europe also offers the markets that are necessary for a range of high-level financial and trafficking crimes to be profitable. The relative profitability of markets in that region is illustrated by cocaine prices. According to a 2001 study, the price per kilogram of cocaine rises from US$2,000 at its point of origin in Colombia to US$22,500 in Spain and to $42,000 in the United Kingdom.[510]

Another attribute of Western Europe holds the same attraction for criminal groups as it does for legitimate businessmen: well-oiled modernity. Arms trafficking expert Paul Eavis has written: "As crime becomes more 'business-like,' it not only becomes more difficult to detect, but criminal groups also profit from many of the conditions and systems established to facilitate legal business, including the Internet and e-commerce channels."[511] Other factors that facilitate the establishment of organized crime in Western Europe are existing immigrant communities, police and official corruption, and existing indigenous crime groups.

In recent years, some changes have occurred in West European organized crime. Organizations still depend on the existence of corrupt law enforcement agents, black markets, and unemployment and on time-tested measures such as blackmail and murder.[512] However, networks have become much more amorphous and ad hoc, and locations and memberships change more quickly. In this way, the crime organization operates more in the manner of a multinational corporation than a clan-based grouping. Various players own and operate various

---

[510] Christopher Aaron, "Globalisation and Organised Crime," *Jane's Intelligence Review*, 1 December, 2001.
[511] Paul Eavis, "The Hidden Security Threat: Transnational Organized Criminal Activity," *RUSI Journal*, 146, no. 6 (December 2001): 36-37.
[512] Alex Schmid, "Troubled Lands Where Criminals Are King," *UNESCO Courier*, 54, no. 2 (February 2001). <http://www.unesco.org/courier/2001_02/uk/doss8.htm>

links on the chain, and their cooperation blurs the distinction between indigenous local groups and non-indigenous international groups. Albanian groups, for example, have been trained by the Turkish mafia and now are entering the territory of Italian and Russian groups as facilitators of smuggling routes.[513] In contemporary West European organized crime, few groups are confined to a local context.

The European Union's plan to create an internally borderless economy, where citizens can move their goods, services, and money freely throughout the region, has been instrumental in creating new opportunities for criminal groups. The Schengen Agreement officially lifted internal European borders (the United Kingdom and Ireland, which are not full members of that accord, retain their border controls) and established a common visa policy. Yet immigration policies were not accompanied by a harmonization of law enforcement policies. Law enforcement officials can pursue a suspect across a national frontier, but if German police, for example, wish to seize assets held by a suspected criminal in Belgium or stop a drug shipment they believe is headed for Belgium, they need approval from a Belgian court. This is a layer of bureaucracy that criminals do not face in doing cross-border deals, and the bureaucratic waiting period can allow criminals to slip past law enforcement authorities. As a result of these conditions, a Stratfor report concluded in 2003: "….for IOC [Italian organized crime] groups and organized criminal enterprises from other European Union countries, the so-called 'Schengen Area' of borderless EU states has become the most important criminal market on the planet."[514]

As the Schengen Agreement lifted border controls among member countries of the EU, it toughened controls along the exterior borders of those countries. The increased difficulty of entry from outside the community raised demand for illegal paths of entry. As trafficking groups adjusted to these changes, the human trafficking activity that targets Western Europe has become a more sophisticated and complex operation. According to Mark Baynham of the United Kingdom's National Criminal Intelligence Service, groups involved in human trafficking study their markets, identify customers, put together asylum packages, and promise legal and employment assistance to migrants. Criminal activity supporting human trafficking includes forgery, money laundering, and official corruption. According to Baynham, the price for smuggling a person from Turkey to the United Kingdom ranges from US$1,500 to US$4,500,

---

[513] Eavis.
[514] "Italy: Organized Crime Groups Expand Influence," Stratfor report, 9 May 2003.

and the price from China to the United Kingdom is about US$30,000. Major trafficking routes run from the major hub in Turkey through the Mediterranean Sea, including points in Greece, Italy, and France.[515]

To deal more effectively with transnational crime, the concept of the European Arrest Warrant was introduced in 2001. The program, which would make an arrest warrant in one European Union country automatically valid in all the others, has met substantial political resistance, especially in Italy. Although implementation is scheduled for January 2004, the parliaments of all countries must ratify legislation before that step can be taken. Other new multinational institutions such as the European Anti-Fraud Office and Eurojust, a justice system paralleling the multinational Europol law enforcement agency, have been introduced since 2000.[516] A joint border force also is under consideration, and Italy and Greece have reached agreements with Albania to set up a special anti-trafficking center in that country.

Before September 11, the lenient policies of most European governments toward non-indigenous terror groups was a major attraction for militant groups outlawed in their own countries. Until very recently, neither the North Atlantic Treaty Organization (NATO), the EU, nor the Council of Europe had outlawed groups such as the Kurdistan Freedom and Democracy Congress (KADEK, formerly the Kurdistan Workers Party, PKK) that other countries had labeled as "terrorist." The EU compiled a list of terrorist organizations only in December 2001, and the resulting list contained only 12 groups and 30 individuals. The list has subsequently been expanded, and EU legislation calls for the 15 member countries to freeze the assets of individuals and groups on the list and render assistance to co-members in gathering information to prosecute accused terrorists. The new anti-terrorism legislation may mitigate Europe's reputation as a safe haven for terrorists.

Belgium

Belgium occupies a prominent place in both the terror and criminal networks of Western Europe. There have been indications of ambivalence among government officials toward the international anti-terrorist campaign that was launched after September 11, 2002. A senior

---

[515] Aaron.
[516] Transparency International, "Global Corruption Report 2003."

Belgian minister was quoted in 2002 as saying, "Bin Laden's war is against America, not us."[517] A Belgian member of parliament described Belgium's appeal as a base of operations: "We are not a target, but we are such a quiet country that we could be a good preparation country."[518] According to a 2002 confidential report, terrorist organizations such as al Qaeda, the Armed Islamic Group (GIA) of Algeria, the Wahabi Tabligh, and the militant GIA splinter group called the Salafist Group for Preaching and Combat (GSPC) have established logistical support bases among the 350,000 Muslim inhabitants of Belgium. Reportedly the Saudi-backed Salafi movement has established a "state" in Belgium, which has its own Islamist police.[519]

Conventional crime also has found a comfortable home in Belgium. United Nations arms specialist Johan Peleman has speculated that the status of Antwerp as an international diamond-trading center and Belgium's post-colonial ties with Africa made Belgium a major arms-trafficking center during the Cold War. According to Peleman, the infrastructure established at that time now has fallen into the hands of private individuals and groups. Africa is the source of diamonds used in payment and the main marketplace for illegal arms shipments by these entrepreneurs.[520] Until 2000, Belgium was the primary weapons source for the ETA, and it has been a staging point for high-volume arms smugglers such as Victor Bout, Leonid Minin, and Jacques Monsieur. Bout used Ostend, Belgium, as his base of operations until 1997, Minin was based in northern Italy and used documentation from Belgium, and Monsieur was based in Belgium and used documentation from Belgium.[521] Although Bout has been described as a "merchant of death" and continues arms trafficking operations from his base in Bahrain, the international warrant for his arrest issued by Belgian authorities in early 2002 is not for arms crimes but for passing counterfeit currency. This fact may point to another reason that Belgium is favored by criminal groups: the judicial system is notoriously slow, allowing criminals to stay several steps ahead of law enforcement.

---

[517] Marie Rose Armesto, "Europe's Terrorist Incubator," *The Wall Street Journal*, 2 September 2002. <http://www.hvk.org/articles/0902/62.html>

[518] Diana Muriel, "Thwarting Terrorist Cells in Europe," CNN.com War Against Terrorism report, 23 January 2002. <http://www.cnn.com/2001/WORLD/europe/10/26/inv.thwarting.cells>

[519] *Daily Telegraph* report, cited in *Shape News Summary and Analysis*, 4 June 2002. <http://www.globalsecurity.org/military/library/news/2002/06/mil-020604-shape02.htm>

[520] Alain Lallemand, "Belgium: Hotbed of Arms Trafficking," *Le Soir* [Brussels], 7 March 2002 (FBIS Document EUP20020307000027).

[521] Judy Pasternak and Stephen Braun, "Following the Trail of Arms to Al-Qaida," *Los Angeles Times*, 21 January 2002. http://www.nisat.org; Ian Traynor, "The Gunrunner," *The Guardian* [Manchester], 9 July 2001; and Alain Lallemand, "A Belgian Angolagate?" *Le Soir* [Brussels], 16 June 2001 (FBIS Document EUP20010617000081).

The status of Antwerp as Europe's main diamond trade center has attracted illegal activity besides arms trafficking. In 2001 Belgium's General Intelligence Service reported that illegal diamond trafficking with the UNITA rebel organization of Angola was linked with narcotics trafficking and money laundering. The report cited the South African diamond giant DeBeers and intermediaries in Great Britain and Canada. Diamonds reportedly were smuggled from Angola to London and Antwerp via Tel Aviv.[522]

Diamonds also have been instrumental in arms trafficking to other parts of the world; in 2000, Belgian authorities identified diamonds as the exchange currency in shipments to the Middle Eastern terrorist organization Hizballah. Although not specifically linked to the narcotics trade, such trafficking operations, which have stood the test of time and political change, also have the potential to diversify their clientele and the currency that they accept in payment. Several individuals have based especially lucrative arms smuggling operations in Belgium.

Terrorist and criminal networks also have benefited from the ease with which Belgian identification papers have circulated; in 2000, some 19,000 passports were stolen. The presence of major international organizations such as the North Atlantic Treaty Organization also may reduce the level of identification inspections for entry into the country. A number of non-standard forms of documentation issued by international organizations are allowed. Foreigners from 11 other European countries can enter Belgium with expired passports, and no passport is required for citizens of 17 other European countries. Several individuals arrested in conjunction with the events of September 11 were carrying forged or stolen Belgian passports. Ten suspected al Qaeda operatives currently are in jail in Belgium. Experts have speculated that the assassination of Afghan military leader Ahmed Shah Masood was planned in Belgium.[523]

Cyprus and Monaco

Cyprus and Monaco are magnets for money laundering because they provide fiscal incentives and offshore banking facilities. Both criminal and terrorist groups have found these conditions attractive. Located between France and Italy on the Mediterranean coast, Monaco has been a base for Italian and Russian mafia groups, which take advantage of the principality's strict

---

[522] "Belgium Accused [of] Continuing Sale of UNITA Diamonds," Panafrican News Agency report, 24 April 2001. <http://www.globalpolicy.org/security/issues/diamond/2001/0424belg.htm>
[523] Pepe Escobar, "Tracking al-Qaeda in Europe, part 4," *Asia Times Online*, 13 July 2002. http://www.atimes.com/atimes/Middle_East/DC13Ak02.html

banking secrecy laws. Those laws make almost impossible the tracing of bank accounts to their true owners. Beyond the banking system, Monaco offers an "impenetrable wall of silence" about its residents, frequently frustrating investigators from neighboring countries.[524]

In the divided island of Cyprus, the highly developed telecommunications system and business and tourism sectors of the Greek sector, together with Cyprus's location at the crossroads of trafficking routes at the eastern end of the Mediterranean Sea, make the country very attractive to organized crime organizations. The presence of a substantial merchant marine fleet provides ideal space to conceal smuggled goods.

Both the Turkish northern sector of Cyprus and the officially recognized Greek southern sector are important money laundering and transit centers. In 1997, Turkish Cypriot heroin trafficker Huseyin Baybasin described the Turkish sector of Cyprus as a money-laundering haven for narcotics profits. According to Baybasin, for a total population of 100,000, the Turkish sector has 100 banks, which together with the sector's many casinos offer easy avenues of money laundering.[525] According to another report released in 2000, the Greek sector of the island has 24,000 companies registered, of which only 1,100 are physically present on the island.[526] Such a situation indicates strongly that Cyprus's Greek sector offers substantial illegal financial services. Former Yugoslav president Slobodan Milošević and Osama bin Laden are among figures who reportedly have placed large amounts of money illegally in the banks of Greek Cyprus. A strong link with Russian mafia organizations has been inferred because of the large number of Russian enterprises registered in the sector. According to a 2001 newspaper report, Cyprus also is an important laundering point for profits from the large-scale arms and narcotics trafficking operations in Greece, in which both the Russian and domestic mafia are involved.[527]

More recently, however, the EU has judged Cyprus's money-laundering activities not to be a serious impediment to the country's entry into that organization. The EU has expressed its satisfaction that Cyprus has money-laundering legislation (the Prevention and Suppression of

---

[524] Anne Barraclough, "Monte Carlo, the Russian Mafia and Dirty Money," *The Times of London*, 7 February 2000.
[525] *Turkish Cypriot Press and Other Media*, no. 19/1997 (29 January 1997).
<http://www.hri.org/news/cyprus/tcpr/97-01-29.tcpr.htm>
[526] "Cyprus Criticizes Crime Report, Accuses U.S. Banks of Benefiting from Money-Laundering," *Kathimerini* [Athens], 23 December 2000 (FBIS Document GMP20001225000026).
[527] V. Nikolakopoulos, "The Arms Trade in Greece," *To Vima* [Athens], 5 August 2001, cited in "Illegal Arms Trade in Greece Expanding Rapidly Due to Developments in Balkans," report of International Action Network on Small Arms." <http://www.iansa.org/news/2001/aug_01/trade_greece.htm>

Money Laundering Activities Law, passed in 1996) and is enforcing it sufficiently to meet West European standards.[528]

France

In recent years, France has experienced several well-publicized cases of high-level corruption and financial fraud. The party of France's President Jacques Chirac has been accused of illegal campaign financing and election fraud. Government officials allegedly have had conflicts of interest in their dealings with large private corporations.[529] Wide publication of such incidents can undermine anti-corruption efforts among officials at lower levels.

Although France has taken a leading role in establishment of OECD's Financial Action Task Force (FATF), designed to prevent money laundering in member nations of that organization, in April 2002 a parliamentary committee found "major shortcomings in the country's ability to tackle money laundering." The focus of attention has been in cities along the Mediterranean coast, where the committee found that money launderers have "effective impunity." Reportedly, real estate purchases are the favorite method of laundering money in this region, and Russian crime groups are heavily involved.[530] In 2001 several large French banks came under investigation for participation in a money-laundering network that allegedly involved large banks from Israel, which is on the blacklist of the FATF.[531]

France has not passed laws specifically outlawing trafficking or enslavement of individuals. A 2000 report by the Council of Europe estimated that several thousand individuals from West Africa, Madagascar, India, Sri Lanka, and the Philippines are working in France as "domestic slaves," having been brought into the country by traffickers.[532] Substantial numbers of women also enter France for the sex trade. France also is known as a transit country for Chinese "snakehead" groups that move migrants from China and Russia to Western Europe. French authorities have not been able to uproot the Chinese trafficking routes, partly because the law's

---

[528] Jean Christou, "EU and US Have Opposing Views on Money Laundering Charges," *Cyprus Mail*, 3 October 2001.

[529] Transparency International, "Global Corruption Report 2003." <http://www.globalcorruptionreport.org>

[530] "Riviera Money-Laundering Worries France," BBC News report, 11 April 2002.
<http://news.bbc.co.uk/2/hi/europe/1923138.stm>

[531] Sharon Berger and Zev Stub, "France Investigates Israeli Banks for Money-Laundering," *Jerusalem Post* [Jerusalem], 30 December 2001. <http://www.rense.com/general/18/laun.htm>

[532] Bryant.

relatively light penalties, combined with high potential profits, attract criminals from more dangerous activities such as narcotics trafficking.[533]

After a spate of terrorist attacks in 1995, French authorities have used harsh new antiterrorism laws, strict security regulations, and intensified intelligence gathering to nearly eliminate such incidents in recent years.[534] In this environment, France is not believed to be a potential launching country for international terrorist groups.

Germany

After the events of September 11, investigators discovered that two terrorist cells in Germany (one in Hamburg, one in Frankfurt) had been bases of operations for al Qaeda members. Analysts speculate that militants had been particularly attracted to Germany because immigration laws were lax and Germany had a Muslim community numbering 3 million. Hamburg has a large, well-integrated Muslim community that includes the largest Afghan population in Europe. Because that community was quiescent and moderate, it fell under little surveillance; only one secret service agent in the city was assigned to watch "Islamic extremists," a category that included members of the Albanian Kosovo Liberation Army (Albanian initialism UCK) and the KADEK. In addition, German intelligence agencies had been reduced in the 1990s after the disappearance of Cold War tensions.[535]

In 1996 German border police reported that they apprehended only one in five illegal migrants crossing the border. Germany is a reunion point for illegal migrants arriving via plane and surface transportation, prior to moving toward France and Italy. Germany also is an important transit country for migrants that Chinese snakehead groups smuggle from Russia via the Czech Republic into other countries of Western Europe. Gangs from local Chinese communities aid the snakeheads in this endeavor. Some Chinese narcotics trafficking routes are identical to the migrant trafficking routes.[536] Germany also is on the transit route of trafficked women, primarily from Poland, Ukraine, Russia, and the Czech Republic. A 1997 report

---

[533] Roger Faligot, *La Mafia Chinoise en Europe* (Paris: Calmann-Lévy, 2001), 202.
[534] Hoffman.
[535] Andreas Tzortis, "On the Trail of Terror's German Connection," *The Christian Science Monitor*, 25 October 2001.
[536] Faligot, 137, 309-10.

estimated that at that time 15,000 Russian and East European women were engaged in prostitution in Germany.[537]

Germany has become an important narcotics transit route and destination. The growing population of Albanians in Germany, estimated to include as many as 400,000 people, has provided a formidable network for the narcotics distribution activities. Until the late 1990s, Albanian groups dominated that type of trafficking in Germany, but in recent years Croatian groups have superseded them.[538] According to a 2002 report, Rhein-Main Airport in Frankfort is one of the three Western European airports most used by narcotics couriers from South America.[539]

Great Britain

In recent years, Northern Ireland has experienced a substantial merging of domestic terrorist organizations with conventional criminal activities. Experts have suggested, in fact, that some branches of the religiously affiliated Irish insurgency groups have completely abandoned their political goals in favor of moneymaking activities. Two kinds of trafficking with transnational implications—in arms and in narcotics—have been linked to both criminal and domestic insurgency activities. In some cases, insurgent groups have used narcotics as direct payment for arms, and the trafficking networks of one commodity often are convenient pathways for moving the other.[540]

The terrorist heritage of the region has yielded a worrisome criminal element. Of 78 criminal gangs identified by the Police Service of Northern Ireland (RUC) in 2001, some 43 have current or historical links to republican (Catholic) or loyalist (Protestant) paramilitary organizations, including the Irish Republican Army (IRA). Says a 2001 report in *The Guardian*: "Thirty years of terrorism have left a web of networks in which organized crime can thrive and a climate of fear and secrecy that makes fighting such crime very difficult." Such groups take

---

[537] Global March, "Worst Forms of Child Labour Data: Germany."
<http://www.globalmarch.org/worstformsreport/world/germany/htm>
[538] Mark Galeotti, "Albanian Gangs Gain Foothold in European Crime Underworld," *Jane's Intelligence Review*, 19 October 2001.
[539] Steven Derix and Jos Verlaan, "Investigative Services Want More Operational Powers at Schiphol," *NRC Handelsblad* [Rotterdam], 29 July 2002 (FBIS Document EUP20020730000226).
[540] Richard Evans, "Systematic Transnational Crime: Organised Crime and Terrorist Financing in Northern Ireland," *Jane's Intelligence Review* [London], 1 September 2001.

advantage of arms supplies that have been accumulated by thirty years of smuggling in support of terrorist activity.[541]

According to the RUC, more than two-thirds of gang members in Northern Ireland are involved in narcotics dealing, 55 percent in forgery and counterfeiting, and 50 percent in money laundering. Groups with loyalist roots tend to be more active in narcotics trafficking than those with republican roots. Loyalist groups normally have granted "franchises" to drug dealers on their territory rather than controlling entire markets themselves. Narcotics trafficking has been especially attractive for newer loyalist groups such as the Loyalist Volunteer Force because narcotics can provide a quick cash return. Interdiction is difficult because police forces have been reduced, are under funded, and do not enjoy the confidence of the citizenry. In 2001 the police force reported a budget shortfall of 20 million pounds (about US$32 million).[542]

Police sources believe that both loyalist and republican groups have fostered contacts with foreign organized crime groups, either directly or via the Irish diaspora. Counterfeit tobacco products, for example, have been obtained from groups in Eastern Europe, and some narcotics shipments reportedly have arrived from groups in Spain.

The Real Irish Republican Army (RIRA), a militant splinter group of the IRA, has become increasingly active in other parts of Great Britain, in both criminal activities and activities in support of a terrorist agenda. (Those two types of activity often are one and the same.) Police authorities estimate that 80 percent of RIRA activity in mainland Great Britain is related to conventional crime. Metropolitan Police commissioner David Veness says, "Paramilitaries…[are] coming to the mainland because their ability to exploit the economic marketplace of the island of Ireland is now limited, whereas Great Britain and indeed mainland Europe represent a much more lucrative marketplace."[543]

England has gained a reputation as a safe haven for terrorist groups because of its open immigration policy and tolerant attitude toward a variety of dissenters. Countries such as India, Sri Lanka, Saudi Arabia, Egypt, and Yemen have called unsuccessfully on England to apprehend suspected terrorists from those countries who have taken refuge in London.[544] Great Britain's

---

[541] Rosie Cowan, "The 78 Criminal Gangs Waging War on Ulster," *The Guardian* [London], 23 March 2001.

[542] Cowan.

[543] Evans.

[544] Richard Beeston, "The Bomber from Birmingham: Pressure on Britain to End Safe Haven for Political Extremists," *The Times of London*, 28 December 2000 (FBIS Document EUP20001228000096).

Terrorism Act of 2000 has substantially expanded the authority of police and the home secretary (equivalent to a minister of the interior) to shut down fund-raising, recruitment, and training conducted by suspected terrorist cells under the guise of political or religious activity. Another law makes possible the confiscation of a group's bank assets in England if a conspiracy to commit a terrorist act can be proven.

In recent years, several factors have made Great Britain a hospitable country for transnational criminal groups. Because Great Britain now is a preferred destination for illegal migrants and because traffickers in people are able to comply with such wishes, human trafficking now is the second most profitable criminal activity in the country, next to narcotics trafficking. The country's open economy offers a market for a variety of counterfeit goods as well as narcotics. Great Britain's financial institutions offer the combination of reliability and anonymity necessary for money laundering; regulation of security markets and exchange bureaus is insufficient and inefficient.[545] The country's large and growing ethnic communities offer protection and anonymity. And Great Britain's long, irregular coastline and large number of busy ports offer opportunities to move illegal people and commodities into the country by sea.

All of the above factors have changed the nature of conventional crime. Traditionally, the vast majority of criminal groups in Great Britain have been of domestic origin whose activities had little transnational impact. During the 1990s, major groups have appeared in Great Britain from Colombia, China, Jamaica, South Asia, Turkey, and West Africa. According to a 2000 government report, within a single year Albanian criminal groups gained control of 79 percent of saunas and massage parlors. Both sites are used for narcotics distribution and money laundering, as well as prostitution in central London.

Greece

Several conditions make Greece attractive to non-indigenous organized crime groups: its location between Western Europe and the eastern end of the Mediterranean, the existence of a substantial domestic mafia, and corruption at high levels of government. Greece's long, irregular coastline and many islands make adequate patrolling impossible. Greece lies on the traditional "Balkan route" that brings a wide variety of illegal goods into Europe from the Middle East and

---

[545] Tamara Makarenko, "Destination UK," *Jane's Intelligence Review* [London], 1 December 2001.

beyond. In recent years that route has expanded to include Greece's border with Bulgaria and Macedonia and new transit points on the coast of the Aegean Sea. Albania, which is directly northwest of Greece, has been a chronic source of illegal activity.[546] Greece's seaports also handle a high volume of container traffic that is not under strict customs control.

Greece is both a transit stage and a destination for trafficking women, many of whom come from Russia, Ukraine, Bulgaria, the former Yugoslavia, and Albania.[547] The volume of trafficking for prostitution has increased substantially in recent years. According to one report, at any given time as many as 20,000 trafficked women are working in the sex trade in Greece; another report estimates that 40,000 women are trafficked into Greece annually.[548] Many of the women pass through Greece en route to Western Europe.

According to recent reports, Greece also is an important transit point for the international arms trafficking industry. Albanian, Italian, and Russian organized crime groups and guerrilla organizations in Kosovo are moving arms through various parts of Greece to points elsewhere in Europe.[549] Greek security authorities estimate that 50,000 illegal guns per year enter Greece.[550] In August 2001, a Greek newspaper report stated that "guns and narcotics are shipped to Greece from nations of the former USSR and are then shipped to European nations through Italy. The immense profits of this trade are laundered in Greece and Cyprus, where the Russian mafia has a strong support base. The Russian mafia is also involved in narcotics and prostitution."[551] Interdiction has been difficult because Russian groups have established links with "influential officials" in Greece.[552] Another important source of illegal arms trade in Greece is the large number of weapons (estimated at 550,000) stolen from military stockpiles in Albania during that country's 1997 uprising.[553]

In Greece the illegally traded weapons are primarily light guns, including the Russian Kalashnikov and the Israeli Uzi, although items such as rocket launchers also appear on the black

---

[546] "Organized Crime Threat in SE Europe: U.S. Names Greece, Cyprus," *Kathimerini* [Athens], 23 December 2000. <http://www.alb-net.com/pipermail/albsa-info/2000-December/001071.htm>
[547] U.S. Department of State, *Trafficking in Persons Report 2001*. <http://www.state.gov/g/tip/rls/tiprpt/2001>
[548] U.S. Department of State, *Country Reports on Human Rights Practices*, March 2002. <http://www.state.gov/g/drl/rls/hrrpt/2002/c8697.htm>
[549] Nikolakopoulos.
[550] Yeoryios Sombolos, "2.5 Billion Drachmas Annual Turnover from Arms Trafficking," *Imerisia* [Athens], 22 December 2001. <http://www.nisat.org>
[551] Nikolakopoulos.
[552] Nikolakopoulos.
[553] Sombolos.

market. Sicilian mafia groups have been trafficking in arms, narcotics, and cigarettes in western Greece since at least 1999. This trade often is done in cooperation with Albanian groups, which already had begun exploiting Greece's northwestern coastline with high-speed boats in the 1990s.[554] Romanian groups also have a share of the market in Athens.[555]

Crete is the largest center of the arms trade in Greece, but Albanian traffickers have established significant markets in the Evros River delta and in the city of Ioannina, in northeastern and northwestern Greece respectively. Kalashnikovs and grenades from Albania often remain in the hands of crime organizations in Greece. Smuggled weapons also enjoy a substantial market among ordinary Greeks because of Greece's onerous gun ownership requirements.[556]

In keeping with the increased pragmatism and business acumen of criminal groups, in the mid-1990s criminal organizations of mixed ethnicity began appearing in Greece. In the case of narcotics trafficking, such organizations often include Albanians who concentrate on production in their own country; ethnic Greek Albanians, who smuggle products from Albania into Greece; and Greek nationals, who are in charge of distribution in major urban centers.[557]

Greece's dynamic banking sector has been accused of harboring transnational money laundering activities behind its less-than-transparent disclosure policies and loose government controls. Reportedly, domestic money laundering also occurs in Greece's many nightclubs and casinos; transnational money laundering also may be present.[558]

The involvement of corrupt state officials has been a major reason that Greece attracts criminal activity. In mid-2002, legal briefs in a court case against local mafia figures alleged that the complicity of State Coast Guard and other officials prevented apprehension of criminals who had committed crimes ranging from protection rackets to murder. The Coast Guard is an

---

[554] Kostas Khatzidis, "The Italian Mafia Has Spread Its Tentacles into Greece," *Ta Nea* [Athens], 20 July 2000. <http://www.nisat.org>
[555] "Romanian Arms Traffickers Take Over Athens Market," *VIMAgazino* [Athens], cited in *Ziua* [Bucharest], 10 August 2001. <http://www.nisat.org>
[556] Sombolos.
[557] Observatoire Géopolitique des Drogues, *Annual Report 1995-1996.*
<http://www.ogd.org/rapport/gb/RP00_TABLE>
[558] V.Y. Lambropoulos, "Night Clubs Launder Dirty Money," *To Vima* [Athens], 8 March 2002 (FBIS Document GMP20020308000107).

especially crucial link in Greece's defense against crime because of the many accesses to the country from the sea.[559]

November 17, a small but violent anti-United States terrorist group that surfaced in Greece in the 1970s, was effectively incapacitated in mid-2002 when authorities learned its structure and methodology. The group long had evaded Greek and international law enforcement authorities after having committed a series of attacks, including assassinations, against Turkish, U.S., and multinational targets in Greece. At least one leader of November 17, Savvas Xiros, reportedly had connections in the Islamic fundamentalist Egypt-based Muslim Brotherhood.[560] Greek authorities also have established a link between November 17 and the People's Revolutionary Struggle (ELA), a domestic terrorist group whose main body disbanded in 1995.[561]

Italy

Italy has been home to major crime groups for more than 100 years. In recent years, however, significant groups from other countries have established operations in parts of the country that had not been under the strict control of an indigenous organization. Groups such as the Albanians have gained access through connections with existing ethnic groups in Italy. The domestic mafia, which in many cases has welcomed cooperative ventures with foreign groups, includes four major groups, which altogether include more than 500 individual families. Such structures are intrinsic parts of Italian society. One scholar has explained the state's inability to eradicate criminal groups as the result of Italy's 19th-century origins as a federation in which central authorities needed the loyalty of local power groups to maintain their position. Mafia groups maintained local power by supplying needed services that the state failed to provide. Key elements of this political structure still support the existence of the mafia "families." Another important factor is the rigidity and inefficiency of Italian public administration, which is based on a maze of complex laws that encourage citizens to take action outside the law and officials to

---

[559] Dhionisis Nasopoulos, "The Secret War of the Athens Mobs," *Ta Nea* [Athens], 27 August 2002.
[560] Tekla Szymanski, "Hunting Down a Greek Terrorist Organization," *World Press Review*, 49, no. 9, September 2002. <http://www.worldpress.org/Europe/671.cfm>
[561] "Greece Plans New Arrests Linking November 17 with Other Groups," World Tribune.com report, 22 January 2003. <http://216.26.163.62/2003/eu_greece_01_22.htm>

engage in corruption.[562] The mafia often functions as an adjudicator of disputes when settlement is sought outside the law.

The presence of Albanian, Kosovar, Russian, Serbian, and Turkish criminal groups has been increasingly visible in recent years. Because of its long, loosely patrolled coastline, geographical position, and famously lax enforcement of immigration controls, Italy has received a wave of illegal immigrants from Albania, Eastern Europe, Kurdistan, and Turkey. The 45-mile-wide Strait of Otranto, which separates Italy from Albania, is a favorite route. The Albanian population of Italy has been estimated at 110,000 to 200,000, of which 20 to 40 percent are illegal immigrants. Police authorities have admitted that expulsion orders seldom are enforced. Because of the EU's open border policy, individuals can travel at will once they have penetrated the border of a member country such as Italy. In central and northern Italy, where domestic groups exert less control, non-Italian criminal groups have reached agreements granting them control of specified markets or activities. In the southern strongholds of the Italian mafia groups, foreign groups can negotiate for a franchise or operating tax for activities in which the Italians have relatively little interest, such as migrant trafficking and prostitution. The tax may take the form of narcotics, arms, or cash.[563]

In these circumstances, Albanian, Chinese, Nigerian, and Russian groups have consolidated their presence in northern and central Italy. Although they have maintained a relatively low profile, groups from Russia and other parts of the former Soviet Union have been active since the early 1990s, both independently and in cooperation with indigenous groups. The activities of the Russian groups have centered around acquisition of property in the tourism and leisure industries, money laundering, currency counterfeiting, the trafficking of arms and synthetic narcotics, and trafficking women. Reportedly, contacts between Italian criminals and individuals in Russia's Ministry of Defense brought a supply of Russian arms to the Italian mafia in return for investments in Russian industrial and financial enterprises. Italian justice authorities periodically have sought extradition of Russian crime figures for a variety of transnational deals between the two countries.[564]

---

[562] Letizia Paoli, "Crime, Italian Style," *Daedalus*, Summer 2001, 157.
[563] Alison Jamieson, "Italy's Criminal Gangs Change Their Tactics," *Jane's Intelligence Review*, 1 December 2001.
[564] Jamieson.

Nigerian crime syndicates are active in Italy's narcotics market and in prostitution rings that are present in all of Italy's regions except for the far south and Sicily. Chinese groups located primarily in central and northern Italy are active in extortion, migrant trafficking, and running textile sweatshops.[565]

Albanian groups, considered especially dangerous because of their tight organization and violent tactics, have close contacts with all four major Italian groups. The Albanians have largely taken over the supply of heroin to northern Italian cities, superseding Turkish traffickers. The Albanians have significantly altered the pattern of narcotics distribution in Italy by distributing cocaine from Colombian cartels and marijuana from Albania. Albanian groups also traffic prostitutes from resorts owned by the Italian Camorra group on the islands of Corfu, Rhodes, and Cyprus (see also Albania). In Milan, Albanian groups have violently exterminated Italian and North African groups in their quest to dominate that city's narcotics trade.

The Albanian "invasion" has aroused greater resistance among law enforcement authorities than have the activities of domestic groups. Some major police operations against Albanian groups have been successful. Domestic criminal groups also have shown signs of reacting to the takeover of their territory. Although Albanian-Italian criminal cooperation remains quite lucrative, there is some evidence that Italian groups are uniting to regain power.[566]

Post-September 11 investigations revealed that a cell of North African extremist Muslims had established a logistical base in Milan that provided counterfeit documents, lodging, and money. In this case, Italy's criminal infrastructure and high level of corruption apparently had offered a more favorable setting for terrorist logistical planning than France, for example. The hospitality of Italy is limited, however, by an anti-Islamic tradition that is especially strong in the south.[567]

The Netherlands

The Netherlands offers conditions favorable to illegal trafficking. It boasts a highly developed communications system and two major seaports, Amsterdam and Rotterdam, where a

---

[565] Jamieson.
[566] Galeotti.
[567] Kevin Whitelaw et al., "The Terror That Wasn't," *U.S. News and World Report*, 29 October 2001.

high volume of cargo containers is handled quickly and with relatively lax customs controls.[568] The 58 Chinese illegal migrants found dead in Dover (Great Britain) had been moved through the Netherlands by a Chinese snakehead group. Eight of the nine suspects in that case were Chinese living in Rotterdam.

Heavy volume has compromised the security controls at Amsterdam's Schiphol Airport, making it a center of narcotics and human trafficking from the Middle East, Eastern Europe, and Latin America. According to the district attorney of Amsterdam, more intensive security measures would compromise the economic viability of this vital European air transport node. Schiphol is one of three West European airports favored by narcotics couriers from South America. Criminals at the airport operate in ad hoc groups rather than fixed organizations, relying on "facilitators" to connect them with transnational traffickers in need of their assistance. Facilitators most often are corrupt civil servants or employees of transit companies. The loading and unloading of cargo often is virtually unsupervised and controls over airline passenger lists are ineffective because the Netherlands' privacy legislation prohibits the use of digital databases to monitor passenger traffic.[569]

These conditions, which have made the Netherlands one of the most active narcotics and human trafficking countries in the world, also favor arms trafficking. In 2001, police confiscated rocket propelled grenades, hand grenades, and anti-tank weapons. The Amsterdam arms trade is shared among groups from Turkey and Yugoslavia. According to police sources, Yugoslav criminals have superseded Russians in the Netherlands and are taking a prominent role in arms trafficking. Investigators have theorized about links between the Basque ETA and the splinter Real Irish Republican Army.[570]

Spain

Spain has become a cocaine supply hub for European criminal organizations as well as a major money-laundering center for the profits generated by this trade. Urban centers such as Madrid, Alicante, Seville, Barcelona, and Malaga host transnational crime groups, some of

---

[568] Stephane Alonso, "Fight Against Narcotics Is Symbolic," *NRC Handelsblad* [Rotterdam], 31 August 2002 (FBIS Document EUP20020902000252).
[569] Derix and Verlaam.
[570] Andrew Osborn, "Amsterdam in Shock as Killer Gangs Muscle in on Tourist Haunts," *The Guardian* [London], 23 October 2000. <http://www.guardian.co.uk/international/story/0,3604,415081,00.htm>

which remain in a city only long enough for a single transaction. Several groups have more permanent bases along Spain's southern Costa del Sol, from where they sell their services as traffickers or protectors of narcotics, as money launderers, and as dealers in illegal migrants and women for the sex trade.[571]

A major factor in this high degree of criminal activity seems to be the collusion of high-level political figures. In 2000, investigators alleged that Calabrian (southern Italian) mafia operations enjoyed the protection of Jesus Gil, the mayor of Marbella, located on the Mediterranean coast between Gibraltar and Malaga. Shortly thereafter, the unnamed mayor of Estapona, just west of Marbella on Spain's Mediterranean Sun Coast (Costa del Sol), was accused of assisting a major Turkish heroin trafficker to launder his profits. The establishment of front businesses that legitimize Colombian narcotics trafficking activities presumably requires political collusion or partnerships with local businessmen, many of whom also are politicians. A 2001 report by the Center for Geopolitical Drug Studies summarized the situation on the Costa del Sol: "The Costa del Sol has become a veritable sanctuary for criminal organizations that often enjoy political protection."[572]

Spain now is the main entry point of Colombian drugs into Europe. Historically, smugglers in the province of Galicia, on the Portuguese border, worked with Colombian cartels to move narcotics into Europe, for which the Galicians received one-half the shipment for their own distribution. After the Galician rings were weakened by new domestic and multinational law enforcement efforts in 2000, the Colombians began shifting their routes to the Mediterranean port of Valencia via the Strait of Gibraltar, then to Madrid. The versatility of the Colombians seems to have preserved the profitability of their European markets and the overall role of Spain. Partnerships with local Spanish traffickers makes detection more difficult. Meanwhile, the Galician traffickers have diversified to include increasing amounts of hashish and heroin from Turkey. The restrictions on the Galicians' Colombian connection also stimulated new agreements with Portuguese traffickers when Portugal became a second alternate route for the

---

[571] "The New Route of Colombian Traffickers," *Geopolitical Drug Newsletter*, July-August 2001. <http://www.geodrugs.net/mini-lettres/AEGD5GB.pdf>
[572] "The New Route of Colombian Traffickers."

Colombians.[573] According to a 2002 report, Barcelona Airport is one of the three West European airports most favored by narcotics couriers from South America.[574]

For four decades, Spanish authorities have been battling the Basque Fatherland and Liberty (Euzkadi Ta Askatasuna, ETA) organization, a separatist group that has used terrorist tactics on many occasions. Despite periodic cease-fires, the group has continued to launch attacks on Spanish territory, and authorities continue to make arrests.[575] The ETA is believed to have purchased weapons from the Italian mafia and other arms traffickers.

Al Qaeda also has had a significant presence in Spain. Al Qaeda cell members apprehended in Madrid and Granada in November 2001 were accused of providing logistical support to the September 11 hijackers, including counterfeit credit cards, and a Spanish citizen of Syrian origin allegedly was at the center of a money-laundering network that funded al Qaeda groups in Europe.[576] In January 2003, 16 al Qaeda suspects were arrested in a combined Spanish and French operation in Spanish cities close to the French border, including Barcelona.

Turkey

Although there is little evidence of non-indigenous criminal or terrorist groups having permanent bases in Turkey, the country is a vital transit line for trafficking in narcotics and other commodities. The main factors contributing to this status are porous borders, a weak penal code, and widespread official corruption. Rampant corruption includes police officers, who receive very low salaries, and senior officials, who have been accused of collaborating with organized crime organizations to protect narcotics trafficking. Sources in West European countries have reported that as much as 75 percent of the illegal narcotics entering Western Europe either transit through or originate in Turkey. Frequently such reports have concluded that such heavy traffic could not occur without the knowledge and complicity of the Turkish government. When Turkish narcotics kingpin Huseyin Baybasin was captured, he claimed immunity because his

---

[573] "The New Route of Colombian Traffickers."
[574] Derix and Verlaam.
[575] "Intelligence News Summary," various dates, 2001-2003," Intelligence Network reports. <http://www.intellnet.org/news/index/html?type=category&value=Spain>
[576] "Al-Qaeda Financier Was Former Accountant to Saudi Royals: Lawyer," *Middle East Times* [Nicosia], 19 September 2002. http://www.metimes.com/2K2/Issue2002-38/reg/al_qaeda_financier.htm. See also a series of reports on al-Qaeda links with Spain by Dan Sale, February and March 2003, referenced in Intellnet. <http://www.intellnet.org/news/index/html?type=category&value=Spain>

trafficking activity had been on behalf of his government. Baybasin claimed that Turkey's state security apparatus and Turkish Intelligence Agency (MIT) had fully supported the success of one of the world's largest narcotics syndicates.[577] A scandal that broke in early 1999 revealed a pattern of telephone communication between a member of a criminal clan and officials high in the offices of the president and the National security agencies of Turkey.[578]

Turkey's border controls are weak. Most of Turkey's 73 sea and land border checkpoints lack adequate control measures such as radiation detectors and x-ray equipment. Because Turkey has borders with seven other countries where a wide variety of criminal activity takes place, this inadequate system is tested severely by illegal trafficking groups. As Turkey's traditionalist society has been exposed very rapidly to Western culture and commercialism, reforms of the country's legal system have not kept pace. This failure has enabled citizens to circumvent rules and laws that have failed to adapt effectively to the new conditions. Bribery is a practice that has lubricated the machinery of the parallel commercial system that has evolved under these circumstances. In passing new legislation to deal with such practices, successive Turkish governments have only increased the web of bureaucracy that was a primary cause of the original problem.

Reportedly, a large percentage of Turkey's domestic organized crime evolved from a state-run security apparatus that used armed thugs to protect government officials from Turkey's very active opposition groups, some of which were connected with the outlawed Kurdistan Workers' Party (PKK). By the time the need for this type of extreme security subsided, the force had grown beyond legal control. According to a 2000 report, for example, the fanatical Muslim group Hizbullah (not connected with the Hizballah group of Lebanon) acquired weapons that a regional governor had imported into Turkey for use by a counter-insurgency group opposing the PKK in southeastern Turkey.[579]

---

[577] Tony Thompson, "Heroin 'Emperor' Brings Terror to UK Streets," *The Observer* [London], 17 November 2002. <http://society.guardian.co.uk/Print/0,3858,4548336,00.html>

[578] Alessandro Politi, "The New Dimensions of Organized Crime in Southeastern Europe," *The International Spectator*, 34, no. 4 (October-December 1999).

[579] "Europe: A Finger Points," *The Economist*, 26 February 2000.

Conclusion

In Western Europe, transnational and domestic organized crime groups have taken advantage of some intrinsic weaknesses such as lack of border controls within the Schengen group, geographical location, and corruption. As they operate enterprises with increasing similarity to legitimate businesses, such groups also have taken advantage of the region's increasingly strong and well-integrated communications and transportation infrastructure.

Historical and cultural ties play an important role in the distribution of transnational crime in the region. For example, Portugal and Spain are natural bridgeheads for narcotics trafficking into Europe from Latin America, and a number of large Chinese and Turkish communities provide cover in many West European countries for criminal organizations of the same ethnic background. A more recent trend is cooperation among criminal groups of different ethnic backgrounds, often bringing a group such as the Albanians into territory traditionally dominated by domestic groups such as the Italians. The cooperation of crime groups has been especially evident in Western Europe. The trend parallels the pragmatic globalization of legitimate commerce and is a strong driver in the increased "transnationalization" of criminal activities. However, it must be noted that traditional, violent "turf wars" still occur in the European underworld.

Western Europe also has provided terrorist cells with a favorable environment for planning, recruiting, and fund-raising. As is the case for conventional crime, the region's sophisticated communications and transportation infrastructure offers valuable assistance to such terrorist activities, as does the presence of large immigrant communities from which to recruit. Until recently, the lax immigration and anti-terrorist policies of several West European countries also fostered the preparatory stages of terrorist activities, such as fund-raising and recruiting. In many European countries, the events of September 11 have brought the first stages of a pronounced reversal of those conditions.

WESTERN HEMISPHERE

The Western Hemisphere countries to be examined in this report—Canada, Colombia, Mexico, and the Triborder Area including parts of Argentina, Brazil, and Paraguay—present a variety of conditions favoring transnational crime and some terrorist activity. Law enforcement and border conditions in Canada and Mexico have promoted the trafficking of narcotics and people across the long borders that those countries share with the United States, as well as the presence of large numbers of illegal immigrants within those countries. In the case of Canada, this condition also has resulted in the movement of some terrorists into the United States. Colombia and the TBA have long-standing conditions of lawlessness that have fostered intensive narcotics and arms trafficking and a high level of violence (in the case of Colombia) and a wide variety of trafficking activity, some of which apparently has subsidized terrorist cells from abroad (in the case of the TBA).

Canada

Introduction

Canada has played a significant role as a base for both transnational criminal activity and terrorist activity. This role is magnified by the country's extensive border with the United States and a long tradition of commercial and cultural relations between the countries. At least until recently, a major factor has been Canada's policies toward border enforcement and illegal immigration.

According to a 2001 report by the U.S. Department of State, "Overall anti-terrorism cooperation with Canada is excellent, and stands as a model of how the United States and other nations can work together on terrorism issues."[580] Canada has assisted and cooperated with the United States on all fronts of the current war against terrorism. It has, for example, frozen the assets of suspected terrorists and is working closely with the United States to improve security along their common borders. Canadian and U.S. customs and immigration agencies, police forces, and intelligence agencies have a long history of cooperation on border security. This coordination has been strengthened in recent years through formal arrangements such as the U.S.-Canadian Bilateral Consultative Group on Counterterrorism Cooperation (BCG) and the Smart Border Action Plan.[581]

---

[580]U.S. Department of State, *Patterns of Global Terrorism 2001.*
<http://www.state.gov/s/ct/rls/pgtrpt/2001/html/10248.htm>
[581] Embassy of Canada, Washington, D.C., "The Smart Border Declaration," 11 February 2003.
http://www.canadianembassy.org/border/declaration-en.asp; and Embassy of Canada, Washington, D.C., "Canada-U.S. Cross Border Crime and Security Cooperation." http://www.canadianembassy.org/border/crime-en.asp

According to numerous intelligence and law enforcement reports, however, terrorists and international organized crime groups increasingly are using Canada as an operational base and transit country en route to the United States. A generous social-welfare system, lax immigration laws, infrequent prosecutions, light sentencing, and long borders and coastlines offer many points and methods of entry that facilitate movement to and from various countries, particularly to the United States. These factors combine to make Canada a favored destination for terrorists and international organized crime groups.

Contributing Factors

Three broad factors contribute to Canada's position as a favored destination for terrorists and international criminals. First, as a modern liberal democracy Canada possesses a number of features that make it hospitable to terrorists and international criminals. The Canadian Constitution guarantees rights such as the right to life, liberty, freedom of movement, freedom of speech, protection against unreasonable search and seizure, and protection against arbitrary detention or imprisonment that make it easier for terrorists and international criminals to operate. In addition, a technologically advanced economy and infrastructure facilitate operations and activities as well as providing a myriad of opportunities for abuse.[582]

Second, Canada's geographical features and its location make it uniquely inviting to terrorists and international crime groups. Canada and the United States share a 5,525 mile-long border (7,000 miles including Alaska) that defies full control. There are 130 official land ports of entry between the United States and Canada, and thousands of unguarded points along the border across which individuals and illicit goods can be transported. In addition, there are no man made barriers along the U.S.-Canadian border to restrict crossing.[583]

Third, particular systemic and institutional characteristics make Canada hospitable to international terrorists and criminals. David Griffin, Executive Officer of the Canadian Police Association, explained:

---

[582] Canada, Department of Justice, "Constitution Acts of 1867 and 1982." <http://laws.justice.gc.ca/en/const>; and Canada, Department of Justice, "Canadian Charter of Rights and Freedoms." <http://laws.justice.gc.ca/en/charter/index.html>
[583] Wendell Sanford, Consul of Canada, remarks for an Address: "Canada Post 9/11 – The New True North Strong and Free," University of California, Berkeley, Oct. 9, 2002.

Our proximity to the United States of America makes Canada extremely vulnerable, however it is our lax immigration policy, open borders, weak laws, archaic justice system, an even weaker corrections system and under enforcement that make us extremely attractive to the sophisticated criminal.[584]

In a 1999 Canadian Security Intelligence Service (CSIS) report entitled "Exploitation of Canada's Immigration System: An Overview of Security Intelligence Concerns," CSIS Director Ward Elcock is quoted as saying that "in most cases, [terrorists] appear to use Canadian residence as a safe haven, a means to raise funds, to plan or support overseas activities or as a way to obtain Canadian travel documents which make global travel easier." According to the report, more than 50 terrorist groups are believed to be operating in Canada, including the Algerian Armed Islamic Group, the Egyptian Islamic Jihad, the Tamil Tigers, Sikh extremists, the Kurdistan Workers Party, Hizballah, and extremist Irish groups.[585]

According to a 1999 report by Canada's Special Senate Committee on Security and Intelligence,

> Illegal migration into Canada—primarily through the refugee determination system—persists as a concern from two perspectives. First, it is a means by which terrorists may circumvent Canada's vetting process abroad and enter in search of a temporary or permanent haven. Once in Canada, they may conduct fundraising or other activities or, in a very few cases, organize acts of violence in Canada or against other countries. Second, large volumes of illegal migrants provide the stream in which a few terrorists can ultimately gain entry to the United States by circumventing Canadian and United States border controls.[586]

Canada has arguably the most generous asylum system of any country in the world. Aliens have a substantially higher chance of gaining asylum in Canada than in the United States. In 1999, Canada granted asylum to 54 percent of applicants, compared with 35 percent in the United States. This condition, combined with easy entry into the United States from Canada, explains why Canada is a primary transition point for smuggled aliens.[587]

---

[584] David Griffin, "Organised Crime in Canada," *Police* Magazine, January 2001. <http://www.polfed.org/magazine/01_2001/01_2001_orgcrime.htm>
[585] Canadian Security Intelligence Service Director Ward Elcock, in Jonathan Dube, "Safe Haven for Terror?" *ABCNEWS.com*. Jan. 14, 2000. <http://abcnews.go.com/sections/world/DailyNews/canada_terrorism000114.html>
[586] Canada, Senate, Special Committees on Terrorism and Public Safety, "Response to Recommendations of the Senate Special Committees on Terrorism and Public Safety," January 1999. <http://www.parl.gc.ca/36/1/parlbus/commbus/senate/com-e/secu-e/rep-e/repsecintjan99-e.htm>
[587] Jeffrey Gettleman, "Canadians Begin to Say No to Immigrants From China," *Los Angeles Times*, Sep. 11, 1999.

Perhaps until recently, there has also not been widespread concern that Canada could be the victim of a terrorist attack. Sensitivity to civil liberties combined with this low threat perception has made both the adoption and the enforcement of tougher immigration laws and strong counter terrorism measures more difficult. The fact that the 2002 bill designed to make Canada's immigration laws less favorable to terrorists and international criminals is entitled the "Immigration and Refugee Protection Act" serves as an indication of the prevailing concern for or priority placed upon civil liberties in Canada.

Crimes committed in Canada are not considered relevant to asylum requests unless they would bring more than ten years of imprisonment. [588] This provision means that most of the criminal means by which terrorists raise funds—such as fraud, theft, and counterfeiting—would not disqualify them for asylum, even if they are found guilty. The same can be said for a portion of the illegal activities engaged in by international organized criminal groups.

Upon arriving at a Canadian port of entry, an individual claiming refugee status normally is released, with no provision for monitoring, rather than being detained pending investigation, as is the practice in Great Britain and the United States.[589] As their claim is under consideration, such claimants can receive work permits, welfare payments, and housing and health care from the government.[590] Deportation orders seldom are carried out for those whose refugee claims are denied.[591]

As of April 2003, Canada's Immigration and Refugee Board had a backlog of 53,000 asylum cases. A 2003 report by Canada's Auditor-General said Canada has lost track of 36,000 people who have been ordered to leave the country over the past six years. The report also notes that only 44 of Canada's 272 staffed points of entry have immigration officers available to conduct the second level of screening required for suspect individuals, and the 44 points that do have immigration officers able to perform this screening are not staffed 24 hours a day. When

---

[588] These features are identified in the course of interviews conducted by the Public Broadcasting Service's documentary program *Frontline*, with Bill Bauer, former member of the Canadian Immigration and Refugee Board; Elinor Caplin, Canada's Minister of Immigration; and David Harris, former chief of strategic planning for the Canadian Security Intelligence Service (CSIS). "Is Canada a Safe Haven for Terrorists?" *Frontline*, PBS, 2001. www.pbs.org/wgbh/pages/frontline/shows/trail/etc/canada.html#harris

[589] "Is Canada a Safe Haven for Terrorists?" *Frontline*, PBS, 2001. www.pbs.org/wgbh/pages/frontline/shows/trail/etc/canada.html#harris

[590] "Is Canada a Safe Haven for Terrorists?" *Frontline*, PBS, 2001. www.pbs.org/wgbh/pages/frontline/shows/trail/etc/canada.html#harris

[591] United States, Congress, 106th House of Representatives, The Committee on the Judiciary, Hearing Before the Subcommittee on Immigration and Claims, "Threat to the United States," 26 January 2000.

no immigration officer is available to do the second screening, the person is allowed into Canada and asked to go to another border crossing. [592]

Terrorist Activity

Terrorist groups operating in Canada generate funds from activities such as drug trafficking and arms smuggling, as well as through charitable donations. Islamic terrorist groups have engaged in both petty crime and organized criminal ventures to raise funds. The Royal Canadian Mounted Police has determined, for example, that profits from a number of auto theft rings in Ontario and Quebec have gone to support the Lebanese terrorist group Hizballah.[593]

Specific instances of crime in Canada supporting terrorist activities have been documented. In October 2002, the *National Post* reported that the CSIS had determined that Hizballah had laundered of tens of thousands of dollars through Canadian banks, while drawing on the accounts to shop for military equipment. According to the CSIS documentation, Hizballah agents had sought blasting devices, night-vision goggles, powerful computers, and camera equipment to record attacks against Israeli forces.[594]

In December 1999, an al Qaeda-trained terrorist, Ahmed Ressam, was arrested as he tried to cross into the United States with more than 100 pounds of powerful explosives intended to blow up a terminal at Los Angeles International Airport. In Canada, Ressam reportedly supplemented his monthly welfare payments by stealing cash, credit cards, traveler's checks, and passports in Montreal. Ressam was convicted once for theft, but he never was jailed.

Transnational Criminal Activity

According to the Canadian Royal Mounted Police's annual reports from 1999 through 2002, most of the major international organized crime groups are represented in Canada, including Asian, Eastern European, Italian, and Latin American organizations. The activities of these groups include drug trafficking, fraud, counterfeiting, money laundering, migrant and

---

[592] Bill Curry and Andrew McIntosh, "Ottawa Loses Track of 36,000 Deportees," *National Post* [Toronto], 9 April 2003.

[593] Stewart Bell, "Hezbollah Uses Canada as Base: CSIS Agency Wiretaps Show Suspected Operatives Using Laundered Money to Buy Materiel," *National Post* [Toronto], 31 October 2002.

[594] Bell, "Hezbollah Uses Canada as Base."

contraband smuggling, and illegal gaming.[595] Asian and East European based organized crime groups are the most active in Canada.

In 1999 Canada's Criminal Intelligence Service (CISC) reported that Asian organized crime groups operating in British Columbia included triads from Hong Kong and Taiwan; the mainland Chinese Big Circle Boys; the Lotus group, comprised mostly of Canadian born Chinese; and numerous other Vietnamese and Chinese gangs. Big Circle is the most active Asian organized crime group operating in Canada. These criminal organizations engage in a variety of enterprises, regularly sharing expertise and personnel. Asian groups continue to expand their association with other organized crime groups and criminal gangs at the regional, national, and international level. An example of the cooperation between groups is the use of Big Circle personnel by triad groups for enforcement.[596] Big Circle is not itself a triad group, but many of its members belong to triads in the typical pattern of overlapping membership among Chinese groups.

Based primarily in the urban centers of Vancouver, Calgary, Edmonton, Toronto and Montreal, Asian based organized crime groups are engaged in trafficking cocaine; the trafficking, production and exporting of marijuana; the importation and distribution of Southeast Asian heroin; and, recently, the production of the "designer drug" ecstasy.[597]

According to authorities, the importation of heroin is among the most profitable and prolific crimes committed by Asian groups in Canada. The importation of heroin with a purity as high as 99 per cent from Thailand and China is primarily controlled by the Big Circle in the Greater Toronto area. Vietnamese gangs are primarily responsible for its distribution.

Asian groups also are involved in large-scale trafficking in migrants, using Canada as both a destination country and as a conduit to the United States. The Akwesasne Mohawk Territory, Walpole Island and the Niagara area are the routes favored for trafficking both goods and people into the United States.[598]

The two largest Hong Kong triads, 14K and Sun Yee On, have increased their presence in Canada in recent years and made substantial property investments during the 1990s. Prominent

---

[595] Royal Canadian Mounted Police, "RCMP Fact Sheets 2000-2001: Fact Sheet No. 9: Organized Crime." www.rcmp-grc.gc.ca/pdfs/facts_2001_e.htm#factsno9www.rcmp-grc.gc.ca/pdfs/facts_2001_e.htm#factsno9
[596] Margaret E. Beare, *Criminal Conspiracies: Organized Crime in Canada* (Nelson: Canada, 1996), 84.
[597] "Asian-Based Organised Crime," in Criminal Intelligence Service Canada, *Annual Report 2002.* <http://www.cisc.gc.ca/AnnualReport2002/Cisc2002/asian2002.html>
[598] "Asian-Based Organised Crime."

14K members from Hong Kong and Macau have immigrated to Canada during this time, and Sun Yee On triad members have settled in Toronto, Edmonton, and Vancouver.[599]

East European organized crime groups, which include organizations from the former Soviet Union, Bulgaria, the former Yugoslavia, Hungary, Poland, and Romania, also are expanding their activities in Canada. Groups from the former Soviet republics tend to be the strongest. East European groups are particularly active in the urban centers of Ontario, Quebec, British Columbia, and the Maritime Provinces; they engage primarily in financial fraud through a variety of credit card schemes and Internet fraud, theft, contraband smuggling, illicit drug importation, vehicle theft and illegal export, and money laundering.[600] Pragmatic relationships often are established with Asian groups and domestic motorcycle gangs to fulfill particular enterprises.

Colombian cartels are responsible for the majority of the cocaine trafficked into Canada. These cartels are reported to have formed affiliations with Eastern European and Italian organized crime groups to distribute cocaine within Canada's borders. Canada is a destination and a transit point to the United States for women, children, and men trafficked for purposes of sexual exploitation, labor, and the drug trade. Trafficked migrants originate primarily in China's Fujian Province,[601] Southeast Asia, Eastern Europe, and Russia.[602]

The Royal Canadian Mounted Police Performance Report to Parliament for the years 1999-2000 describes organized trans-border criminality of all types as thriving, with many organized crime groups now engaging in the trafficking of migrants. The links between organized crime groups and the trafficking of people are being "strengthened" as smugglers form agreements to transport illegal migrants from all over the world into Canada. According to a Toronto newspaper report, "Collaboration between trafficking organizations is evident, whereby ethnic and national groups interact, facilitating the provision of transport, safe houses, local contacts and travel documentation."[603] The majority of illegal migrants continue to enter Canada

---

[599] "Asian Organized Crime," in Federation of American Scientists, *International Crime Threat Assessment 2000.* <http://www.fas.org/irp/threat/pub45270chap3.html#r14>

[600] "East European-Based Organized Crime," in Criminal Intelligence Service Canada, *Annual Report, 2002.* <http://www.cisc.gc.ca/AnnualReport2002/Cisc2002/european2002.html>

[601] Jennifer Bolz, "Chinese Organized Crime and Illegal Alien Trafficking: Humans as a Commodity," *Asian Affairs,* 22, no. 3 (Fall 1995).

[602] U.S. Department of State, *Trafficking in Persons Report 2002.* <http://www.state.gov.g/tip/rls/tiprpt/2002>

[603] Andrew Mitrovica, "Gangs Unite to Capitalize on Human Smuggling," *The Globe and Mail* [Toronto], January 8, 2001.

by regular commercial international flights.[604] Chapter II of the Report of the Special Senate Committee on Security and Intelligence explains how this is often done. Illegal migrants move into Canada by "losing" the identification they used to board an airplane, claiming refugee status when they arrive, and disappearing into a Canadian trafficking system upon their release. The trafficking system then either brings them underground in Canada or moves them across the United States border.[605]

Smuggling illegal migrants is a multibillion-dollar business. Total earnings in Canada were estimated in 1995 at around US$3.2 billion per year. Alien smugglers are rarely prosecuted in Canada; for those who are, sentencing is much lighter than it is for narcotics trafficking. Migrants pay traffickers as much as US$50,000, much of which is repaid by labor in sweatshops or participation in another illegal activity.[606]

Recent Developments

In response to the terrorist attacks of September 11, 2001, and revelations that terrorists have found safe haven within its borders, Canada has taken diplomatic and legislative steps to reduce the attractiveness of Canada as a destination or base for terrorists and international criminals. Among those steps was the Smart Border Declaration of 2001, which established a joint action plan for tightening border controls on both sides of the Canada-United States line. To minimize commercial delays, the plan includes a pre-screening system to allow frequent border crossers to enter and exit Canada quickly.[607] In addition, in late 2002 Canada finally added Hamas, the Islamic Army of Aden, Harkat-ul-Mujahedeen, Asbat Al-Ansar, Palestinian Islamic Jihad, Hizballah, and Jaish-e-Mohammed to Canada's list of terrorist groups, making fundraising for these groups illegal.[608]

In December 2001, the Canadian Parliament passed the Anti-Terrorism Act, which made perpetrating, financing, or contributing to terrorist activity a crime. The Act increases the

---

[604] "Asian-Based Organized Crime."
[605] Canada, Senate, Special Senate Committee on Security and Intelligence.
[606] Bolz.
[607] "Canada: Immigration, Asylum and US," *Migration News*, 10, no. 1 (January 2003). http://migration.ucdavis.edu/mn/Archive_MN/jan_2003-06mn.html; and "New Screening Process Will Speed Traffic into Canada," *Canadian Press Newswire*, Dec. 6, 2001.
[608] Stewart Bell, "Liberals Relent, Hezbollah Outlawed: Graham Says It's Due to Recent Evidence," *National Post* [Toronto], December 12, 2002.

government's investigative powers, criminalizes fundraising and providing logistical support for terrorist activity in Canada or abroad, and provides recourses for freezing or seizing assets belonging to supporters or members of terrorist organizations.

Because Canada's immigration laws are arguably the foremost factor in making Canada hospitable to terrorists and international criminals, the changes to the existing system included in the Immigration and Refugee Protection Act, passed in June 2002, will make it more difficult for such individuals to gain entry or stay in Canada.[609] The major changes in the law are the introduction of in-depth CSIS screening upon arrival in Canada rather than after a significant delay; establishment of nine factors, including misrepresentation of identity and connections with a terrorist or criminal group, as grounds for denial of entry into Canada; increased penalties for immigration offenses such as smuggling; measures to discourage fraudulent immigration applications; reduction of the appeal rights of individuals identified by authorities for deportation for having committed a crime; and increased authority to arrest foreign nationals suspected of a crime or terrorist act.

Together these new laws have the ability to reduce the incentives and ability for terrorists and international criminals to operate in Canada. However, enforcement will be the key. Whether these new laws are effective in reducing the use of Canada as an operational base and transit country for terrorists and international criminals will depend in large part on whether a new balance between civil liberties and security concerns will yield effective prevention. As a possible first indication of future trends, in October 2002 three Filipinos received a two-year sentence for trafficking Chinese migrants into Canada, although the new Immigration and Refugee Protection Act calls for up to a ten-year sentence for such a crime.[610]

In September 2001 Bill Bauer, former member of the Canadian Immigration and Refugee Board, described the judicial approach to human trafficking that preceded the new legislation: "No judge who has tried a trafficker—and very few are ever arrested, let alone tried—has imposed a fine greater than $5,000."[611] The 2001 annual report by the CISC explains that investigation and prosecution of those involved in human trafficking often is difficult because

---

[609] Canada, Citizenship and Immigration, "Bill C-11 Immigration and Refugee Protection Act: What Is New in the Proposed Immigration and Refugee Protection Act," July 2001.
www.cic.gc.ca/english/irpa/c11%2Dnew.htmlwww.cic.gc.ca/english/irpa/c11%2Dnew.html
[610] "Three Sailors Sentenced for Smuggling Chinese Migrants," *National Post* [Toronto], 31 October 2002.
[611] Ron Claiborne, "A Border Breached: Canada's Immigration Laws Draw New Scrutiny," 26 September 2001.
www.abcnews.go.com/sections/world/DailyNews/claiborne_border010926.html

the trafficking organizations are transnational networks with subordinate members who shield their leaders.[612] In order to change the current situation, the profit/risk calculations of the human traffickers must be altered. Only severe penalties can offset the very high potential profits of trafficking migrants into North America.

The new Immigration and Refugee Protection Act has been criticized because it does not change the definition of "serious criminal" as applied to resident aliens. To fall into that category under the new law, an individual still must have received at least a ten-year prison sentence. Thus, for example, Ahmed Ressam would not be subject to deportation because he had only been convicted of petty thefts.

Conclusion

Canada has a well-deserved reputation as a protector of human rights, including the rights of non-citizens who are entering or leaving the country. That protection, together with Canada's very long, loosely monitored border with the richest country in the world and its well-developed commercial, communications, and transportation infrastructures, has promoted the presence of criminal and terrorist groups and individuals. For terrorist groups, Canada has been a safe haven, transit point, and place to raise funds; for criminal groups Canada has provided a route for the trafficking of humans and various illegal commodities, many of which reach the United States.

Canada's new legislative initiatives have the potential to reduce the country's appeal to terrorist organization, international organized crime groups and alien smugglers, as well as their ability to operate. However, the economic necessity of expedient movement of persons and goods across the US-Canadian border and Canada's liberal democratic identity may continue to limit the adoption of security measures necessary to completely halt the operations of these groups.

---

[612] Canada, Criminal Intelligence Service, *Annual Report on Organized Crime in Canada, 2001: Asian-Based Organized Crime.* www.cisc.gc.ca/AnnualReport2001/

Colombia

Introduction

Although Colombia has a long democratic tradition, it also has a history of political violence that has included six interparty wars in the nineteenth century and two more in the twentieth century. By far the most violent country in the Western Hemisphere, Colombia—which also is the leading cocaine-producing country—remains mired in a morass of drug-related guerrilla, state, and paramilitary violence. Experts generally credit the regime of President Alvaro Uribe (inaugurated in 2002) with beginning to reduce violence during Uribe's first year in office.

In recent decades, three different types of nonstate subversive organization—guerrillas, paramilitary groups, and drug mafias—have been pitted in violent conflict against each other, the government, or both. Major left-wing guerrilla groups have been waging violent conflict since the 1960s. Beginning in the 1980s, this insurgency was exacerbated by the anti-guerrilla activities of a right-wing paramilitary organization, the United Self-Defense Forces of Colombia (Spanish initialism ACCU), which now forms the center of a fast-growing umbrella organization. At the same time, organized crime has fuelled warfare by a variety of mutually beneficial support activities carried on with the other groups. These relationships have created a certain interdependency between narcotics trafficking groups on one side and guerrilla and paramilitary groups on the other. Although the government dismantled the country's two major cartels in the 1990s, many smaller groups emerged and have continued to operate with impunity. Colombian narcotics groups have established significant ties with foreign organizations for the sale of narcotics, the laundering of money, and the acquisition of arms.

Contributing Factors

Geographical Factors

Colombia's location at the gate of South America, bordering Panama and the Caribbean Sea, traditionally has facilitated trafficking in narcotics and other types of contraband. Colombia is the only South American country with coastlines on both the Caribbean and the Pacific Ocean.

Trafficking and illegal transit also are facilitated by the fact that the borders with all of Colombia's five neighboring countries traverse largely unpopulated jungle regions.

Institutional Factors

Beginning in the 1970s, a booming narcotics trade spread corruption in Colombia's military and law enforcement agencies, undermining public confidence in those institutions.[613] By the 1980s, all three types of violent groups (guerrillas, paramilitaries, and narcotics traffickers) were challenging government authority. The justice system especially has sagged under the weight of corruption and narco-terrorism in the decades that followed. As Colombia's homicide rate was rising sharply in the 1980s and the 1990s, by 1996 conviction rates for homicide dropped from 11 percent to 4 percent of total incidents.[614] A complex interdependency exists between Colombian guerrillas and narcotics traffickers, based on the guerrillas' protection of cultivation and processing operations and the sources from which traffickers make their purchases. Because the fundamental interests of the two groups are irreconcilable, however—the traffickers are capitalists, whereas the guerrillas' ideology is anti-capitalist—the two have been in conflict.[615]

Scholars generally agree that alliances exist among narcotics traffickers, large landowners, multinational corporations, industrial groups, and agencies and individuals of the state. The last group includes corrupt politicians, members of Congress, judicial and other government officials, and members of the military.[616] Many members of the armed forces are known to cooperate with narcotics traffickers. Aside from corrupt connections, Colombia's military as an institution has not viewed narcotics traffickers as a threat to society, and traffickers often have supported the military's counterinsurgency efforts.

The narcotics earnings and narco-terrorism that have accompanied Colombia's drug industry have strengthened the tradition of domestic and international companies creating private

---

[613] Harvey F. Kline, "Colombia: Lawlessness, Drug Trafficking, and Carving Up the State," in Robert I. Rothberg, ed., *State Failure and State Weakness in a Time of Terror* (Washington, D.C.: Brookings Institution Press, 2003), 176.
[614] Mauricio Rubio, "Violence, Organized Crime, and the Criminal Justice System in Colombia," *Journal of Economic Issues*, 32, no. 2 (June 1998): 605-10.
[615] Nizani Richani, *Systems of Violence: The Political Economy of War and Peace in Colombia* (Albany, New York: State University of New York Press, 2002), 109.
[616] Richani, 56.

security forces.[617] Since their government authorization in 1994, these military-dominated forces have proliferated throughout the country, adding another layer of paramilitary activity and often themselves becoming involved in criminal activities.[618]

According to political economist Nizih Richani, contraband and narcotics trafficking have thrived in Colombia because of a combination of dire economic conditions and a four-decade insurgency that has prevented the state from extending its authority over all of Columbia's national territory. The state's presence is especially weak in the five states containing the largest coca plantations. According to Richani, the ongoing success of guerrilla forces has offered protection and encouragement to peasant and commercial farms that shift from conventional crops to coca cultivation.[619]

Government corruption has played a significant role in supporting criminal activities in Colombia. The 2002 Corruption Perceptions Index (CPI) of Transparency International (TI) placed Columbia 57th among the countries evaluated.[620] According to TI, "Colombia has suffered the tragic consequences of endemic theft by politicians and public officials for decades."[621] In its *Global Corruption Report*, TI cites a World Bank survey of 2002, which found that 50 percent of state contracts in Colombia involve bribes. TI concludes, "….this behavior [has] exacerbated underdevelopment and lawlessness in the countryside."[622]

Economic Factors

Analysts believe that many Colombians have resorted to growing coca (the base crop for cocaine production), trafficking in drugs, and joining armed groups as a result of poverty and high unemployment (13.8 percent at the end of 2001, but as high as 35 percent among youths 18 to 24 years old) and social factors such as the massive internal displacement of the rural population. In 2001 Colombia's per capita gross domestic product was only US$1,821, and an

---

[617] Richani, 50-51.
[618] "Colombian Self-Defense," Americas.org report, November 2000.
<http://www.americas.org/News/Features/200011_Private_Security/Colombia.asp>
[619] Richani, 95.
[620] Transparency International, *Corruption Perceptions Index 2002*. <http://www.transparency
.org/cpi/2002/cpi2002.en.html>
[621] Eduardo Wills Herrera and Nubia Urueña Cortés, "South America," in Transparency International, *Global Corruption Report 2003*, 108.
[622] Herrera and Cortés, 108.

estimated 55 percent of the population was below the poverty line.[623] Armed groups and narcotics traffickers are believed to recruit many young members who are unemployed or displaced. (Colombia is third in the world in number of internal refugees.)[624]

In 1999 the estimated total value of contraband originating from, arriving in, or transiting Colombia reached US$2.2 billion, after having doubled over the previous decade. This amount accounted for 25 percent of the value of the country's total imports and 50 percent of its total exports. This significant economic contribution explains why contraband has the protection of powerful groups that include politicians, business organizations, customs authorities, and the mainly Japanese and Korean multinational corporations that provide the contraband goods.[625]

Narcotics

Colombia remains the world's leading producer and distributor of cocaine base and cocaine, manufacturing nearly 80 percent of the world's cocaine hydrochloride in 2002.[626] Colombia also is the primary supplier of heroin to the United States. In addition to the large amounts of cocaine base produced domestically, Colombian traffickers import that substance from Peru and Bolivia and process it into cocaine hydrochloride. Both Colombia's Caribbean and Pacific coasts are major transshipment points for large shipments of cocaine and cannabis, much of which is carried to Mexico and other destinations on fishing vessels and speedboats. The major production region is eastern Colombia; organizing cartels are centered in Bogota, Cali, Medellin, and other cities. Most of the Colombian heroin that reaches the United States comes via couriers on commercial airlines.[627]

In addition to supporting independent narcotics traffickers and cartels, the drug trade is a major source of funding for guerrilla group Revolutionary Armed Forces of Colombia (Spanish initialism FARC) and the paramilitary United Self-Defense Forces of Colombia (Spanish initialism AUC). A second guerrilla group, the National Liberation Army (Spanish initialism

---

[623] Economist Intelligence Unit, *Colombia: Country Profile 2002* (London: 2002), 31, 65; and U.S. Central Intelligence Agency, *The World Factbook 2002* (Washington, D.C.: 2002), 114.
[624] Julia E. Sweig, "What Kind of War for Colombia?" *Foreign Affairs*, 81, no. 5 (September-October 2002): 125.
[625] Richani, 101.
[626] Eric Green, "U.S. Says Colombia Remains World's Leading Producer of Cocaine: State Dept. Details Illicit Drug Activities in Americas and World," U.S. Department of State International Information Programs report, 3 March 2002. <http://164.109.48.86/topical/global/drugs/03030302.htm>
[627] U.S. Department of State, Bureau for International Narcotics and Law Enforcement Affairs, *International Narcotics Control Strategy Report 2003*, IV-24.

ELN) has been active in narcotics trafficking to a lesser degree only since 1998. According to military information, in 2001 at least 32 of the FARC's 61 fronts and 7 of the ELN's 41 fronts were known to derive income from the drug trade.[628] Since 1999, the FARC reportedly has sought to establish a monopoly position over access to coca and sales of cocaine base to cartels in much of southern Colombia.[629]

The FARC also is believed to be involved in opium poppy cultivation, the techniques of which were learned from Afghani and Pakistani traffickers. Colombian police sources report that dozens of Afghans, using false Pakistani passports, have been involved in processing heroin in Colombia.[630] However, although Colombia is the largest producer of opium poppy in South America, its highest output in 2001 was only 2 percent of the world's total, and output has begun to decline.[631]

Despite extensive involvement in the narcotics trade, Colombia's guerrilla and paramilitary groups are not close partners of the country's drug cartels. The organizations cooperate only when both sides have something to gain. Political scientist Patricia Bibes explains the relationship: "The guerrillas provide security assistance and defense to the drug traffickers, and the drug traffickers provide financial aid to the guerrillas in return."[632] However, according to law enforcement expert James Van de Velde, by the mid-1990s "taxation" and protection of drug farmers and traffickers had become the primary financial support of guerrilla organizations.[633]

Paramilitary Groups

Right-wing paramilitary organizations emerged in Colombia, with subtle backing from the military, to protect the interests of regional elites. However, the existence of paramilitaries

---

[628] Angel Rabasa and Peter Chalk, *Colombian Labyrinth: The Synergy of Drugs and Insurgency and Its Implications for Regional Stability* (Santa Monica, California: Rand, 2001), 32.

[629] "Colombian Rebel Connection to Mexican Drug Cartel," U.S. Department of State statement, 29 November 2002. <http://164.109.48.86/topical/global/drugs/00112901.htm>

[630] Martin Arostegui, "Search for Bin Laden Links Looks South," United Press International report, 12 October 2001. <http://www.autentico.org/oa09505.html>

[631] "Opium Poppy Cultivation in Colombia Down by 25 Percent, Says ONDCP," U.S. Department of State International Information Program report, 13 May 2003. <http://164.109.48.86/topical/global/drugs/03051301.htm>

[632] Patricia Bibes, "Colombia: The Military and the Narco-Conflict," *Low Intensity Conflict & Law Enforcement*, 9, no. 1 (Spring 2000): 41.

[633] James R. Van de Velde, "The Growth of Criminal Organizations and Insurgent Groups Abroad Due to International Drug Trafficking," *Low Intensity Conflict & Law Enforcement*, 5, no. 3 (Winter 1996): 471.

has only exacerbated conflict. At times the state has attempted to deal with its leftist guerrilla groups by enlisting the help of paramilitary organizations.[634]

Beginning in the 1980s, the ACCU and the umbrella AUC to which it belongs have funded themselves increasingly by narcotics trafficking.[635] Estimates of funding amounts vary widely. According to Colombian military sources, eight of the AUC's 19 fronts derive income from this source.[636] According to the U.S. Drug Enforcement Administration (DEA), AUC leader Carlos Castaño is linked to Colombia's current top drug cartel, the Henao Montoyo organization.[637]

The AUC is the fastest-growing armed organization in Colombia. Its constituent ACCU claims to have 15,000 troops. Many members are former police and military personnel who were discharged for human rights abuses. The AUC's strongholds are in rural areas where federal forces are few.

Transnational Narcotics Ties

In 2001 the commander of the Colombian Armed Forces reported that Russian criminal organizations had sent 10,000 AK-47 rifles to the FARC through Brazilian narcotics dealer Fernando Da Costa. In return, the FARC helped Da Costa to move large shipments of cocaine from Colombia to Brazil. Prior to his arrest in 2001, Da Costa allegedly also channeled arms from Paraguay-based Lebanese importer Fuad Jamil to FARC and other groups, including Hizballah.[638] According to another report, the FARC received a similar shipment of Russian AK-47s from the arms trafficking organization of Vladimiro Montesinos, who was then head of Peru's National Intelligence Agency.[639]

---

[634] Nizih Richani, *Systems of Violence: The Political Economy of War and Peace in Colombia* (Albany, New York: State University of New York Press, 2002), 102-03.

[635] Richani, 108.

[636] Rabasa and Chalk, 32.

[637] U.S. Department of State, Bureau for International Narcotics and Law Enforcement Affairs, *International Narcotics Control Strategy Report 2002*. <http://www.state.gov.g/inl/rls/nrcrpt2002/html/17944.htm>

[638] Louis Esnal, "Nexos con Montesinos" [Nexus with Montesinos], *La Nacion* [Buenos Aires], 24 April 2001, 2; and Eleonora Gosman, "Temen una Guerra entre bandas de narcos en Brasil" [Drug Cartel Wars Are Feared], *Clarín* [Buenos Aires], 24 April 2001.

[639] Bruce Michael Bagley, *Globalization and Transnational Organized Crime: The Russian Mafia in Latin America and the Caribbean*, School of International Studies, University of Miami, 31 October 2001 ,http://www.mamacoca.org/feb2002/art_bagley_globalization_organized_crime_en.html#fn1>

Arrests made by Mexican authorities in November 2000 established links between the FARC and Mexican cocaine traffickers. Evidence showed that the FARC had tried to supply cocaine to the Mexican Tijuana cartel in exchange for cash and possibly weapons.[640] The Cárdenas-Guillén cartel of northern Mexico is known to have maintained a pipeline for Colombian cocaine, which the group shipped across the border into the United States. In May 2003, AUC and FARC operatives reportedly had arrived in Mexico to maintain Mexican drug routes after the arrest of key Mexican figures.[641]

The Aruba-based Mansur clan runs a trafficking empire that was founded by the Cali cartel and a Cosa Nostra clan. According to a lawsuit filed in 2000 against the Philip Morris Tobacco Company by the governors of 25 of Colombia's states, the Mansur company sold tobacco products to traffickers in exchange for narcotics profits. When those products were smuggled into Colombia, the pesos earned by the subsequent sale of the products went into the Colombian bank accounts of the narcotics traffickers who had generated the initial profits. This transaction was the final stage in the money laundering operation known as the Black Market Peso Exchange, which connected profits from the United States market with the Colombian cartels.[642] A Syrian-Lebanese clan leader, Mohamed Ali Farhad, has been linked to money laundering activities of the Mansur company and has been investigated for using profits from arms and narcotics trafficking to fund Islamic fundamentalist groups, including Hizballah.[643]

Non-Indigenous Organized Crime

According to official documentation, Colombia has been a transit or base point for the operations of some foreign criminal groups. Solntsevo, one of Russia's largest criminal organizations, established ties with Colombian narcotics traffickers in 1992. In the early 1990s, Solntsevo granted the Cali cartel of Colombia the right to distribute cocaine throughout Russia and to use Russia as a base for distribution in Eastern Europe.[644] In the second half of the 1990s, Colombian narcotics traffickers began receiving small-scale weapons from Russia in exchange

---

[640] "Colombian Rebel Connection to Mexican Drug Cartel."

[641] "Colombian Paramilitary Group Denies Connections with Drug Trafficking," *El Universal* [Mexico City], 5 May 2003 (FBIS Document LAP20030505000102).

[642] "The Black Market Peso Exchange." <http://scolar.vsc.edu:8003/VSCCAT/ACR-1669>

[643] Fabio Castillo, "The Hizballah Contacts in Colombia," *El Spectador* [Bogota], 9 December 2001 (FBIS Document LAP20011210000036).

[644] "The Russian Connection," *Cambio 16* [Madrid], 6 October 1997 (FBIS Document 98L01001A).

for a percentage of the Colombian narcotics output. In 1999 and 2000, Russian crime groups are believed to have strengthened their alliances with new Colombian cartels such as Costa, Norte del Valle, and Los Llanos.[645]

Terrorist Groups

The Department of State's Bureau for International Narcotics and Law Enforcement Affairs calls the FARC "the hemisphere's largest and oldest terrorist group."[646] Although some exchanges have occurred with a branch of the Irish Republican Army,[647] the FARC's terrorist activities largely have been confined to domestic acts such as the hijacking of a domestic commercial flight, the kidnapping of a presidential candidate, the kidnapping and assassination of a former minister of culture, and the kidnapping of three U.S. contractors whose plane crashed in FARC-dominated territory. In 1999 the FARC also killed three American missionaries working in Colombia. The smaller ELN has kidnapped wealthy Colombians for ransom and bombed and extorted multinational and domestic oil companies.[648]

Occasional reports have indicated the presence of Islamic fundamentalist terrorists in Colombia. Mohamed Abed Abdel Aal, a leader of the al Qaeda-affiliated Egyptian Islamic Jihad (Jama'a Islamiyya), who was arrested in Colombia in 1998, allegedly had participated in transactions with Colombian guerrillas involving arms, drugs, and money.[649] In January 2000, Colombian intelligence officials reportedly believed that another Egyptian terrorist suspect, Muhammed Ubayd Abd-al-Al, could have taken refuge in Maicao, Colombia. Maicao, a city near the border of Venezuela, has an Islamic community whose size has been estimated between 4,670 and 8,000. That community comprises the largest and best organized Arab community in Colombia. It is known that a well-established black market for weapons and money laundering exists in Maicao and the neighboring Venezuelan state of Zulia.[650]

---

[645] Alirio Fernando Bustos, "Cayó official de la Armada, su principal enlace: La avanzada de la mafia rusa" [A Retired Navy Officer, Its Principal Liaison, Is Arrested: The Advance of the Russian Mafia], *El Tiempo* [Bogota], 8 February 1999.
[646] U.S. Department of State, *International Narcotics Control Strategy Report 2003*, IV-19.
[647] Center for Defense Information Terrorism Project, "Globalizing Terrorism: The FARC-IRA Connection," 5 June 2002. <http://www.cdi.org/terrorism/farc-ira-pr.cfm>
[648] Council on Foreign Relations and Markle Foundation, "FARC, ELN, AUC: Colombia, Rebels." <http://www.terrorismanswers.com/groups/farc.htm>
[649] "Egyptian Suspect in Luxor Attack Arrives in Ecuador," *The Daily Telegraph* [London], 21 October 1998.
[650] Castillo.

Individuals of Arab descent—possibly affiliated with the radical group Hizballah—reportedly control 70 percent of local commerce in Maicao. According to a Colombian journalist, Hizballah cells in the city have used the money-laundering networks of narcotics traffickers to disguise money that will finance worldwide terrorist operations. Nationalized Arabs who serve as money-laundering couriers have easily obtained Colombian citizenship. The only requirement is two witnesses to verify that an individual was born in Colombia.[651]

Conclusion

Transnational criminal groups and, to a lesser extent, terrorist organizations have taken advantage of the chronically corrupt and violent environment that Colombia presents. Political and judicial reform have not been possible in a system that is controlled by a small elite and has strong links to elements of a thriving narcotics trade. Narcotics-related corruption in the military and law enforcement agencies has undermined public confidence in those institutions. In this environment, powerful guerrilla and paramilitary forces control parts of the country and are increasingly linked with narcotics trafficking activities. The sale of narcotics, the arming of illegal organizations, and the laundering of profits from narcotics sales are activities that bring indigenous groups into cooperation with transnational criminals. There is evidence that some of the exchanges of narcotics, arms, and money also have involved Middle Eastern terrorist organizations.

Mexico

Introduction

Mexico's suitability as a safe haven for transnational criminal and terrorist groups is determined by a variety of factors. Those conditions include geographic proximity and ease of access to the United States; the presence of extra-regional immigrant communities; the volume and sophistication of domestic commercial activity; the volume and ease of trans-border movements of goods, persons and cash; the presence of an established criminal infrastructure; the regulatory environment, transparency, and corruptibility of Mexican institutions; and the capabilities of local law enforcement agencies. From the specific perspective of terrorist

---

[651] Castillo.

organizations, the most important factors are opportunities for the clandestine movement of persons; fundraising and money laundering opportunities; and the existence, vulnerability, and perceived value of potential targets in Mexico.

Mexico's status as the second-largest supplier of U.S. merchandise imports (after Canada), the single largest source of immigrants to the United States, and the most popular foreign tourist destination for Americans imply a level of shared vulnerability rivaled by few other pairs of contiguous nations. Since the mid-1980s, rapid growth in travel between Mexico and the United States and the expansion of trans-border commerce under the North American Free Trade Agreement (NAFTA) have dramatically increased the interdependence of the two nations in security matters, placing new emphasis on factors such as border controls and distribution of drug precursor chemicals.[652]

Factors in Organized Crime and Terrorism

Border Control

Mexico is a major travel destination and air travel hub for Latin America, as well as the biggest source of overland passenger vehicle and pedestrian traffic entering the United States. Under these conditions, flaws in Mexico's visa and border control systems attract the attention of criminal groups. Increased cross-border vehicle traffic, which began in the mid-1990s, has facilitated a variety of transnational criminal activities including the bulk movement of illicit drugs and cash across the United States-Mexico border. Commercial traffic in particular has grown rapidly since the passage of NAFTA. According to the U.S. Department of Transportation, the annual number of truck crossings from Mexico into the United States grew from 2.8 million in 1994 to 4.3 million in 2001. However, the volume of personal vehicle traffic between Mexico and United States, which by 1999 reached 90 million northbound personal vehicle crossings, also has been a significant factor in making extensive border screening impractical.[653]

Tractor- trailers and cars with hidden compartments frequently are used to smuggle drugs out of Mexico into the United States; then the same vehicles are packed with the profits from the

---

[652] David Beard, "NAFTA: Bad Flows in Along with the Goods," *Salt Lake Tribune*, 19 April 1997, A1.
[653] U.S. Department of Transportation, Bureau of Transportation Statistics. <http://www.transtats.bts.gov>

street sale of the drugs and returned to Mexico. Car thieves, smugglers, and money launderers know that vehicles heading south encounter less scrutiny at the border than northbound vehicles because the attention of U.S. Customs and immigration inspectors is focused on northbound traffic.[654] Mexican criminal organizations historically have relied on corruption and understaffing on both sides of the border to move their illicit cargoes to their destinations. These smuggling activities, which have traditionally been dominated by local Mexican border gangs, are increasingly attracting non-Mexican criminal groups as well.

Mexico is the primary source and transit country for undocumented migrants entering the United States. According to the 2000 United States census, Mexicans represent about 4.7 million (55 percent) of the total undocumented population in the United States. Mexico also is the primary transit zone for illegal migrants moving from Central America to the United States. In 2001 Mexican authorities apprehended more than 151,000 individuals in this category,[655] mostly from Guatemala, Nicaragua, and Honduras. Some of Mexico's extra-regional migrants also arrive at Mexican and Central American ports of entry with the assistance of transnational alien smuggling rings. In 2001, Mexico apprehended 1,843 undocumented migrants classified as non-Latin American.[656] Mexico currently is not a major destination for legal immigrants. After the tightening of asylum policies in the 1990s, only 5,828 immigrants were legally admitted during 2002, mainly from Latin America.[657]

The Indigenous Criminal Infrastructure

The large, sophisticated indigenous criminal organizations in Mexico have attracted attention as potential partners for transnational organized crime and terrorist organizations seeking to establish a foothold in the Western Hemisphere. In addition to possessing vital local knowledge, Mexico's criminal gangs and syndicates offer a variety of criminal "skill-sets," such

---

[654] Edward M. Guillen, Chief of Financial Operation, U.S. Drug Enforcement Administration, statement to House Subcommittee on Criminal Justice, Drug Policy, and Human Resources, 23 June 2000."
<http://www.usdoj.gov/dea/pubs/cngrtest/ct062300.htm>

[655] Instituto Nacional de Estadística, Geografía e Informática [Mexico City], *Estadísticas Sociodemográficas, Atención y Control de Indocumentados, 2002* [Sociodemographic Statistics: Illegal Alien Processing and Control].
<http://www.inegi.gob.mx/estadistica/espanol/sociodem/gobernacion/gob_04.html>

[656] George W. Grayson, *Mexico's Forgotten Southern Border* (Washington, D.C.: Center for Migration Studies, 2002).

[657] "Documentación de Inmigrantes" [Documentation of Immigrants], Mexico City: National Migration Institute, 2003. <http://www.inm.gob.mx>

as border smuggling and document falsification skills, which could be harnessed by a foreign partner. Mexico's narcotics trafficking organizations are known to collaborate with extra-regional partners as well as with the Colombian cartels. At least two of the larger drug syndicates, the Arellano Felix and Carrillo Fuentes organizations, have worked with Russian organized crime partners.[658]

Russian criminal organizations have discovered that linkages with one or more of the seven principal Mexican criminal organizations allow them to obtain drugs at low prices and under relatively secure circumstances. In order to maintain a low profile, Russian mafia groups in Mexico often operate out of resorts, hotels, or houses protected and owned by their Mexican associates. Beginning in the late 1990s, the growing importance of the Pacific route as the most reliable maritime corridor for Colombian cocaine bound for Mexico created a demand for the types of open-sea transportation services that Russian and Ukrainian mafia organizations were well positioned to provide. Similarly, some of the Mexican alien smuggling networks are believed to have partnerships with Asian, Middle Eastern, Russian, and Ukrainian human smuggling and trafficking rings.[659]

The desire of Mexican criminal groups for foreign partners is counterbalanced by a reluctance to attract the attention of Mexican and United States law enforcement and intelligence agencies. The increasingly strategic outlook of Mexican narcotics trafficking organizations reduces the likelihood that they would cooperate knowingly with extra-regional criminal or terrorist groups.[660] However, smaller criminal gangs emerging in Mexico may be less discriminating in choosing foreign partners.

Institutionalized Corruption

A tradition of official corruption and influence peddling throughout the seven-decade rule of the Institutional Revolutionary Party (Partido Revolucionario Institucional–PRI) has been a significant factor in promoting criminal activity at various levels. Mexico's twentieth-century

---

[658] Ramón Miró, *Organized Crime and Terrorist Activity in Mexico: 1999-2002,* (Report prepared by the Federal Research Division, Library of Congress, under an Interagency Agreement with the Crime and Narcotics Center, Director of Central Intelligence, February 2003).

[659] Bagley; Gretchen Peters, "Drug Trafficking in the Pacific Has a Distinct Russian Flavor," *San Francisco Chronicle,* 30 May 2001; and Federal Bureau of Investigation, Los Angeles Field Office, "19 Linked to Eurasian Crime Ring Named in Federal Complaint for Alien Smuggling," press release, 3 May 2001.

[660] Miró, *Organized Crime and Terrorist Activity in Mexico: 1999-2002.*

history as a centralized authoritarian regime with heavy state regulation of the economy created opportunities for domestic organized crime groups to function as purveyors of contraband, influence, and evasion and protection services. Organized crime groups historically have relied on large-scale bribery of politicians, civil servants, and law enforcement personnel to protect their criminal enterprises. For example, former drug kingpin Juan García Abrego claimed to have spent up to US$50 million per month to buy protection from Mexican law enforcement and judicial officials during the 1980s.[661]

The political influence of organized crime in Mexico peaked during the administration of President Carlos Salinas de Gortari (1988-94). According to organized crime expert Louise Kelley, during the Salinas years "drug traffickers acquired unprecedented influence at high levels of the national government as well as at the level of regional governorships."[662] Lingering public anger at the Salinas-era scandals contributed to the defeat of the PRI during the 2000 presidential elections, which ended seven decades of single party control over the executive branch.

Deep structural reforms introduced by the Salinas administration eliminated the rationale for organized crime activity based on evasion of burdensome government regulations and tariffs. At the same time, the reforms opened up new channels for criminal participation in the newly liberalized economy.[663] According to regional experts, a politicized and poorly regulated privatization effort during the late 1980s and early 1990s allowed investors linked to Mexican and possibly foreign organized crime groups to expand their holdings within the legal economy.[664]

Drug-related corruption and violence have eroded public trust in Mexico's law enforcement agencies. Much of the public animosity toward the police stems from personal experience of solicitation of bribes by police, poor or nonexistent police response to emergency calls, and soaring levels of street crime in major cities. In 2001, Transparency International rated Mexico nineteenth out of 23 countries in perceived police corruption.[665] Several high-profile police scandals have underscored the apparent intractability of the police corruption problem.

---

[661] "Drug Lord, Now in U.S. Custody, Has Key to Mexican Corruption," *Money Laundering Alert*, February 1996. <http://www.moneylaundering.com>

[662] Louise Kelley, "Corruption and Organized Crime in Mexico in the Post-PRI Transition," *Journal of Contemporary Criminal Justice* 17, No. 3, August 2001, 216.

[663] Kelley, "Corruption and Organized Crime in Mexico," 217.

[664] Fabre, Guilhem, *Criminal Prosperity: Drug Trafficking, Money Laundering and Financial Crisis after the Cold War* (London: Routlege-Courzon, 2003); and Kelley.

[665] Kevin Sullivan, "For Many in Mexico, Bribes a Way of Life," *Washington Post*, 30 October 2001.

According to a 2002 poll cited in the newsweekly *The Economist,* public confidence in the police is so low that four-fifths of all crimes in Mexico never are reported.[666]

Criminal Activity

Finance-Related Crime

In the 1980s and early 1990s, market-oriented structural reforms transformed Mexico's economy from a highly protectionist, public-sector-dominated system to a generally open, deregulated "emerging market" with extensive ties to the United States, Asia, and Europe. This transformation provided new opportunities for criminal organizations to engage in cross-border narcotics trafficking, human smuggling, and money laundering. At the same time, liberalization and deregulation of the economy made obsolete many of the tax and tariff evasion services that domestic crime syndicates had provided in the past. Criminal organizations' role as intermediaries between the Mexican state and the Mexican private sector was reduced, while at the same time their activities aimed at the United States expanded as cross-border trade, financial, and demographic links grew.

The privatization of the financial services sector gave Mexico one of Latin America's most extensive banking systems, consisting of a central bank and six types of banking institutions. Money laundering expert Guilhem Fabre points to incremental investment in newly privatized banks and stocks as the "driving force" behind the economic ascent of Mexico's drug traffickers during the 1990s.[667]

Cross-border financial transactions between Mexico and the United States have grown rapidly since the mid-1990s. The volume of such transactions provides criminal organizations ample opportunities to conceal profits from illicit activities among legal money flows. Mexican immigrants traditionally have relied on the same wire remittance services used by criminal organizations to send money earned in the United States back to Mexico to support their families The value of family remittances to Mexico alone increased from US$5.9 billion in 1999 to US$9.8 billion in 2002.[668] This expansion in the volume of remittances poses an ever-growing

---

[666] "Crime in Mexico," *The Economist* [London], 26 June 2003. <http://www.economist.com>
[667] Fabre, *Criminal Prosperity: Drug Trafficking, Money Laundering, and Financial Crises After the Cold War,* 114.
[668] "Remesas," Instituto Nacional de Migración, 2003 [Mexico City]. <http://www.inm.gob.mx>

challenge to law enforcement agencies seeking to combat the illicit money transfer schemes that utilize the same routes.

A common method used by criminal organizations to smuggle illicit proceeds into Mexico is the use of bank deposits and wire transfer services to conduct multiple small transfers to financial institutions in Mexico. In order to avoid mandatory documentation of their large transactions, money launderers break up cash shipments into transfers smaller than the reporting minimum. Accomplices move the cash into the system, concealing the transfers among the billions of dollars of legal remittances sent by Mexican immigrants to their families in Mexico.[669]

Once the United States currency arrives in Mexico, it is converted into pesos in a variety of money service business (MSBs) such as wire remittance services, cashier check companies, and money exchange house.[670] These MSBs, a form of financial service organization that came into existence during the financial reform of the 1980s and 1990s, function as a parallel banking system with the capability to transfer funds into any banking system worldwide.

Narcotics

Mexico's advanced chemical and pharmaceuticals industries, along with its expanding international trade links, have facilitated the diversion of essential chemicals from legitimate industry in Mexico to supply cocaine and heroin processing operations in Colombia and elsewhere. According to the DEA, many of the chemicals necessary for the clandestine manufacture of illicit drugs also are available in Mexico.[671] Legally imported precursor chemicals from the United States, Europe, and Asia are diverted to clandestine narcotics laboratories. Large-scale Mexican drug traffickers have established routes to procure and smuggle precursors from the international market for the manufacture of methamphetamine and amphetamine in Mexico.

---

[669]Ginger Thompson, "Migrants to the U.S. are a Major Resource for Mexico," *New York Times*, 25 March 2002; and Stephen Fidler, "New Migrants Spur Growth in Remittances," *Financial Times* 17 May 2001.

[670] Organisation for Economic Co-operation and Development, Financial Action Task Force on Money Laundering, *FATF-XI Annual Report: 1999-2000*, 26 March 2001. <http://www.fatf-gafi.org>

[671] U.S. Department of Justice, Drug Enforcement Administration, *Mexico Country Brief*, July 2002. <http://www.usdoj.gov/dea/pubs/intel/02035/02035p.html>

According to the DEA, the majority of ephedrine shipments destined for Mexico are supplied by sources in China, India, the Czech Republic, the United Arab Emirates, Thailand, and Switzerland. In addition, large quantities of the essential chemical potassium permanganate have been diverted in Mexico to supply cocaine-processing laboratories in Colombia. Between 1999 and 2002, at least seven seizures of Mexican-origin potassium permanganate, totaling more than 50 tons, were reported in Colombia.[672] Another essential chemical, acetic anhydride, is manufactured in Mexico for multiple uses in legitimate industry. However, supplies of acetic anhydride are diverted from legitimate sources and made readily available to supply heroin-processing laboratories in Mexico.

Although Mexico has signed international chemical-control treaties such as the 1988 United Nations Convention Against Illicit Traffic in Narcotic Drugs and Psychotropic Substances and passed a Comprehensive Chemical Control Law in 1997, the DEA reports that implementation and enforcement of some provisions remains problematic. In addition, jurisdictional conflicts among agencies with anti-narcotics authority significantly impede chemical investigations. Few significant chemical prosecutions have occurred in Mexico since the law was enacted in 1997.[673]

Mexico has also become a profitable drug and alcohol consumption market. According to Mexico's 2002 National Addictions Survey, out of a total population of 100 million about 3 million people have used illicit narcotics. Drug retailing organizations that cater to Mexican cocaine and heroin users have become increasingly visible throughout Mexico. One of the largest such organizations, based in the Mexico City suburb of Ciudad Nezahualcóyotle (Ciudad Neza), was disrupted in November 2002, when its kingpins, Delia Patricia Buendía and Carlos Morales Correa, were arrested by Mexican federal police. The Buendía gang, which has ties to the three major Mexican cartels, disposed of "surplus" cocaine belonging to the cartels by selling it in the local Mexico City street market.[674]

---

[672] International Narcotics Control Board, report on the Implementation of Article 12 of the United Nations Convention against Illicit Traffic in Narcotic Drugs and Psychotropic Substances of 1988, 2002. <http://www.incb.org>
[673] U.S. Department of Justice, *Mexico Country Brief.*
[674] Ignacio Alzaga, "Atentados en EU fortalecieron operaciones del cartel de Neza [Attacks on the U.S. Strengthened Neza Cartel Operations], *El Sol de Mexico* [Mexico City], 30 August 2002.

Trafficking in Consumer Goods

Mexico's growing consumer economy provides substantial profit-making opportunities for foreign groups trafficking in stolen, counterfeit, and smuggled goods. Recent research has indicated that counterfeiting and piracy attract transnational criminal and terrorist organizations. Mexico's National Garment Industry Chamber has estimated that 58 percent of clothing bought in Mexico enters the country illegally.[675] Intellectual Property Rights (IPR) crimes, such as music piracy, are also widespread. According to the London-based International Federation of the Phonographic Industry (IFPI), Mexico is among the top ten music piracy centers in the world. According to the IFPI, in 2002 some 91 million illegally reproduced recordings were sold at Mexico's street markets, street booths, public markets, and mobile vendors.[676] In 2002 a "Korean mafia" was identified in Mexico City as one of largest distributors of counterfeit products and pirated intellectual property from Asia.[677]

Terrorist Activity

During the 1970s, Mexico's generous asylum policies toward refugees from right-wing dictatorships in Spain and Latin America made it a hospitable environment for foreign militants and terrorists. One of the legacies of Mexico's 1970s-era policies has been a continuing presence of "political delegations" belonging to guerrilla and terrorist groups. These delegations have found Mexico City to be a convenient base for fundraising activities and a safe haven from which to conduct propaganda and media events. As a result of past policies, at least two foreign terrorist groups, the Basque Homeland and Liberty (Euskadi Ta Askatasuna, ETA) and the Revolutionary Armed Forces of Colombia (FARC), maintain a presence in Mexico despite the fact that they are officially banned. Both groups rely heavily on local support networks within Mexico's radicalized university faculties and expatriate communities. Despite their continuing commitment to violence, neither the FARC nor ETA has so far posed a direct threat to the United States from their bases in Mexico.

---

[675] Elisabeth Malkin, "Mexico Making Headway on Smuggling," *New York Times*, 5 June 2003.
[676] International Federation of the Phonographic Industry, *Commercial Piracy Report 2003.*
<http://www.ifpi.org/site-content/about/mission.html>
[677] Luis Alegre, "Cae red de piratería; retienen a 43 coreanos" [Counterfeiting Network Dismantled; 43 Koreans Detained], *Reforma* [Mexico City], 6 December 2002, 22.

A more immediate threat is posed by the potential transit through Mexico of U.S.-bound terrorists, and by the potential for attacks within Mexico itself. Because of its close proximity to the United States, its porous borders, its strategically significant oil industry, and a large U.S. commercial and tourism presence, Mexico may serve as a transit or target environment for a foreign terrorist operation.

Experts believe that improved security procedures will cause future terrorists to resort to covert infiltration if they wish to enter the United States from Mexico. In a March 2002 report, the Foreign Military Studies Office (FMSO) addressed the potential of a smuggler-assisted terrorist infiltration through Mexico. The FMSO determined that "at this time, no apparent link exists between the international smugglers and any terrorist organization. However, that does not preclude a working relationship of some type from becoming a reality in the future."[678] In addition to smuggler-assisted infiltration, there is an ongoing threat of self-smuggling by terrorists. A U.S. Border Patrol report documented two self-smuggling attempts from Mexico into Texas by individuals affiliated with a Middle Eastern terrorist organization since April 2001.[679]

In addition to the threat of terrorist transit through Mexico, there is also a potential that terrorist attackers could seek mass casualties or economic disruption within Mexico. Mexico possesses several strategic and industrial installations that could potentially attract a terrorist strike.[680] In a March 2003 study, the FMSO listed a number of key installations connected to Mexico's petroleum industry that could potentially be attacked, including offshore oil fields in the Bay of Campeche. Another potentially attractive target is the nuclear power plant at Laguna Verde, an attack upon which potentially would cause substantial casualties and economic damage in Mexico and create radioactive fallout over a substantial area of the southern United States.[681]

---

[678] Thomas S. Davidson II, *Human Smuggling along the U.S.-Mexican Border*," Foreign Military Studies Office, Ft. Campbell, Kentucky, March 2002. http://www.fmso.osis.gov

[679] John Hall, *Veracruz Terrorist Threat*, U.S. Border Patrol, Del Rio Sector, undated report accessed through Open Source Information System, www.fmso.osis.gov.

[680] Foreign Islamic terrorist organizations appear to be probing Mexico's anti-terrorism capabilities. Two separate groups of Middle Eastern nationals were intercepted near Eagle Pass, Texas in April 2001 and May 2002. Photographs confiscated from both sets of aliens featured similar panoramic shots of the harbor of Veracruz as well as photos of Mexican naval vessels. The U.S. Border Patrol strongly suspects that the confiscated photos were taken for surveillance purposes; Hall.

[681] John Cabell, *Bay of Campeche Oil Fields Protection Plan and Actions* (Fort Leavenworth, Kansas, Foreign Military Studies Office, Ft. Leavenworth, Kansas, 31 March 2003) http://www.fmso.osis.gov

Conclusion

Mexico presents opportunities for transnational criminal activity because its long border with the United States has been porous, especially as international traffic has increased dramatically since the mid-1990s. As Mexico evolves toward a free-market society with a growing class of consumers, traffickers profit from a growing demand in consumer goods and narcotics. Increased financial exchanges with the United States, combined with a fast-growing sector of independent financial organizations with international banking capabilities, increase the likelihood of narcotics money being laundered in Mexico. In recent years, Mexico's atmosphere of political corruption has been diminished by substantial reforms. The main question is whether those reforms can keep pace with the internationalism and economic growth that have become typical of Mexico since the mid-1990s.

The Triborder Region

Introduction

The Tri-Border Area (TBA) of Argentina, Brazil, and Paraguay provides a haven that is geographically, socially, economically, and politically highly conducive for allowing the activities of organized crime, Islamic terrorist groups, and corrupt officials. Those groups are supported by drug and arms trafficking, money laundering, and other lucrative criminal activities. As of 2001, money laundering in the TBA reportedly was averaging US$12 billion a year, most of which is through the TBA cities of Ciudad del Este and Foz do Iguaçu. Ciudad del Este has been a vibrant commercial city featuring both legitimate and illegal transactions. In 2000 the city generated US$12 to US$13 billion in merchandise sales, placing it third in this category among world cities. However, that figure may have fallen since then as a result of stricter Argentine and Brazilian customs procedures. Although the TBA is an active corridor for arms and drug smuggling into Argentina and Brazil, in recent years most drugs reportedly have been moving from Paraguay into these two countries via other Paraguayan drug centers.

The TBA is home to both indigenous crime groups, most notably Brazilian and Paraguayan mafias, and non-indigenous syndicates from Chile, Colombia, Corsica, Ghana, Italy, Ivory Coast, Japan, Korea, Lebanon, Nigeria, Russia, and Taiwan. The thriving business of importing counterfeit CDs and CD-ROMs into the TBA from Asia is linked to organized crime in Korea, Lebanon, Libya, and Taiwan. The Hong Kong mafia is particularly active in large-scale trafficking in pirated products from mainland China to Ciudad del Este, and Hong Kong crime groups maintain strong ties with Hizballah in the TBA.

Islamic terrorist groups, including al Qaeda, Hizballah, Islamic Jihad, and al-Muqawamah, have used the TBA for fund-raising, drug trafficking, money laundering, plotting, and other such activities. Lax immigration controls and official corruption in the TBA have eased the purchase of false identity documents, including passports and visas, for Islamic extremists entering Paraguay.

Efforts of the Argentine, Brazilian, and Paraguayan police forces to fight organized crime and terrorist activities in the TBA are hindered significantly by endemic corruption within the police, the criminal justice system, and the government; by poor pay and inadequate training, equipment, and funding for law enforcement personnel; by human rights abuses; by weak anti-money-laundering laws and enforcement; and, in Argentina and Brazil, by secrecy provisions of banking laws that encourage money laundering.

Factors in Organized Crime and Terrorism

Geographical Factors

The TBA's porous borders are defined by three closely grouped population centers, one in each of the three countries: the Argentine city of Puerto Iguazú, the Brazilian city of Foz do Iguaçu, and the Paraguayan city of Ciudad del Este (formerly Puerto Presidente Stroessner).

In the early 1970s, government planners sought to profit from the tourist attraction of nearby Iguazu Falls by establishing a free-trade zone in the rapidly growing boomtown city of Ciudad del Este, thereby allowing Argentines and Brazilians to purchase cheap electronic products there.[682] The TBA soon gained a reputation as a lawless jungle corner of three countries—Argentina, Brazil, and Paraguay—dominated by the illegal activities of mafias and Islamic terrorist groups. However, in the past two decades the region also has progressed rapidly as a center of legitimate economic activity. The large majority of the diverse population is reported to be peaceful and law-abiding.

---

[682] Sebastian Junger, "Terrorism's New Geography," *Vanity Fair*, no. 508 (December 2002): 196.

Societal Factors

As a result of the construction of the Itaipú Hydroelectric Dam, the population of the TBA increased from about 60,000 in 1971 to more than 700,000 in 2001.[683] The TBA has a highly heterogeneous population. In 2001, Brazil's Federal Police (Polícia Federal—PF) estimated that Foz do Iguaçu's population consists of 65 different nationalities.[684] In 1994 Ciudad del Este's ethnic population reportedly included 7,000 Lebanese, 6,500 Chinese, and 4,000 Koreans.[685] By 2001, however, the city's largest ethnic group was the Chinese, with an estimated 30,000 members.[686]

The TBA has one of the most important Arab communities in South America. Figures on the size of the Arab population in the region vary widely. A 2001 *Jane's* article notes that the region's population includes 23,000 Arabs of Palestinian and Lebanese descent.[687] Many thousands of Lebanese arrived during the civil war in Lebanon in the 1970s. Of the Arab population in Ciudad del Este and Foz do Iguaçu, an estimated 90 percent is of Lebanese origin, many with relatives in Lebanon's Al Beqa'a Valley.[688]

The social structure of communities in Ciudad del Este and Foz do Iguaçu make these two cities ideal for the operation of Arabic-speaking terrorist or criminal groups. Extremists find the opportunity to assemble, form a cell with no risk of leaks, carry out their missions, and return with alibis backed up by many in the community. Estimates of Foz do Iguaçu's Arab population are not considered to be reliable; estimates range from 10,000 to 21,000 Arabs, most of whom are of Palestinian and Lebanese descent. Foz do Iguaçu's Islamic Cultural Center spokesman Mohamed Ismail has noted that only 1 percent of Arab nationals residing in the TBA do not profess the Islamic religion.[689] The Arab community in the TBA is tightly knit, with its own schools and clubs, making outside penetration very difficult. The size and influence of this Arab

---

[683] Mariano César Bartolomé, *Amenzas a la seguridad de los estados: La triple frontera coma 'área gris' en el cono sur americano* [Threats to the Security of States: The Triborder Region as a 'Grey Area' in the Cone of South America], 29 November 2001. http://www.geocities.com/mcbartolome/triplefrontera1.htm]

[684] Bartolomé, 3.

[685] Ricardo Grinbaum, "In Paraguay, Smugglers' Paradise," *World Press Review*, 43, no.1 (January 1996): 25-6.

[686] Bartolomé, 7.

[687] John Daly, "The Suspects: The Latin American Connection," *Jane's Terrorism and Security Monitor*, 1 October 2001.

[688] Bartolomé, 4.

[689] "Muslims Prevail Among Small Religions in Foz," *A Gazeta do Iguaçu* [Foz do Iguaçu], 3 February 2003 (FBIS Document LAP20030211000124).

community may help to explain why the Lebanese government decided in January 1999 to close its embassy in Asunción, Paraguay, and to open a consulate in Ciudad del Este to watch over the interests of the Arab citizens in the TBA.[690]

Economic Factors

Ciudad del Este is an oasis for informants and spies; peddlers of contraband (largely cheap East Asian goods) and counterfeit products; traffickers in drugs, weapons, and humans (prostitutes, including women and children forced into prostitution); common criminals; mafias; undocumented Arabs; and terrorists. Although Ciudad del Este is filled with street merchants selling cheap trinkets and counterfeit products, one can also purchase items such as an AK-47 for US$375.[691]

Despite its seedy appearance, Ciudad del Este is a world-class center of commerce, attracting many tourists and prosperous banks.[692] Thanks to the presence of organized crime, Ciudad del Este's retail economy ranked third worldwide behind Hong Kong and Miami among cities in volume of cash transactions.[693] In 2001 the estimated annual turnover in Ciudad del Este made the city's economy larger than that of the rest of Paraguay.[694]

The relatively small Arab community in Ciudad del Este is among Latin America's most prosperous and influential. According to some estimates, between 15,000 and 21,000 Arabs of Palestinian and Lebanese descent live and work across the Brazilian border in Foz do Iguaçu and its surrounding hinterlands, while maintaining commercial outlets in Ciudad del Este.

The region's main economic dynamic is business between Ciudad del Este and Foz do Iguaçu. As a result of traditional price differences between Paraguay and Brazil, the Friendship Bridge is crossed daily by large numbers of small-scale entrepreneurs carrying products for sale. Border monitoring of this traffic, which includes many individuals lacking documents, generally has been limited to simple spot-checks.[695]

---

[690] "Arabic Factions 'Bidding' for New Lebanese Consulate," *ABC Color* [Asunción], 31 January 1999, 61 (FBIS Document FTS199902001001342).

[691] Jeffrey Goldberg, "In the Party of God," *The New Yorker*, 79, no. 32 (28 October 2002).

[692] Ricardo Grinbaum, "In Paraguay, Smugglers' Paradise," *World Press Review*, 43, No.1 (January 1996): 25-6.

[693] Sebastian Rotella, "Jungle Hub for World's Outlaws," *Los Angeles Times*, 24 August 1998, 1.

[694] Larry Rohter, "Terrorists Are Sought in Latin Smugglers' Haven," *New York Times*, 27 September 2001, A3.

[695] "Surveillance System on Friendship Bridge," *A Gazeta do Iguaçu* [Foz do Iguaçu], 6 November 2002 (FBIS Document LAP20021121000006).

The traditional status of the TBA as a source of cheap goods has been severely restricted by new regulations issued by Argentina and Brazil. After the implementation of an integrated customs system by the Brazilian Secretariat of Federal Revenue (Secretaria da Receita Federal—SRF) to combat smuggling, commerce between Ciudad del Este and Foz do Iguaçu reportedly decreased by 90 percent, according to information disclosed at a meeting of City Council members of both cities.[696] In an attempt to curb the loss of tax revenues, Argentina's and Brazil's revenue authorities imposed monthly limits on purchases in the region.[697] As a result of these and other measures such as increased security, commercial activity in Ciudad del Este has slowed considerably. Whereas in 1995 the city had 7,000 businesses, the figure in 2000 was only 2,000. During the same period, bank branches in the city were reduced from 21 to 14.[698]

Of the three TBA cities, Argentina's Puerto Iguazú has the least economic activity. The local Chamber of Commerce has reported that 600 of the 1,450 local businesses registered in Puerto Iguazú have closed in recent years.[699]

Immigration Control

The TBA is known for lax immigration controls. According to police in Brazil and Paraguay, false passports, birth certificates, driver's licenses, and other documents are easily obtained through corrupt officials. In 2000 Paraguay's Vice Interior Minister Mario Agustin Sapriza stated that the Immigrations Department of Paraguay had not effectively prevented the TBA from being used by Islamic extremists. He acknowledged that the service must improve to exert greater control, particularly regarding the activities of Islamic terrorism, but said that foreign citizens cannot be stopped from entering the country.[700]

The market for false documentation is especially strong among Arab, Asian, and other migrants who come to live in Paraguay for months or years, then upgrade their documents in

---

[696] "Commerce between Ciudad del Este and Foz do Iguaçu Drops by 90 Percent," *Vanguardia* [Asunción], 3 December 2002 (FBIS Document LAP20021203000105).
[697] Bartolomé, 2.
[698] Bartolomé, 2.
[699] Bartolomé, 4.
[700] Mario Daniel Montoya, "War on Terrorism Reaches Paraguay's Triple Border," *Jane's Intelligence Review*, 13, no. 12 (December 2001): 13; and "Policiais viajam em vôos internos argentinos" [Police Fly on Internal Argentine Flights], 19 September 2001. [http://www.estadao.com.br/agestado/noticias/2001/set/19/207.htm].

order to move on to Argentina, Brazil, or North America.[701] Since 2000, about 30 percent of the false immigration documents seized at Argentina's Puerto Iguazú checkpoint were carried by Chinese who were presumed to be heading to Buenos Aires.[702]

In early October 2001, high-level sources in Argentina's Ministry of Interior called Brazil's immigration control system for the TBA a problem.[703] Argentina places its emphasis on immigration control at the border crossings, whereas Brazil's control operations are located somewhat deeper inside its territory. Brazilian authorities have established controls on the roads several kilometers from Foz do Iguaçu.

Government Corruption

Argentine police official Hugo Antolin Almiron has commented that corruption in Argentina "has penetrated deep within the public offices and has affected every stratum of the society and has further generated various types of misconduct."[704] After the reelection of Carlos Menem as president of Argentina in May 1995, the public increasingly perceived office-holders as highly corrupt. This perception was exacerbated by the government's failure to adopt any of the 40 legislative proposals aimed at goals such as reforming the judiciary and eliminating corruption. The extent of Menem's own corruption was revealed in July 2002 when a witness implicated Menem in covering up the 1994 bombing of the Argentine-Israeli Mutual Association (Asociación Mutual Israeli-Argentina—AMIA), a Jewish community center in Buenos Aires.[705] As president, Menem, whose parents migrated from Syria, appointed a Syrian army colonel to be customs overseer at Buenos Aires' Ezeiza International Airport, which has been described as "a major hub for smuggling in South America."[706] In August 2003, an Argentine court cleared

---

[701] William W. Mendel, "Paraguay's Ciudad del Este and the New Centers of Gravity," *Military Review*, 82, no. 2 (March-April 2002).

[702] Mendel.

[703] "National Border Guard Commander: Tri-Border Area Hotbed of Sleeper Cells," *La Nación* [Buenos Aires], 3 October 2001 (FBIS Document LAP20011003000015).

[704] Hugo Antolin Almiron, "Organized Crime: A Perspective from Argentina." Chapter 14 in Jay S. Albanese, Dilip K. Das, and Arvind Verma, eds., *Organized Crime: World Perspectives*. (Upper Saddle River, New Jersey: Prentice Hall, 2003), 320.

[705] Larry Rohter, "Iran Blew Up Jewish Center In Argentina, Defector Says," *New York Times*, 22 July 2002, A1; "Slow-Motion Justice in Argentina," *New York Times*, 11 March 2003, A24; and Larry Rohter, "World Briefing Americas: Menem Acknowledges Swiss Account," *New York Times*, 25 July 2002, A9.

[706] Martin Edwin Andersen, "Al-Qaeda Across the Americas," *Insight on the News*, 17, no. 44 (26 November 2001): 20-21.

Menem, who again had been a leading candidate for the presidency in the elections of 2003, of charges of involvement in trafficking arms to Ecuador and Croatia between 1991 and 1995.

In December 2000, a parliamentary report by the Drug Traffic Investigating Commission of Brazil's Congress accused a large number of Brazilian officials, including federal deputies (congressmen), former state governors, state deputies, mayors, judges, police officers, and lawyers, of complicity in organized crimes ranging from drug trafficking to arms trafficking to tax evasion.[707] The report concluded that drug-related corruption is so widespread that it is impossible to clean up in the short term without calling in the military and restructuring and rearming the country's police. A 2002 congressional report on Brazil's nationwide surge in highway robberies of truck cargo called for the indictment of 100 politicians, police, and entrepreneurs allegedly involved in the theft of cargo.[708]

Governmental, political, and diplomatic corruption in Paraguay and the TBA allows individuals associated with organized crime and terrorism to bribe judges, purchase entry visas, and engage in any number of other criminal activities that might overlap with legitimate economic activities. An investigation conducted by Paraguay's National Directorate of Civil Aeronautics (Dirección Nacional de Aeronáutica Civil—Dinac) found that an average of 570 foreigners annually enter the country through the Ciudad del Este Airport using irregular documents, after paying bribes averaging US$5,000.[709]

In early November 2001, Paraguayan judge Carlos Cálcena charged that some of Paraguay's consulates had been converted into veritable offices for falsifying documents. During the first 10 months of 2001, the Directorate of Legal Affairs in Paraguay's Ministry of Foreign Affairs opened 10 cases concerning illicit visas.[710]

Recent investigations carried out in the TBA have found that numerous Lebanese citizens residing in Ciudad del Este had entered Paraguay with illicit visas. The most well known case was that of Ahmad Assad Barakat, a leading Hizballah figure in the TBA, who was able to enter Paraguay in 1989 using a visa obtained from the Paraguayan Consulate in Panama although that

---

[707] Andrew Downie, "Corruption's Roots Deep and Wide-Reaching in Brazil," *Christian Science Monitor*, 14 December 2000; "Investigation Shows Pervasive Impact of Drug Trade in Brazil," *America's Insider*, 1, no. 9 (8 December 2000): 6.

[708] Raymond Colitt, "Brazil Tracks Down the Real Culprits Behind Surge in Highway Robberies," *Financial Times* [London], 2 May 2002, 10.

[709] Bartolomé, 18.

[710] Bartolomé, 18.

office not authorized to issue visas.[711] The Paraguayan consul in Miami, Carlos Weiss, had allegedly sold more than 300 passports, visas, and shipping documents to individuals heading to the TBA between 1999 and 2001. Weiss's customers for documents included three Lebanese who were on the FBI terrorist watch.[712]

Police Corruption

The effectiveness of a country's security forces in combating organized crime and terrorism is clearly a factor in determining whether conditions are conducive to allowing these illicit activities to flourish. The efforts of the security forces of Argentina, Brazil, and Paraguay have been ineffective in this regard because they have been of hindered by corruption, human rights abuses, and inadequate funding and training.

The Argentine police have at least three reasons to lack motivation to fight crime. First, their primary duty is to maintain social order, not to investigate serious crime. Second, many police officers are frustrated by the slow-moving legal system and by expanding missions, especially in the area of counter-narcotics. Some police officers take the law into their own hands when they believe that the judicial system's sentences against offenders are too light. Police violence, including beatings, shootings, and rapes, has reportedly greatly increased since the mid-1990s.[713]

The third factor is poor pay, which starts at about US$400 per month. For these reasons, corruption is a serious problem at all levels of the Argentine police.[714] Corruption among police and prison officials receives little attention because whistle-blowing colleagues, judicial officials, and civilian witnesses are intimidated by the prospect of being subjected to retaliation. Threats and beatings aimed at potential witnesses are common. High-level officials have also sought to discredit damaging testimony of subordinates by initiating internal proceedings against whistleblowers.

---

[711] Bartolomé, 17.

[712] Mendel; Larry Rohter, "Terrorists Are Sought in Latin Smugglers' Haven," *New York Times*, 27 September 2001. <www.nytimes.com>; and Bartolomé, 17.

[713] "Delinquent: Tackling Crime Needs Police Reform," *The Economist* [London], 5 October 2002.

[714] U.S. Department of State, *Country Reports on Human Rights Practices 2001*. <http://www.state.gov/g/drl/rls/hrrpt/2001/wha/8278.htm>

For the past 20 years, the Argentine police reportedly have been involved in organized crime. According to María del Carmen Verdú of the Center for the Prevention of Police Repression, "In the last decade, there has not been any major illegal business without police participation, from prostitution to gambling, robbery, or kidnapping."[715] Accusations range from collecting fraudulent payments for services not provided, to theft of vehicles, murder, and rape.[716]

The effectiveness of Brazil's police forces in fighting organized crime and terrorist groups in the TBA is hindered by a general lack of respect for human rights, widespread corruption, and involvement in crime, as well as a general failure of the Brazilian government to address their serious problems. Brazil's state police forces have committed numerous serious human rights abuses. State police forces have committed many extra-judicial killings, tortured and beat suspects under interrogation, and arbitrarily arrested and detained persons. Elements within the military police of some states have been notorious for their vigilantism and death-squad activities. Federal prosecutors have reported that corruption among state police often impedes the apprehension of traffickers. Police also have been implicated in criminal activity of all kinds, including killings for hire, death squad executions, extortion, kidnappings for ransom, and narcotics trafficking.[717]

Brazil's politicians have repeatedly demonstrated a lack of the will needed to implement needed reforms of the police forces, the penal code and criminal justice system, and prisons, and to adopt a gun-control bill.[718] The authorities' failure to investigate, prosecute, and punish police who commit such acts has created a climate of impunity that continues to encourage human rights abuses.

According to the U.S. Department of State, the Paraguayan police has continuing problems with incidents of extra-judicial killings, torture and abuse of convicted prisoners and other detainees, arbitrary arrests and detention, use of force against nonviolent demonstrators, lengthy pretrial detention, corruption and inefficiency in the judiciary, and infringements on

---

[715] "Delinquent: Tackling Crime Needs Police Reform."
[716] "Delinquent: Tackling Crime Needs Police Reform."
[717] Pedro Oviedo, "En la Triple Frontera se lavan doce mil millones de dólares al año del narcotráfico, según un informe official" [In the Triborder Area US$12 billion Is Laundered Per Year From Narcotics Trafficking, According to an Official Report] http://misionesonline.net/paginas/action.lasso?-database=noticias3&-layout=web&-response=noticia.html&id=11349&autorizado=si&-search.
[718] Oviedo.

citizens' privacy rights.[719] By October 2001, as authorities in Paraguay increased surveillance of the country's Arab immigrants, there were charges that police were extorting large sums of money from some merchants in return for not detaining them.[720]

Ciudad del Este's 200-member police force is suspected of corruption.[721] A general lack of confidence in the police may be reflected by the fact that the city's 6,000 shops, 36 banks, and 15 money exchanges all have their private guards.

Organized Crime

Indigenous Groups

Hugo Antolin Almiron has commented that "organized crime in Argentina has a peculiar local character that thrives on the socioeconomic and political conditions prevalent in the country." He adds, however, that international narcotics cartels active in Argentina also are active in trafficking of children, smuggling, marketing of stolen cars, tax evasion, embezzlement, fraud, insider trading, and financial swindles. In his assessment, "organized crime in Argentina exists in an incipient developmental stage, but at the same time it is becoming a major concern."[722] The TBA is of particular concern to the Argentine government in this regard because it serves as a gateway for organized crime to migrate south into the rest of the country.

Until 2001, most of Brazil's arms-for-cocaine trafficking revolved around the country's most notorious cocaine lord, Luiz Fernando Da Costa. Brazil's Parliamentary Commission identified international connections of Da Costa in Paraguay, Peru, and Colombia. Da Costa is known to have purchased arsenals in Paraguay and brought them to a base of operations in Paraguay's Guairá Department. He operated from Paraguay until forced to move to Colombia.[723] According to official reports, prior to his capture in 2001 Da Costa sold arms to FARC rebels in exchange for cocaine.

Organized crime in Brazil appeared to be becoming increasingly violent in 2002 and early 2003. In October 2002, police foiled an attempt by organized criminals to blow up the São

---

[719] U.S. Department of State, *Country Reports on Human Rights Practices 2001.*
<http://www.state.gov/g/drl/rls/hrrpt/2001/wha/8297.htm>
[720] Bill Rogers, "Arabs Accuse Paraguay Police Of Extortion," *Middle East News Online*, 4 October 2001.
[721] Grinbaum, 25-6.
[722] Almiron, 329.
[723] "El prontuario de Fernandinho" [Fernandiño's Handbook] *El Tiempo* [Bogotá], 21 April, 2001; "Muestran a Fernandiño a la prensa" [Fernandiño Is Shown to the Press], *El Tiempo* [Bogotá], 22 April 2001.

Paulo Stock Exchange with a car packed with explosives.[724] In February 2003, drug gangs paralyzed commerce and traffic in parts of the city of Rio de Janeiro and battled police in the streets. In March, organized crime groups assassinated two judges.[725] A powerful São Paulo prison gang has been linked to Da Costa and the Italian Mafia.[726] In February 2003, assassins believed to be members of a criminal organization in Foz do Iguaçu seriously wounded the president of the Foz do Iguaçu City Council.[727]

Paraguay's Ciudad del Este, together with its Brazilian twin city of Foz do Iguaçu, is the epicenter of organized crime in the TBA. In that city, organized crime, corrupt officials, and members of radical Islamic groups have been able to engage freely in money laundering, intellectual property piracy, alien smuggling, and arms and drug trafficking, among other illicit activities. A large percentage of criminal transactions involve bartering drugs for weapons with Colombian armed rebel groups.[728]

One criminal organization operating in the Ciudad del Este area is headed by the feared Elvio Ramón Cantero Aguero, based in Pedro Juan Caballero, located on the Brazilian border northwest of the TBA.[729] In 2002, a police raid of hideouts in Ciudad del Este found a large stock of weapons. Cantero Aguero, however, remained at large.

Former General Lino César Oviedo is reputed by Brazilian and U.S. officials to be head of the so-called Paraguayan Cartel. Included in his estimated worth of US$1 billion are numerous properties in the TBA.[730] In the 1990s, authorities intercepted multi-ton cocaine shipments from Oviedo, originating in the TBA. At the time of his arrest in June 2000, Oviedo was using Foz do Iguaçu and Ciudad del Este as a base of operations for laundering money, with the help of a fellow Paraguayan general, José Tomas Centurión.

---

[724] Stan Lehman, "Brazilian Police Thwart Bomb Plot," *The Columbian*, 22 October 2002, A5.
[725] Peter Muello, "Brazilians Outraged by Slayings of Judges: Organized-Crime Groups Unleash Wave of Violence," *Houston Chronicle*, 27 March 2003, 27.
[726] Raymond Colitt, "Another Judge Killed as Drugs Crime Alarms Brazil," *Financial Times* [London], 25 March 2003, 11.
[727] "Foz City Council President Shot in Attack," Itapiru Radio [Ciudad del Este], 24 February 2003 (FBIS Document LAP20030226000042).
[728] Riyadh Alam-al-Din, "Washington Begins the War on Hizballah in the Border Triangle," *Al-Watan al-Arabi* [Paris], 21 December 2001, 18-19 (FBIS Document GMP20011221000179).
[729] Cesar Palacios and Oscar Florentín, "Paraguay: Police Confiscate Arsenal from Gangster's Home," *Noticias* [Asunción], 6 December 2002 (FBIS Document LAP20021206000030).
[730] "El Caso Lino Oviedo y su conexión con la Argentina" [The Lino Oviedo Case and Its Connection with Argentina], *Página1 2* [Buenos Aires]. <www.pagina12.com.ar/2001/suple/carrio/cap11.pdf>

Non-Indigenous Mafias

Crime syndicates from Brazil China, Colombia, Corsica, Ghana, Italy, Ivory Coast, Japan, Korea, Lebanon, Nigeria, Russia, and Taiwan are known to have operated in Paraguay and the TBA. According to United States law enforcement and intelligence sources, a number of these groups are associated with corrupt Paraguayan business executives, politicians, and military officers tied to the ruling Colorado Party.[731] The Colombian, Italian, and Nigerian mafias have been identified as the main transnational mafias operating in Brazil, although those groups do not appear to have headquarters in that country.[732]

The influence of foreign groups in Brazil has been largely the result of the country's role as a transit country for illegal drug shipments. According to one report, since 1995 monetary reforms have made it more difficult for foreign criminals to find refuge in Brazil, and local groups of varying size now play the most important role in organized crime in Brazil. However, the known presence of foreign mafias from Lebanon, China, and Korea operating in São Paulo and other Brazilian cities casts doubt on this assertion.[733]

The cultural and social demographics of Ciudad del Este are ideal for the operations of Chinese-speaking criminal groups. In the 1990s, Chinese criminal groups such as Fuk Ching, Big Circle Boys, Flying Dragons, and Tai Chen, mostly from mainland China, established a presence in Ciudad del Este in order to profit from the city's Asian imports.[734] Authorities consider these groups to be especially dangerous because they do not limit their activities to predictable locations within the Chinese communities.[735] Chinese criminal groups specialize in providing "protection" to the local Chinese business people, imposing "taxes" on the containers imported by the Chinese businesses, and forcing the Chinese business community to purchase merchandise imported by the groups.[736]

---

[731] Jack Sweeney, "DEA Boosts Its Role in Paraguay," *Washington Times*, 21 August 2001.

[732] Ruy Gomes Silva, "Effective Measures to Combat Transnational Organized Crime in Criminal Justice Processes," presentation to 116th International Training Course, Asia and Far East Institute for Prevention of Crime and Treatment of Offenders, Tokyo, November 2000. <http://www.unafei.or.jp/pdf/103.pdf>

[733] Machado de Morais and Andrea Frota, *Money Laundering in Brazil,* report to School of Business and Public Management, Institute of Brazilian Business and Management Issues, George Washington University, Fall 2000. [http://216.239.51.100/search?q=cache:Ms30X17JQ_YC:www.gwu.edu/~ibi/minerva/Fall2000/Andrea.Morais.pdf+cc-5+brasil+paraguay&hl=en&ie=UTF-8].

[734] Sebastian Rotella, "Jungle Hub for World's Outlaws," *Los Angeles Times*, August 24, 1998, 1.

[735] Rotella.

[736] Bartolomé, 7.

Paraguay's *ABC Color* has reported that Hong Kong-based groups engage in large-scale trafficking in pirated products from mainland China to Ciudad del Este and maintain strong ties with the pro-Iranian Hizballah in the TBA.[737] Chinese and Korean mafias with branches in São Paulo (Brazil), Santa Cruz de la Sierra (Bolivia), San Francisco (California), and Buenos Aires, among other cities, have been identified in the TBA.[738]

As of late 2002, investigators had determined that five Chinese mafias operate in São Paulo: Fu Shin and Fei Jeii from Canton and three others from Beijing, Shanghai, and Taiwan, respectively.[739] The Chinese mafia in São Paulo earns an estimated US$1.6 million annually from extortion or "protection" money from ethnic Chinese businesses in exchange for the right to sell certain contraband merchandise.[740] An estimated 70 percent of the 150,000 Chinese in São Paulo are being extorted.[741] The Chinese mafias have expanded to a number of other Brazilian cities, including Foz do Iguaçu, and to Paraguay's Ciudad del Este.[742]

In 2001 the Paraguayan government made a significant effort to neutralize the activities of the Chinese criminal groups, but with only occasional success. As a result of the Chinese groups' ability to bribe Paraguayan judges, they have been able to operate with impunity, according Jorge Ho, the consul general of Taiwan in Ciudad del Este.[743] Evidence shows that the TBA plays a key role in the expansion plans of these criminal organizations into the duty-free zone of Argentina's San Luis Province.

The Chinese mafia in the TBA is known to collaborate with Islamic terrorist groups in the region. Brazilian investigative reporter Roberto Godoy has reported that at least two organizations with bases in the TBA—the Sung-I and Ming families—have engaged in illegal operations with the Egyptian Gamaa Islamiya (Islamic Group).[744] *ABC Color* reported that

---

[737] "Paraguay: 'Strong Ties' Seen Between Hong Kong Mafia, Tri-border Based Hizballah," *ABC Color* [Asunción], 22 November 2002 (FBIS Document LAP20021122000059).

[738] Bartolomé, 5.

[739] Aloisio Milani, "Máfia chinesa extorque e executa em São Paulo" [Chinese Mafia Extorts and Executes in São Paulo], *Jornal-laboratório da Faculdade de Comunicação Social Cásper Líbero* [São Paulo], no. 28 (December 2001). [http://biondi.fcl.com.br/facasper/jornalismo/esquinas/noticia.cfm?secao=4&codigo=87].

[740] Milani.

[741] Milani.

[742] Milani.

[743] Bartolomé, 16.

[744] Bartolomé, 8.

black-market activity such as the counterfeit manufacture of mass-distribution items such as toys—has a distribution chain running from Hong Kong to Hizballah extremists in the TBA.[745]

Criminal gangs in Paraguay have known ties to Colombia's FARC. Paraguayan authorities arrested a Colombian citizen in Ciudad del Este in 2000 as he tried to arrange a cocaine-for-weapons swap on behalf of the FARC. Links between crime syndicates in Ciudad del Este and the FARC date from the mid-1990s at least. At that time, Paraguayan General Oviedo protected Brazilian drug trafficker Luiz Fernando Da Costa, who was captured in southern Colombia in April 2001 in the company of FARC rebels.[746]

Tightened security measures by the TBA nations have threatened the interests of criminal organizations with links to extremist groups, resulting in a growing trend of violent attacks against authorities. In 1997 Argentine reporter Hernán López Accago described businessmen in the region paying what amounted to protection money to armed Arab groups in the region.[747] This money is used in financing military operations in various parts of the world. At least one Ciudad del Este businessman was murdered because he failed to pay the tax. The convicted murderer, Armando Kassen, who was president of the Paraguayan Arab Chamber of Commerce, fled to Beirut.[748]

In the late 1990s, members of the Russian mafia reportedly began exploring Paraguay, supplementing their presence in Colombia, Argentina, and Brazil.[749] According to Paraguayan police intelligence, Russian mafia groups were seeking out contacts with the mafia of countries belonging to the Southern Cone Common Market (Mercosur), principally those operating from the drug-trafficking zones on the Brazil-Paraguay border northwest of the TBA. The intention of the Russians apparently has been to ally themselves with the capos of the South American mafias in order to facilitate the distribution of cocaine in Europe.

According to regional expert Bruce Michael Bagley, Chechen gangs have established a base in Argentina, primarily to use that country as a transit country for Andean cocaine shipments to Europe, arms trafficking to Brazil and Colombia, and money laundering. In the

---

[745] "Hong Kong Mafia Linked to Hizballah in Tri-Border Region," *ABC Color* [Asunción], 22 November 2002 (FBIS Document LAP20021122000047).

[746] Jack Sweeney, "DEA Boosts Its Role in Paraguay," *Washington Times*, August 21, 2001.

[747] "Brazil: Report on Islamic Terrorism in Iguazu Triangle," *al-Watan al-'Arabi* [Paris], 9 January 1998, 22-24.

[748] "Mastermind of Taiyen's Murder Residing in Beirut," *Vanguardia* [Ciudad del Este], 11 November 2002 (FBIS Document LAP20021121000006).

[749] "Paraguay es uno de los países explorados por mafia rusa" [Paraguay Is One of the Countries Explored by the Russian Mafia], *ABC Color* [Asunción], 16 October 1997.

TBA, Argentine intelligence sources have detected contacts between Chechen separatist groups and Islamic terrorists, Chechen groups also may be using these networks for arms smuggling purposes.[750]

Since the mid-1990s, various sources have reported arms-for-cocaine trafficking between the Russian and Brazilian mafias. The Rio de Janeiro newspaper *O Globo* reported in mid-2000 that various Russian mafia criminals have been detected in Brazil and linked to the growing participation of Russian mafia groups in the recruitment of Brazilian women for prostitution in Europe, especially Spain, and Israel, as well as to the appearance of AK-47 military assault rifles and other modern weapons in the shantytowns of Rio de Janeiro controlled by narcotics traffickers.[751] Frequently used in attacks by Rio de Janeiro gangsters, AK-47 and AR-15 semiautomatic rifles have demonstrated the expansion of the Russian mafia's weapons supply operations to the Brazilian underworld.

Narcotics and Arms Trafficking

According to the U.S. Department of State, Argentina is not a major drug producing country, but it serves as a transit country for cocaine flowing primarily from neighboring Bolivia, some heroin en route from Colombia to the U.S. East Coast, and possibly also some cocaine from Peru and Colombia. Brazil is a conduit for amphetamine precursor substances moving from source countries to Europe and the United States. Paraguay also serves as a transit country for Andean cocaine.[752] The TBA is considered to be an important area for the smuggling of drugs into Argentina, Brazil, and Paraguay as well as arms to organized crime groups in Brazil.

Trafficking operations thrive in the TBA in part because more than 100 hidden airstrips in the triangle provide a transport base. However, drug-related border arrests at Puerto Iguazú have declined since 2000 because most drugs are now moving from Paraguay into Argentina or Brazil from points south of the TBA, such as Encarnación. That city has a large Arab population and is known as a main contraband center.[753] The town of Capitán Bado on the Brazilian border,

---

[750] Bagley.

[751] "Mafia rusia en Latinoamérica" [Russian Mafia in Latin America], *La Nación Digital* [Buenos Aires], 25 September 2000.

[752] U.S. Department of State, *International Narcotics Control Strategy Report 2002*. [http://www.state.gov/g/inl/rls/nrcrpt/2002/html/17952pf.htm].

[753] Mendel.

south of Pedro Juan Caballero, is a center for marijuana production and cocaine distribution. The marijuana is transported to Brazil by land; most of the cocaine is flown in clandestine flights aboard small aircraft.[754]

Money Laundering

As of 2000, an estimated US$12 billion was being laundered in the TBA every year.[755] According to official Brazilian data, money launderers used the banks and exchange houses of Foz do Iguaçu and Ciudad del Este to launder US$6 billion of the estimated US$11 billion of fraudulent financial transactions and tax evasion profits generated in the 1999-2001 period.[756]

Argentina's Central Bank estimates that more than US$6 billion is laundered the country's banking system annually.[757] Laundering related to narcotics trafficking, corruption, contraband, and tax evasion is believed to occur throughout the financial system.[758] Although the country's financial crisis recently has limited money laundering through the banking system, the activity continues through other financial mechanisms. Money laundering does not occur in the Argentine sector of the TBA, however, on nearly as large a scale as in the Brazilian and Paraguayan sectors of the region.[759]

The December 2000 report released by the Brazilian Congress's Drug Traffic Investigating Commission states that US$50 billion in tainted money is laundered through Brazil's banks each year.[760] According to the Central Bank of Brazil, 17 percent of the money of the Colombian drug cartels is laundered through that system. Although the city of Campinas is considered the major money-laundering center in the country, substantial activity also has been identified in the TBA. Local Prosecutor Paulo Gomes Junior estimated in 1999 that 40 percent of the local companies in Foz do Iguaçu are fronts created by local mafia to launder money and to

---

[754] Clarinha Glock, "Brazil-Paraguay: A Full Plate for Journalists."
<http://www.impunidad.com/atrisk/brasil_paraguay7_19_01E.html].
[755] Oviedo.
[756] Bartolomé, 9.
[757] Oviedo.
[758] U.S. Department of State, *International Narcotics Control Strategy Report 2002*.
[759] Mario Osava, "Ciudades de América Latina/Brasil: Lavado y fuga de capitales en la frontera con Paraguay" [Cities of Latin America/Brazil: Laundering and Flight of Capital on the Border with Paraguay], Inter-Press Service report, 1999. <http://ips.org/Spanish/mundial/indices/Correo/cor0606051.htm>
[760] Downie; "Investigation Shows Pervasive Impact of Drug Trade in Brazil," *America's Insider*, 1, no. 9, (8 December, 2000): 6.

send it abroad.[761] Foz do Iguaçu currently has 13 exchange houses remaining after 20 were closed in early 2000 for engaging in laundering activities. [762]

In the assessment of the U.S. Department of State, Paraguay is a principal money-laundering center.[763] A December 2000 Argentine report on money laundering in Foz do Iguaçu, Ciudad del Este, and Puerto Iguazú estimated that almost all of Paraguay's money laundering, estimated to total at least US$5 billion annually, is done in Ciudad del Este.[764] All three of the TBA countries have experienced difficulties in countering money laundering. In the cases of Brazil and Paraguay in particular, such failures have had a significant effect on money laundering, and hence on the forms of crime and terrorism that money laundering supports in the TBA.

Argentina's 2000 anti-money-laundering law theoretically strengthened mechanisms for identifying and prosecuting money launderers.[765] However, the Financial Intelligence Unit (Unidad de Información Financiera—UIF) created by that law only went into full operation in February 2003, after initially operating with low funding. That unit is responsible for prevention and control of laundering activities related to narcotics and arms trafficking, political and racial crimes, federal fraud, and sex crimes.[766] Despite these measures, the Central Bank reportedly has been totally ineffective in prosecuting money laundering, and the Management of Control and Injunction (La Gerencia de Control y Requerimiento) has failed to take to trial a single case that he has investigated.[767]

In Brazil, the lack of transparency in national banking laws presents a significant obstacle to the prevention of money laundering.[768] According to the U.S. Department of State, Brazil has only limited capacity to engage in the sophisticated law enforcement techniques required for investigating complex crimes such as money laundering, and the results of such techniques are

---

[761] Osava.
[762] Oviedo.
[763] U.S. Department of State, *International Narcotics Control Strategy Report 2002.*.
[764] Oviedo.
[765] U.S. Department of State, *International Narcotics Control Strategy Report 2002.*
[766] Argentina, "Ley 25246: Creación de la Unidad de Información Financiera" [Law 25246, Creation of the Financial Information Unit], *Boletín Oficial* [Buenos Aires], 10 May 2000. <http://www.imolin.org/argtlaw2.htm>
[767] Oviedo.
[768] de Morais and Frota, 38.

not admissible in Brazilian courts. As a result, Brazil has had only one money-laundering conviction since 1998, despite its status as a regional financial center.[769]

Other Organized Crime Activities

Smuggling stolen luxury cars is a profitable business in the TBA. Cars are stolen in Brazil and Argentina and taken to Paraguay via the TBA, then to Bolivia and beyond. The stolen car business is facilitated by lax border controls and by Paraguayan legislation that requires no documentary backing to legalize private contracts. According to Paraguayan authorities, more than half of the 450,000 vehicles registered annually in Paraguay were acquired illegally. In Brazil, automobile theft is under the jurisdiction of the State Police, which apparently is not very effective in countering it.[770]

The TBA's two principal transit centers for stolen vehicles and smuggled goods are Foz Do Iguaçu and Ciudad del Este. Those cities also form a corridor for trafficking in drugs and arms. Some of the illicit cargo passes along an illegally opened road crossing the Iguazú National Park.[771] The Asunción-Paranaguá Highway, which passes near the falls, is also presumably used by smugglers.

Street vendors, selling fake products and pirated copies of goods ranging from designer-label sneakers to auto parts, have long been a part of life in Brazil. More than half of the business software and music compact disk (CD) market in Brazil is pirated, and as much as 40 percent of the cigarettes consumed in Brazil come from the black market. Industry experts also estimate that one-fifth of the drugs on pharmacy shelves are produced illegally.[772]

According to Carlos Alberto de Camargo, director of the anti-piracy program of the Brazilian Motion Picture Association, "Brazil has good laws on piracy; the problem is enforcement."[773] Officials in the motion picture industry say that a series of national raids by police have apprehended many small pirate operations without affecting overall trade.[774]

---

[769] U.S. Department of State, *International Narcotics Control Strategy Report 2002*.
[770] Silva.
[771] Glock.
[772] Patrice M. Jones, "Pirated Goods Cripple Brazil's Economy, but Solutions Seen as Weak," *Chicago Tribune*, 4 November 2002, 1.
[773] Jones.
[774] Jones.

Brazilian officials have reported that the power behind the black market is organized crime and international terrorism. The Arab community in the TBA has been tied to the black market trade in pirated goods, particularly CDs. In a series of probes, Paraguayan prosecutors have alleged that pirated CDs were a main funding source for Islamic extremist groups such as Hizballah and Hamas.[775]

Paraguay's thriving industry of pirated products is promoted by weak government support for enforcement measures, an obstructionist judiciary, and ineffective customs procedures. These conditions cause copyright and trademark owners to consider Paraguay a nightmare for their enterprises. Ciudad del Este is the pre-eminent route into Latin America for counterfeit CDs and CD-ROMs from Hong Kong, Macau, Malaysia, and Thailand. An estimated US$1.5 billion worth of goods are moved annually.[776] Many Brazilian tourists visit Ciudad del Este to purchase cheap consumer goods. Although an estimated 90 percent of the products sold in Ciudad del Este are counterfeit, their low prices make them popular. Paraguayan legislation, which permits the patenting in Paraguay's National Brand Register of international brand names, facilitates the pirating and sale of contraband merchandise.[777] Much of this criminal activity has been linked to organized criminals based in Korea, Lebanon, Libya, and Taiwan, and the local press has uncovered numerous examples of corruption.[778] In February 2000, the International Intellectual Property Alliance (IIPA) identified Paraguay as the most serious problem among various Latin American countries with intellectual property (IP) infringements.[779]

Islamic Terrorist Activities

The TBA cities of Ciudad del Este and Foz do Iguaçu have served as a base for terrorists who pose potential threats to countries of the Americas. These terrorists have not carried out any known terrorist attacks within the TBA. Instead, they have used it as a base. The 2001 edition of

---

[775] Jones.

[776] Bartolomé.

[777] Bartolomé.

[778] "Paraguay: 'Strong Ties' Seen Between Hong Kong Mafia, Tri-border Based Hizballah," *ABC Color* [Asunción], 22 November 2002 (FBIS Document LAP20021122000059).

[779] James Nurton, "Goodbye to A Difficult Year: The World's Leading IP Practices," *Managing Intellectual Property* [London], June 2002, 56-70.

Patterns of Global Terrorism described the region as a hub for Islamic terrorist groups such as Hamas and Hizballah.[780]

In 2001 Francis X. Taylor, the Department of State's coordinator for counterterrorism, told the U.S. Congress that the TBA has a "….longstanding presence of Islamic extremist organizations, primarily Hizballah, and, to a lesser extent, the Sunni extremist groups, such as the Egyptian Islamic Group (Gamaat i-Islami) and Hamas."[781] Taylor noted that the activities of these organizations include fund-raising and proselytizing among the region's Middle Eastern population, as well as document forgery, money laundering, contraband smuggling, and weapons and drug trafficking. In 2002 Mark Davidson of the U.S. Embassy in Asunción described the TBA as indisputably an area from which Islamic terrorism is financed by money derived from illicit activities.[782]

The bombing of the Israeli Embassy in Buenos Aires in 1992, which killed 29 people, allegedly was carried out by Hizballah and coordinated by Imad Mughniyah. In 1999, Argentine authorities issued arrest warrants for Mughniyah, who was identified in the TBA shortly before the attack.[783] Mughniyah's Islamic Jihad, one of the armed branches of the pro-Iranian Lebanese Hizballah party, claimed responsibility for the 1994 attack against the AMIA in Buenos Aires. Clues indicated that the explosives or detonators used in the 1994 AMIA bombing were taken from Foz do Iguaçu. Mughniyah was indicted for the bombing, based on what investigators called conclusive evidence that the bombing had been explicitly ordered by Hizballah.[784]

Since 1998, the investigation of an alleged role in the 1994 bombing by Iranian diplomats has been stalled, and none of the suspects have been prosecuted.[785] However, in March 2003 an Argentine judge ordered arrest warrants for four Iranian government officials who allegedly helped to organize and carry out the 1994 AMIA bombing.[786]

---

[780] U.S. Department of State, Office of the Coordinator for Counterterrorism, *Patterns of Global Terrorism 2001.* <http://www.state.gov/s/ct/rls/pgtrpt/2001/html/10246.htm>

[781] Anthony Faiola, "U.S. Terrorist Search Reaches Paraguay; Black Market Border Hub Called Key Finance Center for Middle East Extremists," *Washington Post*, 13 October 2001, A21.

[782] Jon Dougherty, "Could Terrorists Strike from Caribbean?" *WorldNetDaily*, 9 January 2002. <http://www.worldnetdaily.com/news/article.asp?ARTICLE_ID=25977>

[783] Faiola.

[784] "Argentina Issues Arrest Warrant for Senior Hezbollah Leader," *Middle East Intelligence Bulletin*, 1, no. 9 (September 1999).

[785] Blanca Madani, "New Report Links Syria to 1992 Bombing of Israeli Embassy in Argentina," *Middle East Intelligence Bulletin*, 2, no. 3 (March 2000).

[786] Larry Rohter, "Argentine Judge Indicts 4 Iranian Officials in 1994 Bombing of Jewish Center," *New York Times*, 10 March 2003, A3.

Paraguay's Vice Interior Minister Mario Agustin Sapriza confirmed in May 2001 that the TBA serves as a base of operations for dormant Islamic extremist cells linked to international terrorism. Sapriza explained that Hizballah, Hamas, and other terrorist organizations use this region to plan their actions, to obtain supplies, and to live for a certain period of time before launching new attacks in other countries.[787]

The commander of Argentina's National Border Guard, Commandant General Hugo Miranda, offered a somewhat more specific report in October 2001, noting that conditions in the TBA favor the area's role as a hotbed of terrorist cells known as sleeper cells. Said Miranda, "We know that both in Ciudad del Este and in Foz do Iguaçu there is a community of Islamic origin. People in this community have ties to fanatical religious groups, and they are in contact with the Middle East countries. They have significant economic resources and the facilities for forging documents, so terrorist cells can be established there.[788]

Islamic Money Laundering and Other Fund-Raising

Blanca Madani, co-president of the World Amazigh Action Coalition (WAAC), has noted that Hizballah has also relied extensively on funding from the Shi'ite Lebanese Diaspora in the TBA.[789] Islamic money laundering in the TBA is concealed by the common practice of the local Arab community of remitting funds to relatives in the Middle East. Some of these remittances are suspected of reaching Arab terrorist organizations, particularly Hizballah.[790]

During the 1999-2001 period, Islamic extremist groups received at least US$50 million from Arab residents in the area of Foz do Iguaçu through Paraguayan financial institutions. An investigation by Paraguay's Secretariat for the Prevention of Money Laundering found that a group of 42 Arabs in Ciudad del Este remitted abroad, mostly to Lebanon, approximately US$50 million, apparently during the 1997-2001 period. It is believed that these funds were derived from arms trafficking and other illicit activities.[791] Paraguayan Interior Minister Julio César

---

[787] "Paraguay: Vice Interior Minister Confirms Presence of 'Dormant Islamic Terrorist Cells,'" *ABC Color* [Asunción], 4 May 2001 (FBIS Document LAP20010505000002).
[788] "National Border Guard Commander: Tri-Border Area Hotbed of Sleeper Cells," *La Nación* [Buenos Aires], 3 October 2001 (FBIS Document LAP20011003000015).
[789] Blanca Madani, "Hezbollah's Global Finance Network: The Triple Frontier," *Middle East Intelligence Bulletin*, 4, no. 1 (January 2002).
[790] Bartolomé, 9.
[791] Bartolomé, 9.

Fanego estimated the total amount to be between US$50 and US$500 million, with most remittances in the range of US$500 to US$2,000.[792] Brazilian security agencies claimed that the financial aid offered in 2000 by groups in the TBA to Islamic and Middle Eastern terrorist organizations, such as Hizballah, Hamas, and the Islamic Jihad, totaled US$261 million.[793]

Links of Hizballah and al Qaeda

Al Qaeda apparently has long had an interest in the TBA. Although it is unclear when al Qaeda established a presence in the TBA, Osama bin Laden reportedly visited the area in 1995.[794] Another top al Qaeda leader, Khalid Sheikh Mohammed, spent 20 days in Foz do Iguaçu in 1998.[795]

In 1999 agents of Argentina's Secretariat for State Intelligence (Spanish initialism SIDE) reported that al Qaeda agents had been identified in the TBA.[796] An alleged plot by Osama bin Laden and Hizballah leader Imad Mughniyah would have destroyed the Jewish Education Center in the Buenos Aires suburb of Palermo.[797] The larger objective reportedly was to conduct simultaneous attacks in Buenos Aires, Ciudad del Este, and Ottawa (Canada), and to draw world attention to undermine the Middle East peace process.

The SIDE also reported a significant shift in the Muslim terrorist groups in the TBA.[798] Until about 1999, pro-Iranian Shiite extremists organizations, such as the Islamic Jihad and the Lebanese Hizballah faction normally worked separately from the orthodox Sunnites. By mid-1999, however, SIDE's sources were finding evidence of collaboration. In the TBA, according to the SIDE's sources, "…the Sunnite organization maintains various contacts with elements

---

[792] Roberto Cosso, "Extremistas receberam US$50 mi de Foz do Iguaçu" [Extremists Received US$50 Million from Foz do Iguaçu], *Folha de S. Paulo* [São Paolo], 31 December 2001.

[793] Riyadh Alam-al-Din, "Washington Begins the War on Hizballah in the Border Triangle," *Al-Watan al-Arabi* [Paris], 21December 2001, 18-19 (FBIS Document GMP20011221000179).

[794] "Brazil: Terrorist Khalid Sheikh Mohamed's Passage Through Brazil Reported," *O Estado de São Paulo* [São Paolo], 9 March 2003 (FBIS Document LAP20030308000052).

[795] Kevin G. Hall, "Accused al-Qaida Terrorist Spent time in Brazil, Police Say," Knight Ridder Tribune News Service, 13 March 2003, 1.

[796] Mario Daniel Montoya, "War on Terrorism Reaches Paraguay's Triple Border," *Jane's Intelligence Review*, 13, no. 12 (December 2001): 12.

[797] Vladimir Jara Vera and Dany Ortiz, "Police Conduct Operation to Intimidate Islamic Extremists," *ABC Color* [Asunción], 23 December 1999 (FBIS Document FTS19991223001521).

[798] "Tríplice fronteira tinha agentes sauditas, diz 'Clarín' [Triborder has Saudi Agents, *Clarín* Says], *Estadão*, 17 September 2001.

suspected of being Hizballah sympathizers or affiliates."[799] However, the Buenos Aires daily *Clarín* reported that the SIDE's reports were received with skepticism by the CIA and Israel's Mossad.[800] In September 2001, a Latin American expert on money laundering, Jude Walter Fanganiello Maierovitch, said that al Qaeda was establishing a base near Ciudad del Este, in an Arab community of 30,000 people.[801] The new base would take advantage of existing al Qaeda links with TBA trafficking in arms, narcotics, and uranium, as well as ongoing money laundering activities, in association with the Russian and Chinese mafias. The base would use religious entities as fronts for training terrorists and providing refuge for Islamic fugitives.

Rio de Janeiro's *O Globo* reported in late October 2001 that the FBI, in close collaboration with the CIA, had discovered evidence that al Qaeda is making the TBA its main center of operations in Latin America. The area allegedly is the headquarters for two separate financial and drug-trafficking depots. The latter supposedly has a direct connection with the FARC.[802]

Conclusion

A deeply rooted system fosters organized crime and terrorist activities in the TBA and elsewhere in Argentina, Brazil, and Paraguay. That system is sustained by societal, institutional, economic, and geographic factors. A combination of those factors has made the TBA a remote enclave that defies effective law enforcement. A primary obstacle to effective crime prevention is widespread corruption in the political and law enforcement systems of the three countries whose territory is included in the TBA. In Brazil and Paraguay, permissive banking systems foster the money laundering that is a vital adjunct of the arms and narcotics trafficking industries. The same conditions that allow domestic crime to flourish are potent attractions for transnational criminal groups and terrorist organizations. Criminal groups from many countries are present in the TBA. Major international terrorist groups, including al Qaeda and Hizballah, appear to have

---

[799]Daniel Santoro, "Bin Laden's Followers in Triborder Area Probed," *Clarín* [Buenos Aires], 18 July 1999 (FBIS Document WA1907180899); Daniel Santoro, "Argentine Intelligence Services' 1999 Report on Usamah Bin-Ladin's Agents in Triborder Area Viewed," *Clarín* [Buenos Aires], 16 September 2001, 8-9, 1 (FBIS Document LAP20010916000021).
[800] Santoro, FBIS Documents WA1907180899 and LAP20010916000021.
[801]Germano Oliveira, "Brazil's Former Drug Czar: Bin-Ladin Establishing Al-Qa'idah Cell on Triborder," *O Globo* [Rio de Janeiro], 19 September 2001 (FBIS Document LAP200109119000051).
[802] Jose Meirelles Passos, "The Shadow of Bin Laden in Latin America," *O Globo* [Rio de Janeiro], 29 October 2001 (FBIS Document LAP20011029000036).

established planning bases in the TBA, from which operations can be conducted in other countries.

BIBLIOGRAPHIES

Africa

Adam, Hussein M. "Somalia: A Terrible Beauty Being Born?" Pages 69-89 in I. William Zartman, ed., *Collapsed States: The Disintegration and Restoration of Legitimate Authority.* Boulder: Lynne Rienner, 1995.

The Advocacy Project, "Girls for Sale: Building a Coalition to Fight Trafficking in Nigeria." <http://advocacy.autoupdate.com/cpage_view/nigtraffick_girlsforsale_6_25.htm>

"AFP Says Diamond Fever Rages Despite Ban on Illegal Mining," Agence France Presse report, 5 October 2001 (FBIS Document 20011005000155).

"Al Qaeda Suspect Handed to FBI." "World in Brief," *Washington Post*, 20 March 2003, A26.

"Arms Trafficking Networks out of Kenya and Somalia, Including Links to Terrorists, Exposed in Fund for Peace Investigation," Fund for Peace news release, 5 December 2002. <http://www.fundforpeace.org>

"Attentats anti-israéliens: pourquoi le Kenya*?"* [Anti-Israeli Attacks: Why Kenya?], *Marchés Tropicaux et Mediterranéens* [Paris]*,* no. 2978 (6 December 2002).

Barone, Michael. "Dirty Diamonds," *U.S. News and World Report* online report, 12 November 2001. <http://www.usnews.com/usnews/opinion/baroneweb/mb_011112.htm>

Block, Robert. "Kenya, Tanzania Officer Fertile Soil for Intrigue," *Wall Street Journal*, 11 August 1998, A12.

Block, Robert. "In South Africa, Mounting Evidence of al Qaeda Links," *Wall Street Journal*, 10 December 2002.

Blunt, Elizabeth. "Ivory Coast to Fight Child Trafficking," BBC News report, 14 June 2001.

"Carlos Verdicts Taint Chissano's Son," February 1, 2003. <http://allAfrica.co>

Collier, Paul. "Economic Causes of Civil Conflict and Their Implications for Policy." <http://www.ilo.org/public/english/bureau/inf/pr/2001/21.htm>

Council on Foreign Relations and Markle Foundation. "Armed Islamic Group: Algeria, Islamists." http://www.terrorismanswers.com/groups/gia.htm

Council on Foreign Relations and Markle Foundation. "Jamaat al-Islamiyya, Egyptian Islamic Jihad: Egypt, Islamists." http://www.terrorismanswers.com/groups/jamaat.htm

Council on Foreign Relations and Markle Foundation. "Terrorism: Questions and Answers: Sudan," 2002. <http://www.terrorismanswers.com/sponsors/sudan.htm>

Cowell, Alan. "Kenya Is on Terrorism Alert After Reported Sighting of Suspect in 1998 Embassy Bombings," *New York Times*, 21 May 2003.

"East Africa: Terrorism's Ties to Drugs." *Strategic Forecast* [Austin, Texas], Daily Global Intelligence Report, 5 October 2001. http://www.stratfor.com

"ECOWAS Experts Discuss Action Plan Against Human Trafficking." <www.newsinghana.com/politics/archive/ ECOWAS-experts-discuss-action.htm>

Economist Intelligence Unit. *Eritrea, Somalia, Djibouti: Country Profile 2001*. London: 2001.

Economist Intelligence Unit. *Kenya: Country Profile 2001*. London: 2001.

Economist Intelligence Unit. *Tanzania, Comoros: Country Profile 2002*. London: 2002.

Farah, Douglas. "Report Says Africans Harbored Al Qaeda: Terror Assets Hidden in Gem-Buying Spree," *Washington Post*, 29 December 2002.

Farah, Douglas. "Taylor Charged with War Crimes During Long Conflict in Sierra Leone," *Washington Post*, 5 June 2003.

Federation of American Scientists, Intelligence Resource Program. "Salafist Group for Call and Combat (GSPC)." <http://www.fas.org/irp/world/para/salaf.htm>

"Fighting the Burden of Drug Trafficking: Nigeria Works to Reclaim Certification," *Washington Times*, 30 September 1999. <http://www.internationalspecialreports.com/africa/99/nigeria/13.htm>

Filkins, Dexter, and Marc Lacey. "Kenya's Porous border Lies Open to Arms Smugglers," *New York Times*, Wednesday, 4 December 2002, A18.

Gamba, Virginia. "Small Arms Foster Social Turmoil: Illegal Trafficking Disrupts African Communities, Spreads Crime," *Africa Recovery*, 12, no. 1, 1998. <http://www.un.org/ecosocdev/geninfo/afrec/vol12no1/smallarm.htm>

"Gangs Against Gangsterism?" *Jane's Foreign Report*, no. 2520 (12 November 1998).

Gastrow, Peter. "Main Trends in the Development of South Africa's Organised Crime," *African Security Review*, 8, no. 6 (1999). http://www.iss.co.za

Gastrow, Peter. *Organised Crime in the SADC Region: Police Perceptions*. Institute for Strategic Studies, monograph no. 60, 2001.

Gastrow, Peter, and Mark Shaw. "In Search of Safety: Police Transformation and Public Reponses in South Africa," *Daedalus*, 130, no. 1 (Winter 2001): 259-75.

Gberie, Lansana. "War and Peace in Sierra Leone: Diamonds, Corruption and the Lebanese Connection," Diamonds and Human Security Project, *Occasional Paper* no. 6, November 2002.

Global March. "Worst Forms of Child Labour Data 2002: Morocco."
<http://www.globalmarch.org/worstformsreport/world/morocco.html>

Goredema, Charles. "Diamonds and Other Precious Stones in Armed Conflicts and Law Enforcement Co-operation in Southern Africa," *ISS Occasional Paper*, no. 57, May 2002.
<http://www.iss.co.za/PUBS/PAPERS/57/Paper57.html>

Govender, George. "Prevention and Combating of Organised Crime in South Africa." Pages 50-64 in M. Hough and A. Du Plessis, eds., *Conference Papers: The Grim Reaper: Organised Crime in the 1990s—Implications for South and Southern Africa*. Institute for Strategic Studies, Publication no. 36, 1999.

Griffiths-Fulton, Lynne. "Small Arms and Light Weapons in the Horn of Africa," *Ploughshares Monitor*, Summer 2002. <http://www.ploughshares.ca>

Hanlon, Joseph. "Metical Special Investigation: Drugs Now Biggest Business," *Metical* [London], 28 June 2001. mozambique-news@geo2.poptel.org.uk

Harman, Danna. "Why Radicals Find Fertile Ground in Moderate Kenya," *Christian Science Monitor*, Friday, 6 December 2002, 7-8.

Hiltermann, Joost. "Liberia: New Arms Embargo Failing: Weak Export Controls Largely to Blame," Human Rights Watch report, 5 November 2001.
<http://www.hrw.org/press/2001/11/liberia1105.htm>

"A Human Rights Report on Trafficking of Persons, Especially Women and Children: Morocco." <http://209.190.246.239/ver2/cr/Morocco.pdf>

"Human Trafficking Thriving in Kenya," *Nairobi Daily Nation*, 20 February 2002 (FBIS Document AFP20020220000100).

International Actions Network on Small Arms. "Kalashnikovs for Chickens: Small Arms Boom in East Africa," 7 May 2001. <http://www.iansa.org/news/2001/may_01/chicken.htm>

International Labor Organization. "ILO Reports on Child Trafficking in West and Central Africa," 15 June 2001. <http://www.ilo.org/public/english/bureau/inf/pr/2001/21.htm>

International Organization for Migration. "New IOM Figures on the Global Scale of Trafficking: Africa," *Trafficking in Migrants*, special issue, April 2001.

Kelley, Kevin J. "Africa News Service: Daadab an 'Arms Centre," Fund for Peace report, 19 November 2000. <http://www.fundforpeace.org/media/inthenews/itn10001119.php>

"Kenya: Communications." In *Africa South of the Sahara, 2003*. 32nd edition. London: Europa, 2003.

Kenya. Ministry of Finance and Planning. *Second Report on Poverty in Kenya. Vol. I: Incidence and Depth of Poverty*. Nairobi: 2000.

Ketterer, James. "Networks of Discontent in Northern Morocco," *Middle East Report*, no. 218 (Spring 2001). <http://www.merip.org/mer/mer218/218_ketterer.htm>

Khalid M. Medani. "Financing Terrorism or Survival? Informal Finance and State Collapse in Somalia, and the US War on Terrorism," *Middle East Research & Information Project* [Washington], 32, no. 223 (Summer 2002).

Kinnes, Irvin. "From Urban Street Gangs to Criminal Empires: The Changing Face of Gangs in the Western Cape, National and Local Trends" Institute for Strategic Studies, monograph no. 48, 2000.

Labrousse, Alain. Interview with Frederic Dorce, *Jeune Afrique Economie* [Paris], 16 December 2002-19 January 2003 (FBIS Document AFP20030108000224).

Lacey, Marc and Benjamin Weiser, "After Attack, Kenya Traces Qaeda's Trail in East Africa," *New York Times*, Saturday, 1 December 2002, A1.

Le Sage, Andre. "Prospects for Al Itihad & Islamist Radicalism in Somalia," *Review of African Political Economy*, 28, no. 89 (September 2001).

Majtenyi, Cathy. "Small Arms: Only a Regional Approach Can Stop the Trade," *The East African* [Nairobi], 26 November 2001.

McNeil, Donald G., Jr. "A New Scrutiny of Somalia as the Old Anarchy Reigns," *New York Times*, Sunday, 10 February 2002.

Menkhaus, Ken. "Political Islam in Somalia," *Middle East Policy*, 9, no. 1 (March 2002).

Menkhaus, Ken. "Somalia: In the Crosshairs of the War on Terrorism," *Current History*, 101, no. 655, May 2002, 195-202.

"Mombasa Main Conduit for Drug Trafficking," International Action Network on Small Arms report, 18 June 2001. <http://www.iansa.org/news/2001/jun_01/mombasa.htm>

"Mozambique: A Flood of Mud," *Africa Confidential* [London], 43, no. 25 (December 20, 2002).

Muiruri, Stephen. "How Illegal Migrants Use Kenya's Airports," 13 August 2002.
<http://fpmail.friends-partners.org/pipermail/stop-traffic/2002/002266.htm>

Mutua, Martin. "Kibaki Opens Parliament, Vows to Fight Corruption," *East African Standard*
[Nairobi], 19 February 2002. <http://allafrica.com/stories/200302190693.html>

Muyita, Solomon. "Uganda Major Point in Arms Trafficking," *New Vision* [Kampala], 15 July
2001. <http://allafrica.com>

Namburete, Antonio Paolo. "Organised Crime in Mozambique and Its Impact Within the
Regional and International Context," Pages 26-36 in M. Hough and A. Du Plessis, eds., *The
Grim Reaper: Organised Crime in the 1990s—Implications for South and Southern Africa.* Cape
Town: Institute for Strategic Studies, 1999.

Nelson, Craig, and Philip Sherwell. "Business as Usual for Africa's 'Merchant of Death,'" *The
Sunday Telegraph* [London], 22 July 2001.
<http://www.iansa.org/news/2001/jul_01/busi_usual.htm>

"New Ambitions in the Fight Against Drugs," *Geopolitical Drug Newsletter* [Paris], October
2001. <http://www.geodrugs.net/mini-lettres/AEGD6GB.pdf>

"Nigeria: Defence Minister Denounces Increased Number of Small Arms in Country," BBC
report, 14 January 2002. <http://www.clw.org/atop/newswire/nw011402.htm>

Observatoire Geopolitique des Drogues. "Kenya," in *Annual Report 1997.*
<http://www.ogd.org/rapport/gb/RP11_7_KENYA.htm>

Park, Steve. "'Victor B' Watched for Taliban Ties," *Washington Times*, 22 July 2002.
http://www.washtimes.com/world/20020722-330000642.htm

Porzio, Giovanni. "Somalia Ready for the Fireworks," *Milan Panorama*, 7 February 2002, 44-46
(FBIS Document EUP20020203000135).

"Repairing Our Broken Dream," *East African Standard* [Nairobi], 29 December 2002, as quoted
in *Africa Research Bulletin, Political, Social, and Cultural Series* [Oxford, United Kingdom], 39,
no. 12 (24 January 2003).

"Responding to War and State Collapse in West Africa," United States Institute for Peace special
report, 21 January 2002.

Sengupta, Somini. "Chaos in West Africa: Unending Wars," *New York Times*, 5 May 2003.

Shaw, Mark, and Peter Gastrow. "Stealing the Show? Crime and Its Impact in Post-Apartheid
South Africa," *Daedalus*, 130, no. 1 (Winter 2001).

Smucker, Philip, and Faye Bowers. "Iraq Regime Linked to Terror Group*," Christian Science Monitor,* 18 April 2003, 1.

Sullivan, Robert E. "Burgeoning Small Arms Trade Has High Profits and Losses," *Earth Times*, March 2001. <http://globalpolicy.igc.org/security/smallarms/2001/03sc.htm>

"Trafficked Children Registered," report of AllAfrica.com, 4 February 2003. <http://allafrica.com/stories/200302040508>

Trofimov, Yaroslav. "In Mombasa Streets, Bin Laden Is 'Hero,' And U.S. Is Hated," *Wall Street Journal*, Monday, 2 December 2002, A1.

Turetzky, Marc David. "Egypt, Mubarak, and the Rise of Islamic Fundamentalist Terrorism, 1981-1994: An Empirical Analysis of the Mubarak Regime's Punitive Counter-Terrorist Policy," *Michigan Journal of Political Science*, no. 24 (Winter 1998). <http://www.umich.edu/~mjps/24/turetzky.html>

United Nations. Office for the Coordination of Humanitarian Affairs. "East Africa: Small Arms Exacerbating Regional Insecurity." Integrated Regional Information Network Report, 30 November 2001. <http://www.reliefweb.int/w/rwb.nsf/s/23C43ACB12FDC40085256B14005B3462>

United States. Office of the President. *International Crime Threat Assessment*. Washington, D.C.: 2000. http://clinton4.nara.gov

U.S. Department of State. *Patterns of Global Terrorism 2002*. <http://www.usis.usemb.se/terror/rpt2002/index.html>

U.S. Department of State. *Trafficking in Persons Report 2002*. <http://www.state.gov/g/tip/rls/tiprpt/2002>

U.S. Department of State. Bureau for International Narcotics and Law Enforcement Affairs. *International Narcotics Control Strategy Report 2002*. Washington: 2002. <http://www.state.gov/g/inl/rls/nrcrpt/2002>

U.S. Department of State, Bureau for International Narcotics and Law Enforcement Affairs. *International Narcotics Control Strategy Report 2003*. Washington, D.C.: Department of State, 2003.

U.S. Department of State. Bureau of Intelligence and Research. "Arms and Conflict in Africa." http://www.state.gov.s/inr/rls/fs/2001/4004.htm

U.S. Department of State and Federation of American Scientists, Intelligence Resource Program. "Salafist Group for Call and Combat (GSPC)." <http://www.fas.org/irp/world/para/salaf.htm>

"Washington Possibly Examining Militancy Threat in West Africa," Stratfor report, 14 November 2002. http://www.stratfor.com

Wax, Emily. "Marines Comb Borders As Worries Rise in Kenya," *The Washington Post*, 17 May 2003.

Weiser, Benjamin. "Details Given, and 5 More Charged, in Tanzania Bombing," *New York Times*, 17 December 1998.

"West African Arms Trafficking and Mercenary Activities Supported by the Liberian Government and Logging Companies," Global Witness report, 31 March 2003. <http://www.globalwitness.org/text/press_releases/display2.php?id=186>

Williams, Phil, and Doug Brooks. "Captured, Criminal, and Contested States: Organised Crime and Africa in the 21st Century," *South African Journal of International Affairs*, 6, no. 2 (Winter 1999).

Former Soviet Union and Eastern Europe

Adamoli, Sabrina. "Organised Crime and Money Laundering Trends and Countermeasures: A Comparison Between Western and Eastern Europe," in PetrusC. van Duyne, Vinzenzo Ruggiero, Miroslav Scheinost, and Wim Valkenburg, eds., *Cross-Border Crime in a Changing Europe*. Huntington, New York: Nova Science Publishers, 2001.

Akopyan, Armen. "Joint Fight Against Crime," *Ayots Askar* [Erevan], 23 March 2002 (FBIS Document CEP20020323000069).

"Albania: Cash-for-Guns Plan Misfires," Institute for War and Peace Reporting *Balkan Crisis Report*, 379 (4 November 2002). <http://www.iwpr.net>

"Albania: Smuggling Continues Despite Multinational Efforts," *RFE/RL Crime and Corruption Watch*, 2, no. 30 (30 August 2002). <http://www.rferl.org/corruptionwatch>

American University. Transnational Crime and Corruption Center, Vladivostok Centre for Research on Organized Crime. "Summary of Crime in the Region 2001." <http://www.crime.vl.ru>

Aminyeva, Yana, and Viktoria Chernysheva. "Organized Crime in the Far East: Press Survey for Maritime Province, January 2000," *Organized Crime and Corruption Watch*, Summer 2000.

Aminyeva, Yana, and Viktoria Chernysheva. "Organized Crime in the Far East: Press Survey for Maritime Province and the Khabarovsk Region, February 2000," *Organized Crime and Corruption Watch*, Summer 2000.

Aminyeva, Yana, and Viktoria Chernysheva. "Organized Crime in the Far East: Press Survey for Maritime Province and the Khabarovsk Region, March 2000," *Organized Crime and Corruption Watch*, Summer 2000.

Anisko, Sergey. "Belarus Chechens Display Patriotism: Local Power Departments Claim That Chechen Mafiya Sends Half the Money It Earns to the Homeland," *Segodnya* [Moscow], 12 January 1998 (FBIS Document 19980113001126).

Antichenko, Viktor. "The State: It Is I and My Daughter," *Novaya Gazeta* [Moscow], 17 June 2002 (FBIS Document CEP20020620000337).

"Armenian Anticorruption Drive Creates Doubt," *RFE/RL Crime and Corruption Watch*, 2, no. 30 (30 August 2002). <http://www.rferl.org/corruptionwatch>

Armenian Center for National and International Studies. "ACNIS Roundtable on Anti-Corruption Strategies," 27 September 2002. <http://www.acnis.am/pr/corruption>

"Arrest Illegal Capital but Grant No Amnesty," *Asia-Plus* [Dushanbe], 18 April 2002 (FBIS Document CEP20020427000054).

Arsov, Darko. "Money Laundering: The Most Sophisticated Form of Organized Crime," *Ministry of Finance Bulletin* [Skopje], December 2001. <http://www.finance.gov.mk/gb/bulletins>

Atayev, Artur. "There Is No Organized Crime," *Nezavisimaya Gazeta* [Moscow], 5 March 2002 (FBIS Document 20020305000162).

Australia. Ministry for Defence. "Report of the Experts Team Visit to Ukraine," 28 November 2002.

"Azerbaijani Women Mainly Trafficked to Turkey, United Arab Emirates," Trend News Agency [Baku] report, 14 June 2002 (FBIS Document CEP20020614000274).

Babić, Jasna. "MORH Protects Arms Dealers Who Smuggle Weapons to ETA and IRA," *Nacional* [Zagreb], 24 July 2001 (FBIS Document EUP20010724000372).

Babić, Jasna. "SZUP Document Confirms Existence of Another Crime Organization," *Nacional* [Zagreb], 10 September 2002 (FBIS Document EUP20020910000188).

Baker, Peter. "In Struggling Moldova, Desperation Drives Decisions," *Washington Post*, 1 November 2002.

Baker, Peter. "Renewed Militancy Seen in Uzbekistan," *Washington Post*, 27 September 2003.

The Balkan Times, 29 August 2002. <http://www.balkantimes.com>

"Balkans: Organized Crime in the Region," *RFE/RL Crime and Corruption Watch*, 2, no. 31 (6 September 2002). <http://www.rferl.org/corruptionwatch>

"Banned Islamic Movement Still a 'Real Threat' to Uzbek Security—Kazakh Paper," *BBC Monitoring Central Asia Unit*, based on report in *Karavan* [Almaty], 1 March 2002.

Barnett, Neil. "The Criminal Threat to Stability in the Balkans," *Jane's Intelligence Review*, 1 April 2002.

Baumanis, Romans, and Arnolds Karklis. "Public-Private Cooperation Urgently Needed to Halt Transit of Counterfeits by Organized Crime and Terrorist Groups." Coalition for Intellectual Property Rights report, 10 December 2001. <http://www.cipr.org>

Beare, Margaret. "Russian (East European) Organized Crime Around the Globe." Paper read at Transnational Crime Conference, Canberra, 9 March 2000.

"Belarus: Interior Minister Reveals 6,000 Crimes Committed by Police Staff in 2002," *Belapan* [Minsk], 29 November 2002 (FBIS Document CEP20021129000363).

"Belarus Sells Arms to Regimes Harboring Terrorists, Says *NS*," International League for Human Rights, *Belarus Updates*, 4, no. 42 (October 2001). <http://www.ilhr.org>

Beregovoy, Anatoliy. "Asian Eclipse: The Standoff Between the Kazakhstani Authorities and Opposition Has Come to a Head," *Nezavisimaya Gazeta* [Moscow], 4 April 2002 (FBIS Document CEP20020405000042).

Berniker, Mark. "Tajikistan Strives for Growth amid Risk and Poverty," *Eurasianet* report, 11 June 2003. <http://www.eurasianet.org>

Blank, Steven. "Kyrgyzstan: Strategic Pivot," *Central Asia/Caucasus Analyst*, 18 December 2002. <http://www.cacianalyst.org>

Bondarenko, Mariya. "The North Caucasus Is the Hottest Region When It Comes to Drugs, Too," *Nezavisimaya Gazeta* [Moscow], 15 April 2002 (FBIS Document CEP20020416000232).

Borisov, Timofey. "Has Gelayev Got His Eye on the Chechen Leadership? But Before That He Tried Out the Route from Ichkeria to Dagestan," *Rossiyskaya Gazeta* [Moscow], 15 May 2002 (FBIS Document CEP20020515000283).

"Bosnia Suspends Military Exports," VOA News report, 29 October 2002. <http://voanews.com>

Bregu, Zylyftar. "Albania: Authorities Rocked by Drugs Scandal," Institute for War and Peace Reporting, 22 March 2002. <http://www.iwpr.net>

British Helsinki Human Rights Group. "Sex Slaves: Trafficking in Human Beings from Moldova to Italy." <http://www.bhhrg.org>

"Bulgaria: NGO Alleges Money Laundering by Grain Traders," *RFE/RL Crime and Corruption Watch*, 2, no. 31 (6 September 2002). <http://www.rferl.org/corruptionwatch>

Burant, Stephen R. *Hungary: A Country Study*. Washington, D.C.: GPO, 1990.

Burrell, Ian. "Sex, Drugs and Illegal Migrants: Sarajevo's Export Trade to Britain," *The Independent*, 21 January 2002. <http://www.independent.co.uk>

"Central Asia: Governments Slowly Changing Approach to Human Trafficking," *Eurasianet* report, 6 July 2003. <http://www.eurasianet.org/departments/rights/articles/cav070603.shtm>

Coalition for Intellectual Property Rights. "Latvian Government Incinerates 25 Million Cigarettes," press release, 10 December 2001. <http://www.cipr.org/activities>

Cohen, Ariel. "Ukrainian and Russian Organized Crime: A Threat to Emerging Civil Society." Pages 285-302 in Sharon L. Wolchik and Volodymyr Zviglyanich, eds. *Ukraine: The Search for a National Identity*. Lanham, Maryland: Rowman and Littlefield, 2000.

Collins, Jan K. "Doing Business in the Baltic." <http://www.research.moore.sc.edu>

Cornell, Svante E. "The Nexus of Narcotics, Conflict, and Radical Islamism in Central Asia," Cornell Caspian Consulting, *Caspian Briefs*, no. 24 (June 2002).

Cornell, Svante E., and Regina A. Spector. "Central Asia: More Than Islamic Extremists," *The Washington Quarterly*, 25, no. 1 (2002).

"Corruption," *Moldova Gateway*, 2000. <http://www.gate.md/Article/267>

"Corruption Gap May Work in Latvia's Favor," *Radio Free Europe/Radio Liberty News Release*, 9 April 2001. <http://www.rferl.org>

Council of Europe and Commission of the European Communities. "Final Recommendations and Guidelines for Action Addressed to the Government of Estonia," 13 February 1998.

Council of Europe. European Committee on Crime Problems, Select Committee of Experts on the Evaluation of Anti-Money Laundering Measures. "First Report on Latvia," 19 January 2001. <http://www.coe.int>

Council of Europe, European Committee on Crime Problems, Select Committee of Experts on the Evaluation of Anti-Money Laundering Measure. "Second Round Evaluation Report on Slovak Republic," 8 April 2003. <http://www.coe.int>

"Crime Rate in Kyrgyzstan Impedes Socio-Economic Reforms," *Pravda.ru*, 21 August 2001. <http://www.english.pravda.ru>

"Croatian Press Speculates on Underworld Groups' Ties to Establishment," *Nacional* [Zagreb], 24 September 2002 (FBIS Document EUP20020923000505).

"Czech Republic: Top Attorney Calls for Radical Solution to Widespread Corruption," *RFE/RL Crime and Corruption Watch*, 2, no. 13 (4 April 2002). <http://www.rferl.org/corruptionwatch>

Cvijanović, Zeljko. "Serbia: Government Facing Mafia Dilemma," Institute for War and Peace Reporting, *Balkan Crisis Report*, no. 342 (12 June 2002). <http://www.iwhr.net>

Daniels, Anthony. "Market Reform and Moldova," British Helsinki Human Rights Group report, 7 March 2001. <http://www.bhhrg.org>

Davlatov, Vladimir. "Rakhmonov Warns of Afghan Terror Threat," Institute for War and Peace Reporting, *Report on Central Asia*, no. 127 (28 June 2002). <http://www.iwpr.net>

Demurian, Avet. "Armenia Escapes Drugs Epidemic," Institute for War and Peace Reporting, *Caucasus Reporting Service*, no. 130 (23 May 2002). <http://www.iwpr.net>

Diab, Hassan Haidar. "Panic in Slovakia Due to Possible Release of Josip Lončarić," *Večernji List* [Zagreb], 21 November 2001 (FBIS Document EUP20011121000202).

Dobbs, Michael. "Pivotal Alliance Frayed Before Serb's Death," *Washington Post*, 14 March 2003.

Dosybiev, Daur. "Kazakhstan: Police Corruption Worsens," Institute for War and Peace Reporting, *Report on Central Asia*, no. 128 (5 July 2002). <http://www.iwpr.net>

"Drug War for $1.2 Billion," *Trud* [Sofia], 6 February 2001 (FBIS Document EUP20010206000047).

Dziedzic, Michael, Laura Rozen, and Phil Williams. "Lawless Rule Versus Rule of Law in the Balkans," *United States Institute of Peace Special Report*, no. 97 (December 2002).

"The End of the Vory?" *Jane's Intelligence Review*, 1 March 2002.

Eshanova, Zamira. "Central Asia: Border Issues an 80-Year-Old Headache for Region," *Turkestan Newsletter*, 20 October 2002.

Eshanova, Zamira. "Central Asia: Report Says Police Have Improved Little since Soviet Era," *Eurasia Insight*, 18 December 2002. <http://www.eurasianet.org>

Estonia. Ministry of Justice. "Status Report of the Republic of Estonia under the Baltic Anti-Corruption Initiative," March 2002. <http://www.anticorruptionnet.org>

European Union. "Activities of the European Union, Summaries of Legislation," 1 February 2002. <http://europa.eu.int>

Finckenhauer, James O., and Yuri A. Voronin. *The Threat of Russian Organized Crime.* Washington, D.C.: U.S. Department of Justice, 2001.

"Focus on the Balkans," *Trafficking in Migrants*, no. 22 (Autumn 2000).

"Foreign Investors Call on New Government to Crack Down on Corruption," *RFE/RL Crime and Corruption Watch*, 2, no. 27 (25 July 2002). <http://www.rferl.org/corruptionwatch>

Galeotti, Mark. "Albanian Gangs Gain Foothold in European Crime Underworld," *Jane's Intelligence Review*, 1 November 2001.

Gerlin, Andrea. "Sex Trafficking Is Flourishing in Balkans," *Philadelphia Inquirer*, 15 April 2002. <http://www.philly.com>

Giragosian, Richard. "A Troubling Trend in Armenia," *RFE/RL Newsline*, 7, no. 3 (7 January 2003).

Global March Against Child Labour. "Worst Forms of Child Labor Data: Kyrgyzstan." <http://www.globalmarch.org>

Glonti, Georgi. "Problems Associated with Organized Crime in Georgia," report for Institute of Legal Reform [Tbilisi], 2000.

Glonti, Georgi. "Trafficking in Human Beings in Georgia and the CIS," *Demokratizatsiya*, 9, no. 3 (Summer 2001).

Gorobets, Alexander. "Italy Confirmed Connection of Top Ukrainian Officials with Illegal Arms Sales," *Pravda.ru*, 1 October 2002. <http://www.english.pravda.ru>

"Government Publishes Report on Widespread Corruption in Slovakia," TASR news service [Bratislava], 8 September 2002 (FBIS Document EUP20020908000132).

Hedl, Drago. "Links Between Organized Crime and Croatia's Top Brass," *Alternativna Informativna Mreža (AIM)* [Zagreb] report, 11 April 2001. <http://www.aimpress.org>

Hignett, Kelly. "Hungary Takes on the Mafia," *Jane's Intelligence Review*, 1 January 2001.

Hughes, Donna M. "The 'Natasha' Trade: Transnational Sex Trafficking," *National Institute of Justice Journal*, no. 246 (January 2001).

Hughes, Donna M. "Short Report on Trafficking in Women from Ukraine Research Project," National Institute of Justice, Research Partnership with Ukraine report, August 2001. <http://www.ojp.usdoj.gov/nij/international/programs/ukr_short>

"Human Rights Group Says Corruption, Abuse of Power Still High," reported in *Basapress* [Chisinau], 21 May 2002 (FBIS Document CEP20020521000255).

Human Rights Watch. "Arms Trade, Human Rights, and European Union Enlargement: The Record of Candidate Countries," 8 October 2002. <http://www.hrw.org>

Human Rights Watch. *World Report 2002.* http://www.hrw.org

International Action Network on Small Arms, "Central and Eastern Europe Remains Important Source and Transit Route for Arms: Country Analysis," 2 July 2002. <http://www.saferworld.org.uk>

International League for Human Rights. *Belarus Update,* 2, no. 42 (October 2001). <http://www.ilhr.org>

International Organization for Migration. "Azerbaijan: Trafficking in Women," IOM press briefing, 4 October 2002. <http://www.iom.net>

Jerinić, Dragan. "Bosnia: Serb Minister Resigns over Customs Scandal," Institute for War and Peace Reporting, *Balkan Crisis Report,* no. 343 (14 June 2002). <http://www.iwpr.net>

Johnson, Mark. "Nukes and the Russian Mob," *Journal of Commerce*, 13 (March 1998).

Kaliyev, Rustam. "How the Mafias Were Formed," pt. 1 of "Russia's Organized Crime: A Typology," *Eurasia Insight*, 17 June 2002. <http://www.eurasianet.com>

Kalnins, Valts. "Corruption: The Battle Is Not Finished," *Diena* [Riga], 30 August 2002 (FBIS Document CEP20020830000048)

Kanani, Agim. "Albania: Breaking Cycle of Prostitution," Institute for War and Peace Reporting, *Balkan Crisis Report*, 19 April 2002. <http://www.iwpr.net>

Kanani, Agim. "Albania: Cash-for-Guns Plan Misfires." Report of Institute for War and Peace Reporting, *Balkan Crisis Report,* 4 November 2002.

Kaplan, Robert. "Crime and Democracy in Bulgaria," *The Globalist*, 23 June 2001. <http://www.theglobalist.com>

Kattoulas, Velisarios. "Russian Far East: Crime Central," *Far Eastern Economic Review*, 30 May 2002.

"Kazakhgate under Way," International Eurasian Institute for Economic and Political Research report, 5 June 2002. <http://www.iicas.org>

Kelmendi, Adriatik. "Kosovo Prostitution Racket Flourishes," Institute for War and Peace Reporting, *Balkan Crisis Report*, no. 230 (28 March 2001). <http://www.iwpr.net>

Kelmendi, Adriatik. "The Security Zone Between Montenegro and Kosovo Has Become a Paradise for Petrol Smugglers," Institute for War and Peace Reporting, *Balkan Crisis Report,* 28 February 2002. <http://www.iwpr.net>

Khmelik, Natalya. "Military Bookends," *Sovershenno Sekretno* [Moscow], 1 August 2002 (FBIS Document CEP20020813000393).

Konstantinova, Elizabeth. "Bulgarian Gangs Provide Key Link in European Trafficking Chain," *Jane's Intelligence Review*, 1 November 2002.

"Kosovo" Fuel Smugglers Flourishing." Report of Institute for War and Peace Reporting, 28 February 2002. <http://www.iwpr.net>

Krajewski, K. "Drug Trafficking in Poland," in Petrus C. van Duyne, Vinzenzo Ruggiero, Miroslav Scheinost, and Wim Valkenburg, eds., *Cross-Border Crime in a Changing Europe*. Huntington, New York: Nova Science Publishers, 2001.

Kupchinsky, Roman. "Cesium Sale Thwarted in Lithuania," *RFE/RL Crime and Corruption Watch*, 2, no. 22 (6 June 2002). <http://www.rferl.org/corruptionwatch>

Kuzio, Taras. "Ukraine's Virtual Struggle Against Corruption and Organized Crime," *RFE/RL Crime and Corruption Watch*, 2, no. 31 (6 September 2002). <http://www.rferl.org/corruptionwatch>

"Kyrgyz Security Official Again Warns of Imminent IMU Threat," *Central Asia and Caucasus Analyst*, 3 July 2002.

"Kyrgyzstan Must Act Against Terrorism and Religious Extremism," *Slovo Kyrgyzstana* [Bishkek], 18 October 2002 (FBIS Document CEP20021028000208).

Landesman, Peter. "Arms and the Man," *New York Times Magazine*, 17 August 2003.

Larsson, Frederic. "Trafficking in Women to Bosnia and Herzegovina," *Trafficking in Migrants*, Autumn 2000.

Latvia. Ministry of Justice. "Status Report of the Republic of Latvia under the Baltic Anti-Corruption Initiative," April 2002. <http://www.anticorruptionnet.org>

"Latvian Officials May Have Interest in Russian Crime Group," *Neatkagiga Rita Avize* [Riga], 22 February 2001 (FBIS Document CEP20010222000055).

"Latvia's Anticorruption Effort Gets High Marks," *RFE/RL Crime and Corruption Watch*, 1, no. 6 (6 December 2001). <http://www.rferl.org/corruptionwatch/2001>

"Law Enforcement in Kosovo," *Jane's Intelligence Review*, 1 April 2002.

Layne, Mary. "Estimating the Flow of Illegal Drugs Through Ukraine, National Institute of Justice Research Partnership with Ukraine conference paper, September 2001. http://www.ojp.usdoj.gov/nij/international/programs/ukr_est

Ledeneva, Alena V., and Marina Kurkchiyan, eds. *Economic Crime in Russia.* The Hague: Kluwer Law International, 2000.

Liklikadze, Koba. "What Money Laundering Has to Do with Terrorism," *24 Saati* [Tbilisi], 18 October 2002 (FBIS Document CEP20021021000156).

Linotte, Daniel, and Gianluca Rampolla. "Fighting Corruption in Georgia: The Need for a Long-Term and Comprehensive Perspective," *Central Asia/Caucasus Analyst*, 25 April 2001. <http://www.cacianalyst.org>

"Lithuania." Activities of the European Union, Summaries of Legislation, 1 February 2002. <http://europa.eu.int>

Lithuania. Ministry of Finance. "Supplementary Memorandum of Economic Policies of the Government and the Bank of Lithuania for the Period May-December 2002." http://www.finmin.lt/engl/smcpp

Lithuania. Ministry of the Interior. Financial Crime Investigative Service. "Money-Laundering Prevention: Legal Acts." <http://www.fmtt.lt/eng.mlp>

Lomas, Ulrika. "Hungary Bans Anonymous Accounts in Response to FATF Listing," *Tax-News* [Brussels], 3 September 2001.

Loriya, Yelena. "Nikolay Reznichenko: Tourists Used to Walk along the Gunman's Paths," *Izvestiya* [Moscow], 24 May 2002 (FBIS Document CEP20020524000290).

Lvov, Mikhail. "The Northwest: The Criminal Element," Freelance Bureau [Moscow] Internet report, 10 June 2002 (FBIS Document CEP20020613000225).

"Macedonia Has the Largest Transit of Drugs for the Albanian Narco Mafia," 6 November 2001. <http://www.realitymacedonia.org.mk>

"Macedonian Government Confirms Ethnic Albanians Buying Arms from Drug Funds," *Nova Makedonija* [Skopje], 20 February 2002.

"Main Anti-Organized Crime Department Comments on Crime Statistics," Interfax News Agency [Moscow] report, 23 July 2002.

"Major Drug Busts Made by Hungarians, Russians, Romanians," *RFE/RL Crime and Corruption Watch*, 2, no. 35 (4 October 2002). <http://www.rferl.org/corruptionwatch>

Makarenko, Tamara. "Crime, Terror and the Central Asian Drug Trade," *Harvard Asia Quarterly*, Summer 2002.

Makarenko, Tamara. "Kyrgyzstan and the Global Narcotics Trade," *Eurasia Insight*, 8 December 1999. <http://www.eurasianet.org>

Makarenko, Tamara. "Ukrainian Mafia Moves into the International Crime Arena," *Jane's Intelligence Review*, 1 February 2002.

Matejickova, Maša. "Ivan I. Miško on His Contacts with S. Mogilyev, Strong Man of the Ukrainian Mafia in the World," *SME* [Bratislava], 11 January 2000 (FBIS Document FTS20000115000458).

McConnell, Artie. "Islamic Radicals Regroup in Central Asia," online report of *Eurasia Insight*, 15 May 2002. <http://eurasianet.org>

McMahon, Robert. "Yugoslavia: Arms Expert Traces Belgium-to-Liberia Arms Trafficking," Radio Free Europe/Radio Liberty report, 11 January 2002. <http://rfe/rl.org>

Meyer, Henry. "Russian Mafia Extends Tentacles Across the Globe," Agence France Presse [Paris] report, 15 August 2002.

Mois, Jüri. "Organised Crime and Illegal Immigration in Estonia," speech to Baltic Assembly, 14th session, 27 May 1999. <http://www.baltsam.org/activity>

"Much Remains to Be Done in Fight Against Corruption in Latvia," *Diena* [Riga], 30 August 2002 (FBIS Document CEP20020830000048).

Mutschke, Ralf. "Links Between Organized Crime and 'Traditional' Terrorist Groups," testimony to U.S. House Judiciary Committee, Subcommittee on Crime, 13 December 2000. <http://www.russianlaw.org/Mutschke>

Nadiroglu, R. "Ben Ladin's Ties to Arms Are Much More Extensive Than It Appears," Internet report of *Zerkalo* [Baku], 6 December 2002 (FBIS Document CEP20011206000417).

Namoradze, Zaza, Goka Gabashvili, and George Papuashvili. "Georgia Appeals to Public to Help Fight Corruption," *Open Society News*, no. 8 (Spring 2001). <http://www.soros.org/open_society_news>

Nelson, Todd H. "Russian Realities: Nuclear Weapons, Bureaucratic Maneuvers, and Organized Crime," *Demokratizatsiya*, 8, no. 1 (Winter 2000).

"New Bribery Scandal," *RFE/RL Crime and Corruption Watch*, 1, no. 6 (6 December June 2001). <http://www.rferl.org/corruptionwatch>

Nikolov, Jovo. "Crime and Corruption after Communism: Organized Crime in Bulgaria," *East European Constitutional Review*, 6, no. 4 (Fall 1997). <http://www.law.nyu.edu/eecr>

Nuclear Threat Initiative. "Kazakhstan Overview," February 2002. <http://www.nti.org>

Observatoire Géopolitique des Drogues. *The World Geopolitics of Drugs, 1998/1999*. Dordrecht: Kluwer, 2001.

Olcott, Martha Brill, and Natalia Udalova. "Drug Trafficking on the Great Silk Road: The Security Environment in Central Asia," Carnegie Endowment for International Peace *Working Papers*, no. 11 (March 2000).

Organisation for Economic Cooperation and Development. Financial Action Task Force on Money Laundering. "Members and Observers: PC-R-EV Committee." http://www1.oecd.org/fatf

Organisation for Economic Cooperation and Development. Financial Action Task Force on Money Laundering. "Report on Money-Laundering Typologies 2001-2002." <http://www1.oecd.org/fatf/pdf/TY2002_en.pdf>

Organisation for Economic Cooperation and Development. Financial Action Task Force on Money Laundering. "Review to Identify Non-Cooperative Countries or Territories," 21 June 2002. <http://www1.oecd.org/fatf-gafi.org/pdf/NCCT2002>

Organisation for Economic Cooperation and Development, Financial Action Task Force on Money Laundering. "Annual Review of Non-Cooperating Countries or Territories," 20 June 2003. <http://www1.oecd.org/fatf/pdf/NCCT2003_en.pdf>

"Organized Crime in St. Petersburg: Press Survey, February 2000," *Organized Crime and Corruption Watch*, Summer 2000.

Orttung, Robert. "Russia's Southern Regions: Threats and Opportunities," East-West Institute Policy Brief, 1, no. 2 (June 2002).

Osser, Bernard. "In the East, the Specter of Another Iron Curtain," *Le Figaro* [Paris], 8 March 2002 (FBIS Document EUP2002031000003).

Osyka, I. "Organised Economic Crime Problems in the Ukraine," in Petrus C. van Duyne, Vinzenzo Ruggiero, Miroslav Scheinost, and Wim Valkenburg, eds., *Cross-Border Crime in a Changing Europe*. Huntington, New York: Nova Science Publishers, 2001.

"'Overindulgence' in Bribery," *RFE/RL Crime and Corruption Watch*, 2, no. 27 (25 July 2002). <http://www.rferl.org/corruptionwatch>

"Pakistani Islamists Active in Kazakhstan?" *RFE/RL Newsline*, 6, no. 129 (12 July 2002).

Panfilova, Viktoriya, and Roman Ukolov. "Anti-Terror No Bar to Drug Traffickers: Hopes for a Diminution in the Flow of Dope Have Not Been Justified," *Nezavisimaya Gazeta* [Moscow], 4 February 2002 (FBIS Document CEP20020204000277).

"Paper Accuses Communist Authorities of Protecting Oil, Arms Smugglers," *Tara* [Chisinau], 13 June 2002 (FBIS Document CEP20020617000276).

Pasztelanski, Rafal. "You Should Not Mess Around with 'Wolf,'" *Zycie* [Warsaw], 28 August 2002 (FBIS Document EUP200208300000246).

Petruseva, Anna. "Macedonia: Threats Follow Corruption Report," Institute for War and Peace Reporting, *Baltic Crisis Report,* 21 August 2002. <http://www.iwpr.net>

Peuch, Jean-Christophe. "Georgia: Corruption Seen as the 'Norm,'" Radio Free Europe/Radio Liberty report, 5 October 2001. <http://www.rferl.org/nca/features/2001/05/1005200115630.asp>

Picarelli, John T., and Phil Williams. "Structure and Scope of Ukrainian Organized Crime," American Society of Criminology conference, 15 November 2000. <http://www.asc41.com>

"Poland: Country Used to Launder Large Amounts of Money," *RFE/RL Crime and Corruption Watch*, 2, no. 41 (3 December 2002). <http://www.rferl.org/corruptionwatch>

Popa, Razvan. "We Have Secured Our Eastern Border, but We Are Attacked to the South: Bulgaria Is Throwing Waves of Illegal Immigrants to Us Across the Border," *Adevarul* [Bucharest], 25 July 2002 (FBIS Document EUP20020725000182).

Pritchard, Eleanor. "Smuggled Smokes a Problem," *Central European Review*, 2, no. 25 (26 June 2000). <http://www.ce-review.org>

"Racovat, Moldova: Immigrant Trafficking," Network of East-West Women report, 21 June 2000. <http://lists.partners-intl.net/pipermail/women-east-west>

Radu, Paul Cristian. "Romania Tackles Human Traffickers," Institute for War and Peace Reporting, *Balkan Crisis Report*, no. 357 (9 August 2002). <http://www.iwpr.net>

Rasidoglu, A. "Corruption Has Taken on a Menacing Character," *Zerkalo* [Baku], 22 June 2002 (FBIS Document CEP20020710000409).

Rawlinson, Paddy. "Russian Organised Crime and the Baltic States: Assessing the Threat," University of Wales Centre for Comparative Criminology and Criminal Justice, *Working Paper*, 38/01.

Rawlinson, Patricia. "Baltic States Battle Organised Crime," *Jane's Intelligence Review*, 1 November 2001.

Repetskaya, A., and V. Shakina. "Organized Crime in Irkutsk: Press Survey, February 2000," *Organized Crime and Corruption Watch*, Summer 2000.

Ristić, B. "Whose Arm Runs Serbia?" *Glas Javnosti* [Belgrade], 3 November 2002 (FBIS Document EUP20021104000406).

Rosen, Nir. "Mafia Fuels Balkans Turmoil," Institute for War and Peace Reporting, *Balkans Crisis Report*, no. 333 (26 April 2002). <http://www.iwpr.net>

"Russian CD Piracy on Kremlin Property," *RFE/RL Crime and Corruption Watch*, 2, no. 31 (6 September 2002). <http://www.rferl.org/corruptionwatch>

"Russian Counterfeiting on the Rise," *RFE/RL Crime and Corruption Watch*, 2, no. 28 (8 August 2002). <http://www.rferl.org/corruptionwatch>

"Russian Customs Officials Seize over 27 Tonnes of Enriched Uranium," TVS [Moscow] report, 8 October 2002.

Ryabtsev, Denis. Interview with Emanuil Yordanov, minister of the interior of Bulgaria, *Segodnya* [Moscow], 6 December 2000.

Scheinost, Miroslav. "Transnational Organised Crime and Cross-Border Trafficking in Human Beings in the Czech Republic," in Petrus C. van Duyne, Vinzenzo Ruggiero, Miroslav Scheinost, and Wim Valkenburg, eds., *Cross-Border Crime in a Changing Europe*. Huntington, New York: Nova Science Publishers, 2001.

Shelley, Louise. "Crime and Corruption: Enduring Problems of Post-Soviet Development," *Demokratizatsiya*, 11, no. 1 (Winter 2003).

Shelley, Louise. "Organized Crime and Corruption Are Alive and Well in Ukraine," World Bank Group, *Transition Newsletter*, January-February 1999. <http://www.worldbank.org/transitionnewsletter>

Shelley, Louise. "Organized Crime in the Former Soviet Union: The Distinctiveness of Georgia," in Institute of Legal Reforms [Tbilisi], *Legal Aspects of Struggle Against Organized Crime and Corruption in Georgia*. Tbilisi: 1999.

Shpakova, Sasha. "A War Against Drug Trafficking in Kyrgyzstan," *Central Asia/Caucasus Analyst*, 25 April 2001. <http://www.cacianalyst.org>

Sinitsyn, Fedor. "Corruption in the Federal Migration Service of Russia," *Organized Crime and Corruption Watch*, Spring-Summer 2001.

"Smuggling Continues Despite Multinational Effort," *RFE/RL Crime and Corruption Watch*, 2, no. 30 (30 August 2002). <http://www.rferl.org/corruptionwatch>

Southeast European Legal Development Initiative. "Corruption Indexes: Regional Corruption Monitoring in Albania, Bosnia and Herzegovina, Croatia, Macedonia, Romania, and Yugoslavia," April 2002.

Spirin, Yuriy. "Heroin Heroes," Stringer News Agency report, 12 February 2002 (FBIS Document CEP20020219000161).

Stanimirović, Sinisa. "Serbia: Corruption Clampdown," Institute for War and Peace Reporting, *Balkan Crisis Report*, no. 315 (6 February 2002). <http://www.iwpr.net>

Starostin, Dmitriy. "Osmium Worries the FSB," *Vremya Novostey* [Moscow], 27 September 2002. <http://www.nti.org>

Stoecker, Sally W. "The Rise in Human Trafficking and the Role of Organized Crime," *Demokratizatsiya*, 8, no. 1 (Winter 2000).

Sultanoglu, S., and N. Majidova. "Azerbaijan Is One of the World Leaders in Corruption," *Zerkalo* [Baku], 10 September 1999. <http://www.aliyev.com>

"Suspected Accomplice Says She Spent Years Collecting Bribes Related to Ministry Contracts," *RFE/RL Crime and Corruption Watch*, 2, no. 27 (27 July 2002). <http://www.rferl.org/corruptionwatch>

Tabyshalieva, Anara. "Kyrgyz Turmoil over a Border Agreement," *Central Asia/Caucasus Analyst*, 22 May 2002, 9-10.

Tessadori, Vincenzo. "Drugs for Weapons: The Market of Terror," *La Stampa* [Turin], 24 June 2002 (FBIS Document EUP20020624000015).

Titorenko, Larissa G. "The Walls That Have Yet to Fall: Belarus as a Mirror of CIS Transition," *Demokratizatsiya*, 8, no. 2 (Spring 2000).

"Top Attorney Calls for Radical Solution to Corruption," *RFE/RL Crime and Corruption Watch*, 2, no. 13 (4 April 2002). <http://www.rferl.org/corruptionwatch>

"Trafficking in Prostitutes Is Urgent Problem in Latvia," LETA (news agency) report, 7 June 2002 (FBIS Document CEP20020607000086).

"Trafficking in Women in the Baltic States: Legal Aspects," *Trafficking in Immigrants*, special issue, 2001.

Transparency International. "Corruption Perceptions Index 2002." <http://www.transparency.org/cpi/2002/cpi2002en.html>

U.S. Agency for International Development. "Combating Human Trafficking in Bulgaria," 25 April 2003. <http://www.usembassy.bg/prog/aps.htm>

"U.S. Asks Russia to Crack Down on CD Piracy," *RFE/RL Crime and Corruption Watch*, 2, no. 28 (8 August 2002). <http://www.rferl.org/corruptionwatch>

U.S. Department of State. *Trafficking in Persons Report 2002*. <http://www.state.gov/g/tip/rls/tiprpt/2002>

"The U.S. Department of State's Human Trafficking Report," *RFE/RL Crime and Corruption Watch*, 2, no. 23 (14 June 2002). <http://www.rferl.org/corruptionwatch>

U.S. Department of State. Bureau for International Narcotics and Law Enforcement Affairs. *International Narcotics Control Strategy Report 1996*. <http://www.state.gov.g/inl/rls/nrcrpt/1996>

U.S. Department of State. Bureau for International Narcotics and Law Enforcement Affairs. *International Narcotics Control Strategy Report 2001*. http://www.state.gov/g/inl/rls/nrcrpt/2001

U.S. Department of State. International Information Programs. "Hungary, Israel Removed from Money Laundering Blacklist," report of 21 June 2002. <http://usinfo.state.gov.topical/econ/mlc/02062101.htm>

"Ukrainian, Polish Border Chiefs Discuss Illegal Migration, Border Checkpoints," Ukrainian television report [Kiev], 12 July 2002 (FBIS Document CEP20020713000058).

United Nations. Economic Commission for Europe. "Moldova: Anti-Trafficking Policies." <http://www.unece.org>

United Nations. Office for Drug Control and Crime Prevention. "The Case of Poland," 1 October 2002. <http://www.undcp.org>

University of Exeter. Department of Politics. "Organised Crime in Estonia." http://www.ex.ac.uk/politics

University of Exeter, Department of Politics. "Organised Crime in Russia." <http://www.ex.ac.uk/politics>

"Up to Code," *The Warsaw Voice*, no. 21 (2002). <http://www.thepolishvoice.pl>

Volkhonsky, Boris. "Moldovan President Offers Dniester Region Compromise, but Europe Pushes Him Toward Tough Stance," *Kommersant* [Moscow], 6 February 2002 (FBIS Document CEP20020206000176).

Voss, Michael. "'Slave Trade' Thrives in Bosnia: High Unemployment Makes Women Easy Prey," University of Rhode Island Trafficking in Women from Ukraine Research Project, 8 March 2001. <http://www.uri.edu/artsci/wms/hughes/ukraine/slavebosnia>

Weir, Fred. "Baltics Step from Russia's Shadow into Western Club," *The Christian Science Monitor*, 20 November 2002, 13.

Williams, Phil. "Drugs and Guns," *Bulletin of the Atomic Scientists*, 55, no. 1 (January-February 1999). <http://www.bullatomsci.org>

Wrase, Michael, and Waltraud Kasener. "Belgium Smuggled Weapons to Iraq," *Welt am Sonntag* [Hamburg], 27 October 2002 (FBIS Document EUP20021027000097).

Yarmish, A.N. *Organized Criminal Groups in Ukraine: Traditional and Typical*. Kharkov: National University of Internal Affairs, 2002.

"Yugoslav Arms-Export Scandal Grows," *Radio Free Europe/Radio Liberty Newsline*, 6, no. 207, part II (1 November 2002).

Zalisko, Walter. "Russian Organized Crime: The Foundation for Trafficking." http://www.monmouth.com/~wplz/Index1

South Asia

"Advani's Security Beefed Up," *The Times of India* [Mumbai], 13 February 2002. <http://timesofindia.indiatimes.com/cms.dll/xml/uncomp/articleshow?msid=882143>

Armentrout, Debra. "Child Trafficking Continues to Threaten Young Women in India," Digital Freedom Network report, 15 November 2002. http://www.dfn.org/news/india/trafficked.htm

"The Arms Race in Bangladesh: Issues and Challenges," *The Daily Star* [Dacca], 29 July 2001. <http://www.dailystarnews.com/law/200107/05/right.htm>

Bhattacharya, Saurabh. "Sex Workers See Freedom in Rules and Regulations," Inter Press Service report, 15 December 1997. <http://www.oneworld.org/ips2/dec/india3.html>

"… But What About Remote-Control Operations?" *The Times of India* [Mumbai], 27 March 2000.

Chalk, Peter. "Light Arms Trading in SE Asia," *Jane's Intelligence Review*, 1 March 2001.

Chandran, Suba. "Drug Trafficking and the Security of the State: Case Study of Pakistan," Institute for Defence Studies and Analyses [New Delhi] report, 1997. <http://www.idsa-india.org/an-sep8-7.html>

Charles, Molly. "The Drug Scene in India," presentation to Drug Abuse: A Symposium on Social Processes, Narcotics and the State, Mumbai, August 2001. <http://www.india-seminar.com/2001/504/504%20molly%20charles.htm>

Charles, Molly. "The Growth and Activities of Organised Crime in Bombay," *International Social Science Journal*, 53 (2001).

Chossudovsky, Michael. "The Role of Pakistan's Military Intelligence (ISI) in the September 11 Attacks." <http://globalresearch.ca/articles/CHO111A.html>

"Crime and Migration: The Body Trade," *Far Eastern Economic Review*, 26 October 2000.

"Daily Details Bangladesh as Transit Point for Arms Smuggling," *Dainik Janakantha* [Dacca], 16 July, 2000 (FBIS Document SAP20000722000010).

Development Resource Center [Mumbai]. "Grassroot Merchants of Illicit Goods in Gujarat," presentation to Drug Abuse: A Symposium on Social Processes, Narcotics and the State," Mumbai, August 2001. <http://www.india-seminar.com/2001/504/504%20drc.htm>

Fanney, Rob. "Bangladesh: Harakat-ul-Jihad-ul-Islami," *Jane's World Insurgency and Terrorism* 16 (14 November 2002).

Federation of American Scientists. Intelligence Resource Program. "Sikh Terrorists," 8 August 1998. <http://www.fas.org/irp/world/para/sikh.htm>

Ganguly, Dia. "Justice and Force in Bangladesh," *World Press Review*, 12 December 2002. <www.worldpress.org/Asia/861.cfm>

Ghosh, Nirmal. "LTTE's Global Shadow Economy Behind Violence," *The Straits Times*, 24 May, 2000.

Human Rights Watch. "World Report 2001." <http://www.hrw.org/wr2k1/>

Human Rights Watch. "World Report 2002." <http://www.hrw.org/wr2k2>

Human Rights Watch. "World Report 2003." <http://www.hrw.org/wr2k3>

Hussain, Neila. "Proliferation of Arms and Politics in South Asia: The Case of Bangladesh," Regional Centre for Strategic Studies [Colombo], *Policy Studies*, 7 (May 1999). <http://www.rcss.org/policy_studies/ps_7_1.html>

Hyder, Tariq Osman. "Kashmir: Self-Determination Versus State Terrorism," *The Korean Journal of Defense Analysis*, 14, no. 1 (Spring 2002).

"India 2002-2003," *Jane's World Armies*, 8 April 2002.

International Action Network on Small Arms. "Pakistan Begins Major Campaign to Seize Illegal Weapons," 30 May 2001. <http://www.iansa.org/news/2001/may_01/pak_beg.htm>

International Labour Organization, "Nepal: Trafficking in Girls with Special Reference to Prostitution: A Rapid Assessment," November 2001. <http://www.ilo.org/public/english/standards/ipec/simpoc/nepal/ra/trafficking.pdf>

Iqbal, Nadim. "Drug Abuse Grows on Bumper Poppy Crop in Afghanistan," Inter Press Service report, 15 January 2003. <http://www.aegis.com/news/ips/2003/IP30107.htm>

Jaleel, Muzamil. "India's Demands," *The Observer*, 13 January 2002. <www.observer.co.uk/international/story/0,6903,632110,00.html>

Jaleel, Muzamil. "Kashmiris Tell Indians to Go," *The Observer* [London], 13 January 2002.

Jasparro, Christopher, "Transnational Pressures Destabilize India's Northeast," *Jane's Intelligence Review*, 12 November 2002.

Johnson, Larry. "The Future of Terrorism," *American Behavioral Scientist*, 44, no. 3 (February 2001): 894-914.

Kalliangopoulos, F., and N. Tsoutsias, "Greek Deputy Links Tycoon Kokkalis to Stazi, Tamil Tigers," *Kathimerini* [Athens], 18 April 2002 (FBIS Document GMP200204020000193).

Kumar, Dhruba. "Impact of Terrorism on Democratic Development in South Asia," *Conference on Terrorism in South Asia: Impact on Development and Democratic Process*, 23-25 November 2002, Nepal.

Kumar, Neeraj. "Organized Crime," *PoliceSpeak*, November 1999. <www.india-seminar.com/1999/483.htm>

Lancaster, John. "Reshaping Pakistan along Religious Lines," *Washington Post*, 20 June 2003, A1.

Lancaster, John, and Kamran Khan. "Extremist Groups Renew Activity in Pakistan," *Washington Post*, 8 February 2003.

Lintner, Bertil "A Cocoon of Terror," *Far Eastern Economic Review,* 4 April, 2002.

"LTTE's Drug Trafficking Links," *Daily Reports from Reality of Sri Lanka*, 15 March 2000. <www.realityofsrilanka.com/d153Mar00.htm>

"Mandrax," *Electronic Doctor* [South Africa]. <http://www.edoc.co.za/drughelp/mandrax>

Mazari, Shireen. "India's Unconventional War Strategy," *Defense Journal,* January 1999. <www.defencejournal.com/jan99/rawfacts.htm>

McCarthy, Rory. "Militant Factions Consider Ceasefire," *Guardian Unlimited*, 8 June 2002. <www.guardian.co.uk/pakistan/story/>

Meo, Nick. "All Eyes on India's Most Wanted," *The Sunday Herald* [Glasgow], 27 January 2002. <http://www.sundayherald.com/print21831>

Naylor, R.T. "Bin Laden, Crime and Opportunism," 3 November 2001. <http://www.yorku.ca/nathanson/Publications/Bin%20Laden.htm>

"Pakistan," *Jane's World Armies*, 12 (17 June 2002).

Peiris, G. H. "Secessionist War and Terrorism in Sri Lanka: Transnational Impulses," *International Centre for Ethnic Studies,"* no. 3, April 2002.

Rahman, Maseeh. "Facing into a Storm," *Far Eastern Economic Review*, 11 October 2001.

Raman, B. "India: Omens from Katunayake," *Businessline,* 27 July, 2001.

Rashid, Ahmed. "America's War on Terror Goes Awry in Pakistan," *Yale Global*, 4 June 2003.

Rashid, Ahmed. "The Danger Within," *Far Eastern Economic Review*, 30 May 2002.

Rashid, Ahmed, and Joanna Slater. "Threats and Consequences," *Far Eastern Economic Review*, 6 June 2002.

Rehman, Jalilur. "Outlawed Islamic Militant Party Challenges Musharraf's Ban," *Agence France-Presse*, 26 January 2003.

Reid, Gary. "Revisiting The Hidden Epidemic," *The Centre for Harm Reduction,* 2000. <http://www.ahrn.net/rapidassessment.pdf>

Sahadevan, P. , "Coping with Disorder: Strategies to End Internal Wars in South Asia," *Regional Centre for Strategic Policy Studies*, 17, no. 5 (November 2000).

Sen, Ashish Kumar. "India Plots Against Pakistan," *Deccan Chronicle*, 28 January 2000.

Slater, Joanna. "From Riots to Recrimination," *Far Eastern Economic Review*, 14 March 2002.

"South Asia, Internal Affairs," *Jane's Sentinel Security Assessment*, 15 May 2003.

"State Supported Sectarianism and Terror," *Jane's Sentinel Security Assessment-South Asia*, 10 (3 September 2002).

Subramanian, Nurupama. "Delhi-Chennai-Colombo-Narcotics Racket Flourishes," *Indian Express*, 2 November, 1999. <www.indianexpress.comie/daily/19991102/ige02045.html>

Transparency International. *Corruption Perceptions Index 2002*. <http://www.transparency.org/cpi/2002/cpi2002.en.htm>

U.S. Department of State. *Patterns of Global Terrorism 2001*. <http://www.state.gov/s/ct/rls/pgtrpt/2001>

U.S. Department of State. *Patterns of Global Terrorism 2002*. <http://www.state.gov/s/ct/rls/pgtrpt/2002>

U.S. Department of State. Bureau for International Narcotics and Law Enforcement Affairs. *International Narcotics Control Strategy Report 2002*. http://www.state.gov/g/inl/rls/nrcrpt/2002

U.S. Department of State. Bureau for International Narcotics and Law Enforcement Affairs. *International Narcotics Control Strategy Report 2003*. Washington, D.C.: 2003.

U.S. Drug Enforcement Administration. "India Country Brief," May 2002. <http://www.usdoj.gov/dea/pubs/intel/02022/02022p.html>

"United Liberation Front of Assam (ULFA)," *Jane's World Insurgency and Terrorism* 16 (7 March 2003).

Weerakoon, Gamini. "Illicit Trafficking of Small Arms and Terrorism." Paper presented at United Nations Conference on Disarmament, Akita, Japan, August 22-25, 2000.

Woollacott, Martin. "For Musharraf, Being Decisive Is Not an Option," *Guardian Unlimited*, 31 May 2002.

Southeast Asia

Abdullah, Mustafa. "Analysis of Current Situation on Illicit Drug Trafficking," *UNAFEI Resource Material Series 58* [Tokyo], December 2001. <www.unafei.co.jp>

"All It Takes Now Is Commitment," *Bangkok Post* [Bangkok], 14 April 1999 (FBIS Document SEP19990414000037).

Arquiza, Rey. "Tamil Guerrilas in Philippines Engage in Raising Funds for War in Sri Lanka," *The Philippine Star* [Philippines], 16 August 2000 (FBIS Document SEP20000816000040).

"Asia: A Surfeit of Pills in Thailand," *Economist* [London], 28 April 2001, 42.

"Australia Facing Challenges in Taking Regional Anti-Terrorism Lead," *Strategic Forecasting,* 4 October 2002. <http://www.stratfor.biz>

"Australia, Malaysia Agree to Cooperate Against People-Smuggling, Drugs," *Radio Australia* [Melbourne], 2 November 2001 (FBIS Document SEP20011102000076).

"Australian Ministers Says Malaysia Transit Point for People Smugglers," *Radio Australia* [Melbourne], 12 July 2000 (FBIS Document SEP20000712000097).

Bai-ngern, Chaiyakorn. "Thai Police Investigate Three Alien-Smuggling Gangs," *Nation* [Thailand], 9 June 1999 (FBIS Document FTS19990608002032).

Bai-ngern, Pongsak, and Piyanart Srivalo. "Thailand: Authorities Uncover Money Laundering Ring with Over 40 Companies," *Nation* [Bangkok], 9 November 2001 (FBIS Document FTS20011109000012).

"Bali Bombing Forcing Jakarta to Ease Focus on Aceh Rebels," *Strategic Forecasting,* 12 November 2002. <www.stratfor.biz>

"Bali Bombing: Rift Emerges Within Jemaah Islamiyah," *ICG News Media Release*, 11 December 2002. <http://www.intl-crisis-group.org>

Bonner, Raymond. "Qaeda Meeting in Thailand Reportedly Plotted Attacks on Tourists," *New York Times*, 8 November 2002, sec. A, 10.

Bonner, Raymond. "Southeast Asia Remains Fertile for Al Qaeda," *Washington Post,* 28 October 2002, sec A, 1.

Burton, Paul. "Behind the Bali Bombing," *Jane's Sentinel Online,* 16 October 2002. <http://www.janes.com>

Cahill, Laurena. "Thai Border Customs Officials Adopt Measures to Prevent Money Laundering," *Nation* [Bangkok], 21 March 2001 (FBIS Document SEP20010321000011).

Calica, Aurea. "Analysts Say Philippines' Anti-Money Laundering Law 'Lacks Teeth,'" *Philippine Star* [Manila], 1 October 2002 (FBIS Document SEP20011001000034).

"CCC Study Names 5 Most Corrupt Thai Government Agencies," *Nation* [Bangkok], 16 August 1999 (FBIS Document FTS19990816000169).

Chaiviwan, Suthep. "Gun Running: Transit to Terror," *Bangkok Post* [Bangkok], 14 July 2002 (FBIS Document SEP20020714000011).

Charles, Lourdes. "Thailand Links Drug Money to Terrorism Funding, Disagrees," *Star* [Kuala Lumpur], 18 May 2002 (FBIS Document SEP20020518000005).

Charoenpo, Anucha. "European Union Seeks to Set Up Bangkok Office to Combat Money Laundering in Asia," *Bangkok Post* [Bangkok], 3 April 2001 (FBIS Document SEP20010403000033).

Charoenpo, Anucha. "Laundering Agency to Expand Its Duties," *Bangkok Post* [Bangkok], 31 December 2001. <http:\\scoop.bangkokpost.co.th>

Charoenpo, Anucha. "Terrorists Collecting Cash Here: Money Transferred to al-Qaeda, Hezbollah," *Bangkok Post* [Bangkok], 10 March 2002. <http:\\www.bangkokpost.co.th>

Charoenpo, Anucha. "Thai Police Seek Information on Foreign Criminal Gangs" *Bangkok Post* [Bangkok], 5 July 1999 (FBIS Document FTS19990705000177).

Charoenpo, Anucha. "Wa Army Said Taking Smuggled Cars from Malaysia in Barter Deals with Local Help," *Bangkok Post* [Bangkok], 24 August 2001 (FBIS Document SEP20010824000016).

"Chinese National of Human Smuggling Syndicate Nabbed in Cebu," *Philippine Star* [Manila], 4 September 2001 (FBIS Document SEP20010904000063).

Chouvy, Pierre-Arnaud. "Drugs and War Destabilize Thai-Burma Border Region," *Jane's Intelligence Review*, 1 April 2002. <http:\\www.janes.com>

Chouvy, Pierre-Arnaud. "New Drug Trafficking Routes in Southeast Asia," *Jane's Intelligence Review*, 1 July 2002. <http:\\www.janes.com>

Crispin, Shawn. "Drug Tide Strains Ties," *Far Eastern Economic Review*, 162, no. 36 (9 September 1999): 24-27.

Cueto, Donna. "Marcos Daughter Attempted Funds Transfer—German, RP Gov'ts," *Philippine Daily Inquirer* [Manila], 5 July 2001 (FBIS Document SEP20010705000032).

"Cutting Off Cash to the Terrorists," *Bangkok Post* [Bangkok], 9 September 2002 (FBIS Document SEP20020909000041).

Danao, Efren, and Aurea Calica. "Crame Was Center of Drug Trade in '98," *Philippine Star* [Manila], 30 August 2001 (FBIS Document SEP20010830000035).

Davis, Anthony. "Bangkok as Crime Central: Where International Gangs Are Settling Scores," *Asiaweek*, 26, no. 40 (13 October 2000). <http:\\www.asiaweek.com>

Davis, Anthony. "The Complexities of Unrest in Southern Thailand," *Jane's Intelligence Review*, 1 September 2002. <http:\\www.janes.com>

Davis, Anthony. "Tamil Tigers Continue Procurement," *Jane's Intelligence Review*, 1 May 2002. <http:\\www.janes.com>

Davis, Anthony. "USA Steps Up Support for Thai War on Drugs," *Jane's Intelligence Review*, 1 October 2002. <http:\\www.janes.com>

Dawson, Alan. "Al-Qaeda Links Run Deep," *Bangkok Post* [Thailand], 29 May 2002 (FBIS Document SEP2002529000048).

De Leon, Eva, and Cecille Suerte Felipe. "4 Chinese Arrested in Biggest Drug Bust," *Philippine Star* [Manila], 7 November 1999 (FBIS Document FTS19991107000004).

De Ruyver, Brice, and Koen Van Heddegem. "Human Trafficking Between Belgium and the Philippines," *Tijdschrift voor Criminologie* [Amsterdam], 10 January 2001 (FBIS Document EUP20020823000403).

Desker, Barry. "Islam and Society in Southeast Asia after 9-11," *Institute of Defense and Strategic Studies,* September 2002.

Dinan, Kinsey Alden. "Trafficking in Women from Thailand to Japan," *Harvard Asia Quarterly,* 6, no. 3 (Summer 2002). <http://www.fas.harvard.edu/~asiactr/haq/200203/index.htm>

Doronila, Amando. "The Senate—the Nation's Laundry Machine," *Philippine Daily Inquirer* [Philippines], 24 August 2001 (FBIS Document SEP20010824000031).

Echeminada, Perseus. "Lina: RP-China Anti-Crime Cooperation in the Works," *Philippine Star* [Manila], 25 December 2001 (FBIS Document SEP20011225000035).

Emmanuel, Tony. "Malaysia Used as Transit Point for Smuggling Human Cargo," *New Straits Times* [Kuala Lumpur], 28 February 2000 (FBIS Document SEP20000301000075).

"EU to Target Philippines, Nauru in Money-Laundering Crackdown," *Agence France-Presse* [Paris], 12 October 2001 (FBIS Document EUP20011012000252).

"Free Aceh (Aceh Merdeka)," FAS Intelligence Resource Program Report. <http://www.fas.org>

Garoupa, Nuno. "The Economics of Organized Crime and Optimal Law Enforcement," *Western Economic Association International,* 38, no.2 (April 2000): 278-288.

Gershman, John. "Is Southeast Asia the Second Front?" *Foreign Affairs,* 81, no.4 (July/August 2002): 60-75.

Gunarant, Rohan. "The Singapore Connection," *Jane's Intelligence Review,* 1 March 2002. <www.janes.com>

Hem Raj, Ramend. "Current Situation of Illegal Firearms Trafficking and Human (Women, Children, and Migrants) Trafficking," *UNAFEI Resource Material Series 58* [Tokyo], December 2001. <www.unafei.co.jp>

"Human Rights Report for Indonesia: Trafficking in Persons," *Countries of the World,* July 2002. <www.ncbuy.com/reference/humanrights.html>

"A Human Rights Report on Trafficking of Persons, Especially Women and Children," *The Protection Project*, March 2002, 341.

"Human Trafficking Syndicates' Scheme in Smuggling Filipinos to Europe Uncovered," *Philippine Daily Inquirer* [Manila], 27 June 2002 (FBIS Document SEP20020627000090).

"In the Spotlight: Indonesia's Free Aceh Movement," CDI Terrorism Project Report, 10 May 2002. <http://www.cdi.org>

"Indonesia: Bali Bombing Forcing Military to Address Militia Dilemma," *Strategic Forecasting*, 8 November 2002. <http://www.stratfor.biz>

"Indonesia," Population Resource Center, December 2002. <http://www.prcdc.org/summaries/indonesia/indonesia.html>

"Indonesia Backgrounder: How the Jemaah Islamiya Terrorist Network Operates," *ICG Asia Report*, no. 43 (11 December 2002). <http://www.crisisweb.org>

"Indonesia Plays Increasing Role in Producing, Consuming Designer Drugs," *Radio Australia* [Melbourne], 16 April 2002 (FBIS Document SEP20020416000090).

"Indonesia's Final Days?" *Jane's Intelligence Digest,* 17 October 2002. <www.janes.com>

Jadulco, Boyet. "Ping-Lee Drug Link," *Abante* [Manila], 4 September 2001 (FBIS Document SEP20010904000047).

Jimenez-David, Rina. "Sex Abuse and Sex Trafficking in Malaysia," *Asia Intelligence Wire: Financial Times,* 5 September 2002.

Jinakul, Surat. "Godfathers of Crime," *Bangkok Post* [Bangkok], 28 March 1999 (FBIS Document FTS19990330000025).

Jinakul, Surath [stet]. "Invasion of the Triads," *Bangkok Post* [Bangkok], 7 November 1999 (FBIS Document FTS19991107000013).

Jinakul, Surath, and Songpol Kaopatumtip. "Towards a Terror-Free Thailand," *Bangkok Post* [Bangkok], 2 June 2002 (FBIS Document SEP20020602000027).

Jones, David Martin, and Michael Smith. "Islamists Defeat Asian Way," *World Today,* 58, no. 6 (June 2002): 12-14.

Jost, Patrick M. "The Hawala Alternative Remittance System and Its Role in Money Laundering." Interpol, January 2000.
<http://www.interpol.int/Public/FinancialCrime/MoneyLaundering/hawala/default.asp>

Kitada, Mikinao. "Money Laundering in Asia: Current Situation and Countermeasures Against Money Laundering in Asia," *Law-Asia Conference*, 5 October 2001.

Klaidman, Daniel. "A Good Place to Lie Low," *Newsweek*, 139, no.5 (February 2002): 34.

Lang, Niu. "Thailand Is among the World's 10 Criminal Dens," *Mangu Shibao* [Bangkok], 19 May 1999 (FBIS Document FTS19990519002227).

Laohong, King-O. "Foreign Mafias Take Over Rachada Road Areas as Place to Launder Money and Carry Out White Slavery and Narcotics Trafficking," *Bangkok Krungthemp Thurakit* [Thailand], 4 November 2001 (FBIS Document SEP2001105000049).

Lertcharoenchok, Yindee. "Thai Authorities 'Closing In' on Golden Triangle Warlord," *Nation* [Bangkok], 12 February 1999 (FBIS Document SEP19990212001814).

Lertcharoenchok, Yindee. "Thailand Said Fast Becoming Transnational Crime Center," *Nation* [Bangkok], 22 June 1999 (FBIS Document FTS19990621001844).

Lopez, Leslie. "Asia Terror Probe Focuses on Malaysian—Suspect Who Hosted Hijackers Ordered Material Widely Used to Make Bombs," *Asian Wall Street Journal*, 25 January 2002.

Madanir, Rudy, and Christine T. Tjandraningsih. "Indonesia Issues Terror Decree, Arrests Muslim Leader," *Kyodo* [Tokyo], 19 October 2002 (FBIS Document JPP20021019000087).

"Major Raid in Manila Yields 57 Kilos of Shabu from China," *Philippine Star* [Manila], 27 December 2001 (FBIS Document SEP20011227000058).

"Malaysia Denies Being Springboard for Illegal Immigrants Going to Third Nations," *Bernama* [Kuala Lumpur], 27 February 2002 (FBIS Document SEP20020227000002).

"Malaysia: Kedah Police Cripple Drug-Trafficking Ring," *Bernama* [Kuala Lumpur], 4 August 2002 (FBIS Document SEP2002085000007).

"Malaysia's Former Military Officer Suspected as Leader of Weapons Thieves Group," *New Straits Times* [Kuala Lumpur], 5 July 2000 (FBIS Document SEP20000706000053).

"Malaysia's Illegal Immigrants 300,000 [sic] to Curb Entry," *Star* [Kuala Lumpur], 25 February 2000 (FBIS Document SEP20000225000043).

"Malaysian Police Nab 110 Indonesian Illegal Immigrants," *Star* [Kuala Lumpur], 29 February 2000 (FBIS Document SEP20000229000050).

"Malaysian Police Say Islamic Militants 'May be Hiding on Thai Soil,'" *Nation* [Bangkok], 22 September 2001 (FBIS Document SET20010922000003).

Manggut, Wenseslaus, Edy Budiyarso, and Chandra. "Angry Indonesian Army Chief: Death for Soldiers Stealing, Selling Weapons," *Tempo* [Jakarta], 25 August 2002 (FBIS Document SEP20020905000036).

Marfil, Martin P. "Philippine Government Employees Warned of Suspension Over Drug Links," *Philippine Daily Inquirer* [Manila], 7 September 2001 (FBIS Document SEP20010907000026).

"Marijuana Trafficking Involves International Syndicates," *Medan Analisa* [Banda Aceh], 1 May 2002 (FBIS Document SEP20020501000096).

McBeth, John. "Weak Link in the Anti-Terror Chain," *Far Eastern Economic Review*, 165, no. 42 (4 October 2002): 15.

McBeth, John. "What If He Isn't Guilty," *Far Eastern Economic Review*, 165, no. 44 (November 2002): 16-20.

Mejias, Jhay. "Police Hunt Malaysian Based Syndicate," *Pilipino Star Ngayon* [Manila], 1 November 2001 (FBIS Document SEP20011101000024).

"The Military's Social Safety Net," *Laksamana* [Jakarta], 27 June 2002 (FBIS Document SEP20020702000010).

"Minister: Malaysia Not Threatened by Methamphetamine Drug from Thailand," *Bernama* [Kuala Lumpur], 30 October 2000 (FBIS Document SEP20001031000021).

Miranda, Rose. "Philippines Concerned at UN Report on Bin Ladin's Fund in Operation," *Abante* [Manila], 2 September 2002 (FBIS Document SEP20020902000052).

Mitton, Roger. "Burma-Thailand Relations: Still Lousy After All These Years," *Asiaweek*, 19 October 1999. <http://www.asiaweek.com/asiaweek/intelligence/9910/19>

Mookjang, Pisan. "Current Situation and Countermeasures Against Money Laundering in Thailand," *UNAFEI Resource Material Series 58* [Tokyo], December 2001. <www.unafei.co.jp>

Murphy, Dan. "Southeast Asia Easy Source of Al Qaeda Recruits," *Christian Science Monitor*, 9 October 2002, 7.

Murphy, Dan. "US Pushes Southeast Asian States on Islamic Radicals," *Christian Science Monitor*, 93, no. 223 (12 October 2001): 7.

"Myanmar, Thailand Draw Up Joint Plan to Fight Drugs," Agence France-Press [Paris], 14 December 2002. <http://www.clarinews.net>

Nakashima, Ellen. "Jailed Indonesian Suspect Details Links to Bombings," *Washington Post*, 9 November 2002, sec A, 15.

Nanuam, Wassana, and Subin Kheunkaew. "Thailand: Wa Use Cars Stolen from Malaysia; Thai Criminals Act as Go-Betweens," *Bankgkok Post* [Bangkok], 12 January 2002 (FBIS Document SEP20020112000028).

"Officer Describes Bali as Drug Transit Point," *Jakarta Suara Pembaruan*, 2 March 1997 (FBIS Document FTS19970303000479).

"Organized Crime Moves into Migrant Trafficking," *Trafficking in Migrants Quarterly Bulletin*, no. 11 (June 1996).

Orhant, Melanie. "Abused Thai Women 'Trafficked' to Japan Need Help," *Stop Traffic News*, 24 September 2000. <http://www.friends-partners.org>

Orhant, Melanie. "Human Trafficking: Gangs Make Thailand a Regional Hub: Yakuza Operating," *Stop Traffic News*, 22 September 2000. <http://www.friends-partners.org>

Pamintuan, Ricardo Tiuseco. "Country Paper on Effective Methods to Combat Transnational Organized Crime in Criminal Justice Processes," *UNAFEI Resource Material Series*, 58 [Tokyo], December 2001. <www.unafei.co.jp>

Paz, Reuven. "Middle East Terrorist Groups Use of Western Front Companies to Finance Operations," *Herzliyya International Policy Institute for Counter Terrorism,* 23 October 2000 (FBIS Document GMP200011101000209).

"Philippines Tracks Human Smugglers in France, Italy," *Philippine Daily Inquirer* [Manila], 27 June 2002 (FBIS Document SEP20020627000090).

"Philippines: Rebel Alliance or Aid Ploy?" Stratfor report, 8 May 2003.

"Philippines: Violence Surging Against U.S. Interests," *Strategic Forecasting,* 2 October 2002. <http:\\www.stratfor.com>

Phongpaichit, Pasuk. *Guns, Girls, Gambling, Ganja: Thailand's Illegal Economy and Public Policy*. Bangkok: Silkworm Books, 1998.

Pomonti, Jean-Claude. "Al-Qa'ida's Invisible Presence in Southeast Asia," *Le Monde* [Paris], 1 November 2001 (FBIS Document EUP20011112000434).

Pomonti, Jean-Claude. "Evidence of Al-Qa'ida Financial Transactions in Southeast Asia Viewed," *Le Monde* [Paris], 4 November 2001 (FBIS Document EUP20011112000434).

Pomonti, Jean-Claude. "The Terrorist Network Covers All of Southeast Asia," *Le Monde* [Paris], 20 December 2002 (FBIS Document EUP20021220000074).

"Report on Transnational Crimes in Thailand," *Matichon* [Bangkok], 23 March 2000 (FBIS Document SEP20000323000032).

Reyes, Maritess N. "Philippines on Its Way to Becoming a Narco-State," *Intersect Magazine,* 27 November 2001. <http://www.cyberdyaryo.com/features/f2001_1127_03.htm>

Robinson, Colin. "In the Spotlight: Indonesia's Free Aceh Movement," *Center for Defense Information Terrorism Project,* 10 May 2002. <http://www.cdi.org/terrorism>

"ROK's Yonhap: Illegal Aliens, Their Crimes on Increase: Police Report," *Yonhap* [Seoul], 29 September 2002 (FBIS Document KPP20020929000015).

Roule, Trifin, and Jeremy Kinsell. "Investigators Seek to Break Up Al-Qaeda's Financial Structure," *Jane's Intelligence Review,* 1 November 2001. <www.janes.com>

Rullan, Mercedes. "Five 'Big Circle' Members Arrested, P116-M Shabu Recovered," *Manila Kabayan* [Philippines], 23 December 2001 (FBIS Document SEP20011223000011).

Salah, Muhammad. "UK-Based Paper Traces Origins of Jihad Groups, Afghan Fighters," *Al-Hayah* [London], 20 October 2001 (FBIS Document GMP20011022000102).

Sapsomboon, Somroutai. "Thai Banks Urged to Fight Money Laundering," *Nation* [Bangkok], 21 August 1999 (FBIS Document FTS19990821000135).

Sarifudin, Amir. "Iraqi, Iranian Illegal Immigrants Detained in Malaysia," *Utusan Malaysia* [Kuala Lumpur], 24 February 2000 (FBIS Document SEP20000224000042).

Schulze, Kirsten. "Bringing the TNI in from the Cold," *Jane's Intelligence Review,* 1 June 2002. <www.janes.com>

Sebastian, Leonard. "Getting to the Root of Islamic Radicalism in Indonesia," *Institute of Defence and Strategic Studies,* December 2002.

"Singapore: Internal Affairs," *Jane's Sentinel Security Assessment Southeast Asia,* 8 July 2002. <www.janes.com>

Sipress, Alan. "Bin Laden Named in Asian Terror Plots," *Washington Post,* 27 June 2003, A24.

Song-sik, Cho. "Developments in ROK Organized Crime Viewed," *Sindong-a* [Seoul], 1 March 2001 (FBIS Document KPP2001037000092).

"Southeast Asia: Malaysia, Thailand," *Migration News*, 8, no.7 (July 2001). <http:\\www.migrations.ucdavis.edu>

"Special Report-Case Study: The Liberation Tigers of Tamil Eelam," *Jane's Intelligence Review,*" 1 October 2001. <http://www.janes.com>

Swire, Mary. "New Malaysian Money Laundering Act Now in Force," *Tax-News* [Hong Kong], 28 August 2001. <www.tax-news.com>

"Thai Authorities Confirm Tamil Eelam Activities in Phuket," *Bangkok Daily News,* 20 April 2000 (FBIS Document SEP200004200000560).

"Thai Daily Says Eight Southern Separatist Groups Have Set Up Bases in Malaysia," *Matichon* [Bangkok], 11 July 2002 (FBIS Document SEP20020711000093).

"Thailand 'Source' of Fake Passports," *Bangkok Post,* 21 June 2002. <http://scoop.bangkokpost.com>

"Thirteen Hong Kong Residents Face Execution for Smuggling 17 Tons of Ice," *Tung Fang Jih Pao* [Hong Kong], 10 September 2001 (FBIS Document SEP20010910000038).

U.S. Department of State. *Patterns of Global Terrorism 2002*. <http://www.state.gov/s/ct/rls/pgtrpt/2002>

U.S. Department of State. Bureau for International Narcotics and Law Enforcement Affairs. *International Narcotics Control Strategy Report 2002*. <http://www.state.gov/g/inl/rls/nrcrpt/2002>

Vijayan, K.C. "Methamphetamine Scourge from Thailand Threatens Singapore, Region," *Straits Times* [Singapore], 28 October 2000 (FBIS Document SEP20001030000030).

"Wa Money Laundering, Drug Operation Viewed," *Phuchatkan* [Bangkok], 18 August 1999 (FBIS Document FTS19990818001080).

Xuanliang, Li. "Article on Terrorist Activities by National Separatists, Illegal Religious Groups in China," *Kuang Chiao Ching* [Hong Kong], 16 October 2001 (FBIS Document CPP20011016000099).

Western Europe

Aaron, Christopher. "Globalisation and Organised Crime," *Jane's Intelligence Review*, 1 December 2001.

Alonso, Stephane. "Fight Against Narcotics Is Symbolic," *NRC Handelsblad* [Rotterdam], 31 August 2002 (FBIS Document EUP20020902000252).

"Al-Qaeda Financier Was Former Accountant to Saudi Royals: Lawyer," *Middle East Times* [Nicosia], 19 September 2002. <http://www.metimes.com/2K2/Issue2002-38/reg/al_qaeda_financier.htm>

Armesto, Marie Rose. "Europe's Terrorist Incubator," *Wall Street Journal*, 2 September 2002. <http://www.hvk.org/articles/0902/62.html>

Barraclough, Anne. "Monte Carlo, the Russian Mafia and Dirty Money," *The Times of London*, 7 February 2000.

Beeston, Richard. "The Bomber from Birmingham: Pressure on Britain to End Safe Haven for Political Extremists," *The Times of London*, 28 December 2000 (FBIS Document EUP20001228000096).

"Belgium Accused [of] Continuing Sale of UNITA Diamonds," Panafrican News Agency report, 24 April 2001. <http://www.globalpolicy.org/security/issues/diamond/2001/0424belg.htm>

Berger, Sharon, and Zev Stub. "France Investigates Israeli Banks for Money-Laundering," *Jerusalem Post* [Jerusalem], 30 December 2001. <http://www.rense.com/general/18/laun.htm>

Bryant, Elizabeth. "Europe Home to Thousands of Domestic Slaves," United Press International report, 9 January 2001. <http://fpmail.friends-partners.org/pipermail/stop-traffic/2001-November/001206.htm>

Christou, Jean. "EU and US Have Opposing Views on Money Laundering Charges," *Cyprus Mail*, 3 October 2001.

Cowan, Rosie. "The 78 Criminal Gangs Waging War on Ulster," *The Guardian* [London], 23 March 2001.

"Cyprus Criticizes Crime Report, Accuses U.S. Banks of Benefiting from Money-Laundering," *Kathimerini* [Athens], 23 December 2000 (FBIS Document GMP20001225000026).

Derix, Steven, and Jos Verlaan, "Investigative Services Want More Operational Powers at Schiphol," *NRC Handelsblad* [Rotterdam], 29 July 2002 (FBIS Document EUP20020730000226).

"EU: Third-Country Migrants," *Migration News*, 7, no. 11 (November 2000). <http://migration.ucdavis.edu/mn/archive_mn/nov_2000-08mn.htm>

Eavis, Paul. "The Hidden Security Threat: Transnational Organized Criminal Activity," *RUSI Journal*, 146, no. 6 (December 2001).

Escobar, Pepe. "Tracking al-Qaeda in Europe, part 4," *Asia Times Online*, 13 July 2002. <http://www.atimes.com/atimes/Middle_East/DC13Ak02.html>

"Europe: A Finger Points," *The Economist*, 26 February 2000.

"Europe's Borders: A Single Market in Crime," *The Economist*, 16 October 1999.

Evans, Richard. "Systematic Transnational Crime: Organised Crime and Terrorist Financing in Northern Ireland," *Jane's Intelligence Review* [London], 1 September 2001.

Faligot, Roger. *La Mafia Chinoise en Europe* [The Chinese Mafia in Europe]. Paris: Calmann-Lévy, 2001.

Galeotti, Mark. "Albanian Gangs Gain Foothold in European Crime Underworld," *Jane's Intelligence Review*, 19 October 2001.

Global March. "The Worst Forms of Child Labour Data: Germany." <http://www.globalmarch.org/worstformsreport/world/germany.htm>

"Greece Plans New Arrests Linking November 17 with Other Groups," World Tribune.com report, 22 January 2003. <http://216.26.163.62/2003/eu_greece_01_22.htm>

Hoffman, Bruce. "Is Europe Soft on Terrorism?" *Foreign Policy*, Summer 1999. <http://www.foreignpolicy.com/issue_SeptOct_2001/hoffman.html>

"Italy: Organized Crime Groups Expand Influence," Stratfor report, 9 May 2003.

Jamieson, Alison. "Italy's Criminal Gangs Change Their Tactics," *Jane's Intelligence Review*, 1 December 2001.

Khatzidis, Kostas. "The Italian Mafia Has Spread Its Tentacles into Greece," *Ta Nea* [Athens], 20 July 2000. <http://www.nisat.org>

Kusovac, Zoran. "Stemming the Flow of People-Smuggling at Sea," *Jane's Navy International* [London], 1 May 2001.

Lallemand, Alain. "A Belgian Angolagate?" *Le Soir* [Brussels], 16 June 2001 (FBIS Document EUP20010617000081).

Lallemand, Alain. "Belgium: Hotbed of Arms Trafficking," *Le Soir* [Brussels], 7 March 2002 (FBIS Document EUP20020307000027).

Lambropoulos, V.Y. "Night Clubs Launder Dirty Money," *To Vima* [Athens], 8 March 2002 (FBIS Document GMP20020308000107).

Makarenko, Tamara. "Destination UK," *Jane's Intelligence Review* [London], 1 December 2001.

Muriel, Diana. "Thwarting Terrorist Cells in Europe," CNN.com War Against Terrorism report, 23 January 2002. <http://www.cnn.com/2001/WORLD/europe/10/26/inv.thwarting.cells>

Nasopoulos, Dhionisis. "The Secret War of the Athens Mobs," *Ta Nea* [Athens], 27 August 2002 (FBIS Document GMP20020829000230).

"The New Route of Colombian Traffickers," *Geopolitical Drug Newsletter*, July-August 2001. <http://www.geodrugs.net/mini-lettres/AEGD5GB.pdf>

Nikolakopoulos, V. "The Arms Trade in Greece," *To Vima* [Athens], 5 August 2001, cited in International Action Network on Small Arms, "Illegal Arms Trade in Greece Expanding Rapidly Due to Developments in Balkans." <http://www.iansa.org/news/2001/aug_01/trade_greece.htm>

Observatoire Géopolitique des Drogues. *Annual Report 1995-1996.* <http://www.ogd.org/rapport/gb/RP00_TABLE>

"Organized Crime Threat in SE Europe: U.S. Names Greece, Cyprus," *Kathimerini* [Athens], 23 December 2000. <http://www.alb-net.com/pipermail/albsa-info/2000-December/001071.htm>

Osborn, Andrew. "Amsterdam in Shock as Killer Gangs Muscle in on Tourist Haunts," *The Guardian* [London], 23 October 2000. <http://www.guardian.co.uk/international/story/0,3604,415081,00.htm>

Paoli, Letizia. "Crime, Italian Style," *Daedalus*, Summer 2001.

Pasternak, Judy, and Stephen Braun. "Following the Trail of Arms to Al-Qaida," *Los Angeles Times*, 21 January 2002. <http://www.nisat.org>

Politi, Alessandro. "The New Dimensions of Organized Crime in Southeastern Europe," *The International Spectator*, 34, no. 4 (October-December 1999).

"Riviera Money-Laundering Worries France," BBC News report, 11 April 2002. <http://news.bbc.co.uk/2/hi/europe/1923138.stm>

"Romanian Arms Traffickers Take Over Athens Market," *VIMagazino* [Athens], cited in *Ziua* [Bucharest], 10 August 2001. <http://www.nisat.org>

Schmid, Alex. "Troubled Lands Where Criminals Are King," *UNESCO Courier*, 54, no. 2 (February 2001).

Shape News Summary and Analysis, 4 June 2002. <http:www.globalsecurity.org/military/library/news/2002/06/mil-020604-shape02.htm>

Sombolos, Yeoryios. "2.5 Billion Drachmas Annual Turnover from Arms Trafficking," *Imerisia* [Athens], 22 December 2001. <http://www.nisat.org>

Szymanski, Tekla. "Hunting Down a Greek Terrorist Organization," *World Press Review*, 49, no. 9 (September 2002). <http://www.worldpress.org/Europe/671.efm>

Thompson, Tony. "Heroin 'Emperor' Brings Terror to UK Streets," *The Observer* [London], 17 November 2002. <http://society.guardian.co.uk/Print/0,3858,4548336,00.html>

Transparency International. "Corruption Perception Index 2002." http://www.transparency.org/epi/2002/cpi2002.en.html

Transparency International. "Global Corruption Report 2003." http://www.globalcorruptionreport.org

Traynor, Ian. "The Gunrunner," *The Guardian* [London], 9 July 2001.

Turkish Cypriot Press and Other Media, no. 19/1997 (29 January 1997). http://www.hri.org/news/cyprus/tcpr/97-01-29.tcpr.htm

Tzortis, Andreas. "On the Trail of Terror's German Connection," *The Christian Science Monitor*, 25 October 2001.

U.S. Department of State. Bureau of Democracy, Human Rights, and Labor. *Country Reports on Human Rights Practices*, March 2002. <http://www.state.gov/g/drl/rls/hrrpt/2002/c8697.htm>

U.S. Department of State. *Trafficking in People Report 2001.* <http://www.state.gov/g/tip/rls/tiprpt/2001>

Whitelaw, Kevin, et al. "The Terror That Wasn't," *U.S. News and World Report*, 29 October 2001.

Western Hemisphere

"Al-Qaeda and Argentina," *Jane's Intelligence Digest*, 26 October 2001.

Alam-al-Din, Riyadh. "Washington Begins the War on Hizballah in the Border Triangle," *al-Watanal-Arabi* [Paris], 21 December 2001 (FBIS Document GMP20011221000179).

"An Alarm Call for Latin America's Democrats," *The Economist* [London], 28 July 2001.

Alegre, Luis. "Cae red de pirateria; retienen 43 koreanos" [Counterfeiting Network Dismantled; 43 Koreans Detained], *Reforma* [Mexico City], 6 December 2002.

Almiron, Hugo Antolin. "Organized Crime: A Perspective from Argentina," in Jay S. Albanese, Dilip K. Das, and Arvind Verma, eds., *Organized Crime: World Perspectives*. Upper Saddle River, New Jersey: Prentice Hall, 2003.

Alzaga, Ignacio. "Atentados en EU fortalecieron operaciones del cartel de Neza (Attacks on the U.S. Strengthened Neza Cartel Operations], *El Sol de Mexico* [Mexico City], 30 August 2002.

Anderson, Martin. "Al-Qaeda Across the Americas," *Insight on the News*, 26 November 2002.

"Arabic Factions 'Bidding' for New Lebanese Consulate," *ABC Color* [Asuncion], 31 January 1999 (FBIS Document FTS199902001001342).

Argentina. "Ley 25246 Creación de la Unidad de Información Financiera" [Law 25246, Creation of the Financial Information Unit], *Boletín Oficial* [Buenos Aires], 10 May 2000. <http://www.imolin.org/argtlaw2.htm>

Arostegui, Martin. "Search for Bin Laden Links Looks South," United Press International report, 12 October 2001. <http://www.autentico.org/oa09505>

Arrieta, Carlos G., Luis J. Orjuela, Eduardo Sarmiento, and Juan G. Tokatlian. *Narcotráfico en Colombia: Dimensiones políticas, económicas, jurídicas e internacionales* [Narcotics Trafficking in Colombia: Political, Economic, Juridical, and International Dimensions]. Bogota: Tercer Mundo Editores, 1990.

"Asian-Based Organized Crime," in Criminal Intelligence Service Canada, *Annual Report 2002*. <http://www.cisc.gc.ca/AnnualReport2002/Cisc2002en/asian2002.htm>

Bagley, Bruce Michael. *Globalization and Transnational Organized Crime: The Russian Mafia in Latin America and the Caribbean*, School of International Studies, University of Miami, October 31, 2001 [http://www.mamacoca.org/feb2002/art_bagley_globalization_organized_crime_en.html#fn1].

Bagley, Gretchen Peters. "Drug Trafficking in the Pacific Has a Distinct Russian Flavor," *San Francisco Chronicle*, 30 May 2001."

Bailey, John, and Roy Godson. *Organized Crime and Democratic Governability: Mexico and the U.S.-Mexico Borderlands*. Pittsburgh: University of Pittsburgh Press, 2002.

Barczak, Monica. "Representation by Consultation? The Rise of Direct Democracy in Latin America," *Latin American Politics and Society*, 43, no. 3 (Fall 2001).

Bartolomé, Mariano César. *Amenzas a la seguridad de los estados: La triple frontera coma 'área gris' en el cono sur americano* [Threats to the Security of States: The Triborder Region as a 'Grey Area' in the Cone of South America]. http://www.geocities.com/mcbartolome/triplefrontera1.htm.

Beard, David. "NAFTA: Bad Flows in Along with the Goods," *Salt Lake Tribune*, 19 April 1997.

Beare, Margaret E. *Criminal Conspiracies: Organized Crime in Canada*. Nelson: Canada, 1996.

Bell, Stewart. "Hamas Boasted of Canada Fundraising," *National Post* [Toronto], 14 August 14 2002. (FBIS Document EUP 20020815 000176)

Bell, Stewart. "Hezbollah Uses Canada as Base: CSIS Agency Wiretaps Show Suspected Operatives Using Laundered Money to Buy Materiel," *National Post* [Toronto], 31 October 2002.

Bell, Stewart. "Liberals Relent, Hezbollah Outlawed: Graham Says It's Due to Recent Evidence," *National Post* [Toronto], 12 December 2002.

Bell, Stewart. "LTTE Fundraiser's Case to Test Canada's Ability to Deport Suspected Terrorists," *National Post* [Toronto], 17 December 2001. (FBIS Document EUP20011218000328).

Bell, Stewart, and Marina Jimenez. "Al Qaida Operatives in Canada," *National Post* [Toronto], 12 December 2001. (FBIS Document EUP20011217000340).

Berdal, Mats, and Mónica Serrano, eds. *Transnational Organized Crime and International Security: Business as Usual?* Boulder, Colorado, and London: Lynne Rienner, 2002.

Bergquist, Charles, Ricardo Peñaranda, and Gonzalo Sánchez, eds. *Violence in Colombia: The Contemporary Crisis in Historical Perspective.* Wilmington, Delaware: Scholarly Resources, 1992.

Bibes, Patricia. "Colombia: The Military and the Narco-Conflict," *Low Intensity Conflict & Law Enforcement*, v. 9, no. 1 (Spring 2000).

Bibes, Patricia. "Transnational Organized Crime and Terrorism: Colombia, a Case Study." *Journal of Contemporary Criminal Justice*, 17, no. 3 (August 2001).

"The Black Market Peso Exchange." <http:/scolar.vsc.edu:8003/VSCCAT/ACR-1669>

Bodansky, Jossef. *Bin Laden: The Man Who Declared War on America.* Roseville, California: Prima Publishing/Random House, 2001.

Bolz, Jennifer. "Chinese Organized Crime and Illegal Alien Trafficking: Humans as a Commodity," *Asian Affairs*, 22, no. 3 (Fall 1995).

"Brazil Grapples with Crime, Punishment and Policing," *The Economist* [London], 24 June 2000.

"Brazil: Terrorist Khalid Sheikh Mohamed's Passage Through Brazil Reported," *O Estado de São Paolo* [São Paolo], 9 March 2003 (FBIS Document 20030308000052).

Brieger, Pedro, and Enrique Herszkowich. "The Muslim Community of Argentina," *The Muslim World*, 92, no. 1/2 (Spring 2002).

Bustos, Alirio Fernando. "Cayó official de la Armada, su principal enlace: La avanzada de la mafia rusa" [A Retired Navy Officer, Its Principal Liaison, Is Arrested: The Advance of the Russian Mafia], *El Tiempo* [Bogota], 8 February 1999.

Cabell, John. *Bay of Campeche Oil Fields Protection Plan and Action*s. Fort Leavenworth, Kansas, Foreign Military Studies Office, 31 March 2003 [accessed via Open Source Information System: www.fmso.osis.gov].

Canada. Citizenship and Immigration Canada. "Bill C-11 Immigration and Refugee Protection Act: What Is New in the Proposed Immigration and Refugee Protection Act," July 2001. <http://www.cic.gc.ca/english/irpa/c11%2Dnew.html>

Canada. Department of Justice. "Canadian Charter of Rights and Freedoms." <http://laws.justice.gc.ca/en/charter/index.html>

Canada. Department of Justice. "Constitution Acts of 1867 and 1982." <http://laws.justice.gc.ca/en/const/>

Canada. Department of Justice. "Proceeds of Crime (Money Laundering) and Terrorist Financing Act," 2000. <http://canada.justice.gc.ca/en/>

 "Canada: Immigration, Asylum and US," *Migration* News, 10, no. 1 (January 2003). <http://migration.ucdavis.edu/>

Canada. Senate. Special Select Committee on Security and Intelligence. *The Report of the Special Senate Committee on Security and Intelligence,* Jan. 1999. <http://www.parl.gc.ca/36/1/parlbus/commbus/senate/com-e/secu-e/rep-e/repsecintjan99-e.htm>

Canada. Statistics Canada. *Census of Canada 2001*. www.chass.utoronto.ca/datalib/cc01/cc01.htm

Canadian Broadcasting Corporation, "The Undefended Border." <http://www.cbc.ca/news/indepth/usattacked/>

Canadian Press Newswire. "New Screening Process Will Speed Traffic into Canada," 6 December 2001.

Canadian Security Intelligence Service. *Annual Public Report, 2001, 2000, 1999, 1998.* http://www.csis-scrs.gc.ca/eng/publicrp/pub2001_e.html#3c

Canadian Security Intelligence Service. "Transnational Criminal Activity," November 1998 [http://www.fas.org/irp/threat/back10e.htm].

"El Caso Lino Oviedo y su conexion con la Argentina" [The Lino Oviedo Case and Its Connection with Argentina], *Paginal 2* [Buenos Aires]. <http://paginal2.com.ar/2001/suple/carrio/cap11.pdf>

Castillo, Fabio, "The Hizballah Contacts in Colombia," *El Spectador* [Bogota], 9 December 2001 (FBIS Document LAP20011210000036).

Center for Defense Information Terrorism Project. "Globalizing Terrorism: The FARC-IRA Connection, 5 June 2002. <http://www.cdi.org/terrorism/farc-ira-pr.cfm>

Cheney, Peter. "US Links Charity Official to Terrorism," *The Globe and Mail* [Toronto], 10 October 2002 (FBIS Document EUP20021010000331)

Claiborne, Ron. "A Border Breached: Canada's Immigration Laws Draw New Scrutiny." 26 September 2001. <http://www.abcnews.go.com/sections/world/DailyNews/claiborne_border010926.html>

Cliffe, Lionel, and Robin Luckham. "Complex Political Emergencies and the State: Failure and the Fate of the State," *Third World Quarterly* [London], 20, no. 1 (February 1999).

Clayton, Mark, and Gail Russel Chaddock. "Terrorists Aided by a Leaky US-Canada Line," *The Christian Science Monitor*, 19 September 2001.

Coderre, Denis. "Notes for An Address by the Honorable Denis Coderre, Minister of Citizenship and Immigration, Made at a Meeting at the Renaissance Club, Detroit, Michigan," March 11, 2003. <http://www.cic.gc.ca/english/press/speech/detroit.html>

Colitt, Raymond. "Another Judge Killed as Drugs Crime Alarms Brazil," *Financial Times* [London], 25 March 2003.

Colitt, Raymond. "Brazil Tracks Down the Real Culprits Behind Surge in Highway Robberies," *Financial Times* [London], 2 May 2002.

"Colombian Paramilitary Group Denies Connections with Drug Trafficking," *El Universal* [Mexico City], 5 May 2003 (FBIS Document LAP20030505000102).

Cooke, Melinda Wheeler. "National Security," in Dennis M. Hanratty and Sandra W. Meditz, eds., *Paraguay: A Country Study.* Washington: GPO, 1990.

Cosso, Roberto. "Extremistas receberam US$50 mi de Foz do Iguaçu" [Extremists Received US$50 Million from Foz do Iguaçu], *Folha de S. Paolo* [São Paolo], 31 December 2001.

Council on Foreign Relations. "Terrorism: Questions and Answers: Borders." http://www.cfrterrorism.org/security/borders.html

Council on Foreign Relations and Markle Foundation. "FARC, ELN, AUC: Colombia, Rebels."
<http://www.terrorismanswers.com/groups/farc.htm>

Crane, David. "A Step at a Time Is Way to Go On Security," *Toronto Star*, 24 March 2003.
(FBIS Document EUP2003032400195)

"Crime in Mexico," *The Economist* [London], 26 June 2003. <http://www.economist.com>

Criminal Intelligence Service Canada. *Annual Report on Organized Crime Canada.* Ottawa:
1999, 2000, 2001, 2002. http://www.cics.gc.ca

Curry, Bill, and Andrew McIntosh. "Ottawa Loses Track of 36,000 Deportees," *National Post*
[Toronto], 9 April 2003, A1.

Curzio, Leonardo, "The Evolution of Intelligence Services in Mexico," Pages 163-180 in John
Bailey and Jorge Chabat, eds. *Transnational Crime and Public Security: Challenges to Mexico
and the United States.* San Diego: Center for U.S.-Mexican Studies, University of California,
2002.

Daly, John. "The Suspects: The Latin American Connection," *Jane's Terrorism and Security
Monitor*, 1 October, 2001.

Davidson II, Thomas S., *From Mexico into the U.S.: Third-Nation Immigrants Since 9/11*. Fort
Leavenworth, Kansas, Foreign Military Studies Office, October 2002 [accessed via Open Source
Information System: www.fmso.osis.gov].

Davidson II, Thomas S., *Human Smuggling Along the U.S.-Mexican Border*. Fort Leavenworth,
Kansas, Foreign Military Studies Office, March 2002 [accessed via Open Source Information
System: www.fmso.osis.gov].

Davidson II, Thomas S., *Non-Arab Terrorist Infiltration Through Mexico and Into the U.S.* Fort
Leavenworth, Kansas, Foreign Military Studies Office, March 2002 [accessed via Open Source
Information System: www.fmso.osis.gov].

"Delinquent Politics in Argentina (Argentina's Crime Wave)," *The Economist* [London], 5
October 2002.

"Delinquent: Tackling Crime Needs Police Reform," *The Economist* [London], 5 October 2002.

Delpirou, Alain, and Eduardo Mackenzie. *Les cartels criminels: Cocaïne et heroine, une
industrie lourde en Amérique latine*. [Criminal Cartels: Cocaine and Heroin, a Heavy Industry in
Latin America]. Paris: Presses Universitaires de France, 2000.

de Morais, Machado, and Andrea Frota. "Money Laundering in Brazil." Report for School of
Business and Public Management, Institute of Brazilian Business and Management Issues,

George Washington University, 2000.
<http://www.gwu.edu/~ibi/minerva/Fall2000/Andrea.Morais.pdf>

"Documentacion de Inmigrantes," Mexico City: National Migration Institute, 2003.
Dube, Jonathan. "Safe Haven for Terror?" *ABCNEWS.com.* 14 January 2000.
<http://abcnews.go.com/sections/world/DailyNews/canada_terrorism000114.html>

Dougherty, Jon. "Homeland Insecurity: Could Terrorists Strike from Caribbean?"
WorldNetDaily, 9 January 2002.
<http://www.worldnetdaily.com/news/article.asp?ARTICLE_ID=25977>

Downie, Andrew. "Corruption's Roots Deep and Wide-Reaching in Brazil," *America's Insider*,
1, no. 9 (8 December 2000).

"East European-Based Organized Crime," in Criminal Intelligence Service Canada, *Annual
Report 2002*. <http://www.cisc.gc.ca/AnnualReport2002/Cisc2002/european2002.html>

Economist Intelligence Unit. *Colombia: Country Profile 2002*. London: 2002.

Edmonds, Sarah. "Canada Gaining Reputation as Economic–Crime Haven," *Seattle Times*, 14
February 1999, A15.

"Egyptian Suspect in Luxor Attack Arrives in Ecuador," *The Daily Telegraph* [London], 21
October 1998.

Embassy of Canada, Washington, D.C. *"Canada's Actions Against Terrorism Since September
11."* Washington, D.C.: 2003. <http://www.canadianembassy.org/border/backgrounder-en.asp>

Embassy of Canada, Washington, D.C. "Canada-U.S. Cross Border Crime and Security
Cooperation." <http://www.canadianembassy.org/border/crime-en.asp>

Embassy of Canada, Washington, D.C. "The Smart Border Declaration," 11 February 2003.
<http://www.canadianembassy.org/border/declaration-en.asp>

Epstein, Jack. "Where Tourism Meets Terrorism," *U.S. News & World Report*, 117, no. 6 (8
August 1994).

Esnal, Louis, "Nexos con Montesinos" [Nexus with Montesinos], *La Nacion* [Buenos Aires], 24
April 2001.

Fabre, Guilhem. *Criminal Prosperity: Drug Trafficking, Money Laundering and Financial
Crises after the Cold War*. London: Routlege-Courzon, 2003.

Fabre, Guilhem, "Prospering on Crime: Money Laundering and Financial Crises," Paper
presented at the Conference on Business Practices of Narcotics Trafficking Enterprises.
Washington, D.C.: Library of Congress, 29 January 2003.

Fayt, Carlos. *Criminalidad del terrorismo sagrado: El atentado a la embajada de Israel en Argentina* [The Criminality of Religious Terrorism: The Attack on the Israeli Embassy in Argentina]. La Plata, Argentina: Editorial Universitaria de La Plata, 2001.

Federal Bureau of Investigation. Los Angeles Field Office. "19 Linked to Eurasian Crime Ring Named in Federal Complaint for Alien Smuggling," press release, 3 May 2001.

Fidler, Stephen. "New Migrants Spur Growth in Remittances," *Financial Times* [London], 17 May 2001.

Fields, Jeffrey. "Islamist Terrorist Threat in the Tri-Border Region." Report for Center for Nonproliferation Studies, Monterey Institute of International Studies, October 2002. <http://www.nti.org/e_research/e3_16b.html>

Filho, Expedito, Sílvio Ferreira, and Patrícia Cerqueira. "Rede de clandestinidade" [Clandestine Network], *Epoca* [São Paolo], no. 179 (22 October 2001).

Financial Transactions and Reports Analysis Centre of Canada (FINTAC). www.fintrac.gc.ca.

Finckenauer, James O. "Chinese Transnational Organized Crime: The Fuk Ching." Report for National Institute of Justice, 2000. <http://www.ojp.usdoj.gov/nij/international/chinese.html>

"Foz City Council President Shot in Attack," Itapiru Radio [Ciudad del Este] broadcast, 24 February 2003 (FBIS Document LAP20030226000042).

Friedman, Robert I. *Red Mafiya: How the Russian Mob Has Invaded America*. Boston: Little, Brown, 2000.

Friman, Richard II., and Peter Andreas, eds. *The Illicit Global Economy and State Power*. Boulder: Rowman & Littlefield, 1999.

Geddes, John. "The Terrorists Next Door," *Maclean's* [Toronto], September 24, 2001.

Gettleman, Jeffrey. "Canadians Begin to Say No to Immigrants From China," *Los Angeles Times*, 11 September 1999.

Glock, Clarinha. "Brazil-Paraguay: A Full Plate for Journalists." <http://www.impunidad.com/atrisk/brasil_paraguay7_19_01E.html>

Goldberg, Jeffrey. "In the Party of God," *The New Yorker*, 79, no. 32 (28 October 2002).

Gosman, Eleonora. "Temen una guerra entre bandas de narcos en Brasil" [Drug Cartel Wars Are Feared in Brasil], *Clarin* [Buenos Aires], 24 April 2001.

Government Reform in Mexico: Government Capacity to Assure High Quality Regulation. Paris: Organisation for Economic Co-operation and Development, 1999.

Grayson, George W. *Mexico's Forgotten Southern Border*." Washington: Center for Migration Studies, July 2002.

Green, Eric. "U.S. Says Colombia Remains World's Leading Producer of Cocaine: State Dept. Details Illicit Drug Activities in Americas and World," U.S. State Department International Information Program report, 3 March 2002.
<http://164.109.48.86/topical/global/drugs/03030302.htm>

Griffin, David, "Organised Crime in Canada," *Police Magazine*, January 2001.
<http://www.polfed.org/magazine/01_2001/01_2001_orgcrime.htm>

Grinbaum, Ricardo. "In Paraguay, Smugglers' Paradise," *World Press Review*, 43, no. 1 (January 1996).

Guillen, Edward M. Statement to the [Canada] House Subcommittee on Criminal Justice, Drug Policy and Human Rights, 23 January 2000.

Hall, John. *Veracruz Terrorist Threat*. U.S. Border Patrol, Del Rio Sector [undated, accessed via Open Source Information System].

Hall, Kevin G. "Accused al-Qaida Terrorist Spent Time in Brazil, Police Say," Knight Ridder Tribune News Service, 13 March 2003.

Herrera, Eduardo Wills, and Nubia Urueña Cortés. "South America," in Transparency International, *Global Corruption Report 2003*. Berlin: Transparency International, 2003.

Holmes, Jennifer S. "Terrorism, Drugs, and Violence in Latin America," *Latin American Research Review*, 37, no. 3 (2002).

"Hong Kong Mafia Linked to Hizballah in Tri-Border Region," *ABC Color* [Asuncion], 22 November 2002 (FBIS Document LAP20021122000047).

Hudson, Peter, and Joseph Contreras. "No Magical Solutions: Argentines Have Grown Cynical About Politicians," *Newsweek*, February 3, 2003.

Hudson, Rex A. "Narcotics-Funded Terrorist/Extremist Groups in Latin America." Pages 11-39 in Rex A. Hudson, ed., *A Global Overview of Narcotics-Funded Terrorist and Other Extremist Groups*. Washington, D.C.: Federal Research Division, Library of Congress, 2002.

Instituto Nacional de Estadistica, Geografia e Informatica. *Estadisticas Sociodemograficas, Atencion y Control de Indocumentados, 2002* [Sociodemographic Statistics: Illegal Alien Processing and Control].
<http://www.inegi.gob.mx/estadistica/sociodem/gobernacion/gob_04.html>

Inter-American Development Bank. *Development Beyond Economics: Economic and Social Progress in Latin America, 2000 Report*. Washington, D.C.: Johns Hopkins University Press and The Inter-American Development Bank, 2000.

International Federation of the Phonographic Industry. *Commercial Piracy Report 2003*.

International Intellectual Property Alliance. *2003 Special 301 Report: Brazil*. [http://www.iipa.com/rbc/2003/2003SPEC301BRAZIL.pdf].

International Narcotics Control Board. *Report on the Implementation of Article 12 of the United Nations Convention Against Illegal Traffic in Narcotic Drugs and Psychotropic Substances of 1988*, 2002. <http://www.incb.org>

"Investigation Shows Pervasive Impact of Drug Trade in Brazil." *America's Insider*, 1, no. 9 (8 December 2000).

"Is Canada a Safe Haven For Terrorists?" *Frontline*, PBS, 2001. www.pbs.org/wgbh/pages/frontline/shows/trail/etc/canada.html#harris

Jones, Patrice M. "Pirated Goods Cripple Brazil's Economy, but Solutions Seen as Weak," *Chicago Tribune*, 4 November 2002.

Jordan, David C. *Drug Politics: Dirty Money and Democracies*. Norman: University of Oklahoma Press, 1999.

Junger, Sebastian. "Terrorism's New Geography," *Vanity Fair*, no. 508 (December 2002).

Junior, Policarpo. "Tem famosos no meio: Polícia apura um bilionário esquema de remessa ilegal de dinheiro ao exterior e já tem nomes de gente graúda" [They Have Famous People Among Them: Police Expedite a Billion-Real Scheme for Remitting Illegal Money Abroad and Already Have the Names of Big-Shots], *Veja*, no. 1,755 (12 June 2002). http://veja.abril.com.br/120602/p_046.html/

Kelley, Louise. "Corruption and Organized Crime in Mexico in the Post-PRI Transition," *Journal of Contemporary Criminal Justice*, 17, no. 3 (August 2001).

Klebnikov, Paul. *Godfather of the Kremlin: Boris Berezovsky and the Looting of Russia*. New York: Harcourt Brace, 2000.

Kline, Harvey F. "Colombia: Lawlessness, Drug Trafficking, and Carving Up the State." Pages 161-82 in Robert I. Rotberg, ed., *State Failure and State Weakness in a Time of Terror*. Washington, D.C.: Brookings Institution Press, 2003.

Kline, Harvey F. *State Building and Conflict Resolution in Colombia, 1986-1994*. Tuscaloosa: University of Alabama Press, 1999.

Korzeniewicz, Roberto P. "The Society and Its Environment." Chapter 2 in Rex A. Hudson, ed., *Argentina: A Country Study* (unpublished manuscript, Federal Research Division, Library of Congress, 1998).

Kovadloff, Jacob. *Crisis In Argentina.* American Jewish Community report, June 2002. <http://www.ajc.org/InTheMedia/PublicationsPrint.asp?did=555>

Kozameh, Ernesto Nicolás, Julio O. Trajtenberg, C.P. Nicolás Kozameh Jr., and Ezequiel Trajtenberg. *Guide to the Argentine Executive, Legislative and Judicial System.* <http://www.llrx.com/features/argentina.htm>

"LTTE Fundraiser's Case to Test Canada's Ability to Deport Suspected Terrorists," *National Post* [Toronto], 17 December 2001 (FBIS: EUP20011218000328)

"Latin America: A Safe Haven for Militants?" Stratfor Global Intelligence Report, 4 September 2003.

LeBlanc, Daniel. "Terrorist Fundraisers Will Face Jail," *The Globe and Mail* [Toronto], 3 October 2001 (FBIS Document EUP2001100300043).

Lehman, Stan. "Brazilian Police Thwart Bomb Plot," *The Colombian*, 22 October 2002.

Lymnan, Michael D., "Business Principles of Modern Narcotics Trafficking Operations." Paper presented at the Conference on Business Practices of Narcotics Trafficking Enterprises, Library of Congress, Washington, D.C., 29 January 2003.

Macías, Viviana, and Fernando Castillo, "Mexico's National Public Security System: Perspectives for the New Millennium," Pages 53-70 in John Bailey and Jorge Chabat eds., *Transnational Crime and Public Security: Challenges to Mexico and the United States.* San Diego: Center for U.S.-Mexican Studies, University of California, 2002.

Madani, Blanca. "Hezbollah's Global Finance Network: The Triple Frontier," *Middle East Intelligence Bulletin*, 4, no. 1 (January 2002).

Madani, Blanca. "New Report Links Syria to 1992 Bombing of Israeli Embassy in Argentina," *Middle East Intelligence Bulletin*, 2, no. 3 (March 2000).

"Mafia rusa en Latinoamerica" [Russian Mafia in Latin America], *La Nacion Digital* [Buenos Aires], 25 September 2000.

Mahan, Sue. *Beyond the Mafia: Organized Crime in the Americas.* Thousand Oaks, California: Sage, 1998.

Malkin, Elizabeth. "Mexico Making Headway on Smuggling," *New York Times*, 5 June 2003.

"Mastermind of Taiyen's Murder Residing in Beirut," *Vanguardia* [Ciudad del Este], 11 November 2002 (FBIS Document LAP20021121000006).

McClelland, Susan. "Inside the Sex Trade: Trafficking in Foreign Prostitutes in One of the Fastest-Growing Illicit Activities in the World. Welcome to a Hidden Canada—and Lives of Quiet Desperation," *Maclean's* [Toronto], 3 December 2001. http://www.macleans.ca

McLean, Phillip. "Colombia: Failed, Failing, or Just Weak?" *The Washington Quarterly*, 25, no. 3 (Summer 2002).

McLeod, Ian. "Independent Terrorists Threaten Canada," *Ottawa Citizen*, 7 November 2002 (FBIS Document EUP20021108000333).

Mendel, William W., "Paraguay's Ciudad del Este and the New Centers of Gravity," *Military Review*, 82, no. 2 (March-April 2002).

Merrill, Tim L., and Ramón Miró, eds. *Mexico: A County Study*. Washington: GPO, 1997.

Milani, Aloisio. "Mafia chinesa extorque e executa em São Paolo" [Chinese Mafia Extorts and Executes in São Paolo], *Jornal-laboratorio da Faculdade de Comunicacao Social Casper Libero* [São Paolo], no. 28 (December 2001).

Mingardi, Guaracy. "Money and the International Drug Trade in São Paulo," *International Social Science Journal*, no. 169 (September 2001).

Miró, Ramón. *Legal and Institutional Factors Affecting Alien Smuggling in Mexico*. Report prepared by the Federal Research Division, Library of Congress, under an interagency agreement with the Human Smuggling Team, Illicit Activities Group, Office of Transnational Issues, Central Intelligence Agency, March 2003.

Miró, Ramón. *Organized Crime and Terrorist Activity in Mexico: 1999-2002*. Report prepared by the Federal Research Division, Library of Congress, under an interagency agreement with the Crime and Narcotics Center, Director of Central Intelligence, February 2003.

Mitrovica, Andrew. "Gangs Unite to Capitalize on Human Smuggling," *The Globe and Mail* [Toronto], 8 January 2001.

Montoya, Mario Daniel. "Israel Takes Special Interest in Triple Border Area," *Jane's Intelligence Review*, 13, no. 12 (December 2001).

Montoya, Mario Daniel. "War on Terrorism Reaches Paraguay's Triple Border," *Jane's Intelligence Review*, 13, no. 12 (December 2001).

Moser, Caroline. "Violence in Colombia: Building Sustainable Peace and Social Capital." Pages 9-77 in Andrés Solimano, ed., *Colombia: Essays on Conflict, Peace, and Development*. Washington, D.C.: World Bank, 2000.

Muello, Peter. "Brazilians Outraged by Slaying of Judges: Organized Crime Groups Unleash Wave of Violence," *Houston Chronicle*, 27 March 2003.

"Muestran a Fernandino a la prensa" [Fernandino Is Shown to the Press], *El Tiempo* [Bogota], 22 April 2001.

"Muslims Prevail Among Small Religions in Foz," *A Gazeta do Iguaçu* [Foz do Iguaçu], 3 February 2003 (FBIS Document LAP20030211000124).

"National Border Guard Commander: Tri-Border Area Hotbed of Sleeper Cells,"*La Nacion* [Buenos Aires], 3 October 2001 (FBIS Document LAP20011003000015).

Nurton, James. "Goodbye to a Difficult Year: The World's Leading IP Practices," *Managing Intellectual Property* [London], June 2002.

O'Balance, Edgar. *Islamic Fundamentalist Terrorism, 1979-95: The Iranian Connection* New York: New York University Press, 1997.

"Opium Poppy Cultivation in Colombia Down by 25 Percent, Says ONDCP," U.S. Department of State International Information Program report, 13 May 2003. <http://164.109.48.86.topical/global/drugs/03051301.htm>

Oppenheimer, Andres. *Bordering on Chaos: Guerrillas, Stockbrokers, Politicians, and Mexico's Road to Prosperity*. Boston: Little, Brown, 1996.

Organisation for Economic Cooperation and Development. Financial Action Task Force on Money Laundering. *FATF-XI Annual Report 1999-2000*. <http://www.fatf-gafi.org>

Orjuela, Luis Javier, and Cristina Barrera. "Narcotráfico y política en la década de los ochenta: Entre la repressión y el diálogo." In Carlos G. Arrieta, Luis J. Orjuela, Eduardo Sarmiento, and Juan G. Tokatlian. *Narcotráfico en Colombia: Dimensiones políticas, económicas, jurídicas e internacionales*. Bogotá: Ediciones Uniandes: Tercer Mundo Editores, 1990.

Osava, Mario. "Ciudades de America Latina/Brasil: Lavado y fuga de capitals en la frontera con Paraguay" [Cities of Latin America/Brazil: Laundering and Flight of Capital on the Border with Paraguay], Inter-Press Service report, 1999. <http://ips.org/Spanish/mundial/indices/Correo/cor0606051.htm>

Oviedo, Pedro. "En la Triple Frontera se lavan doce mil millones de dólares al año del narcotráfico, según un informe official" [In the Triborder Area US$12 billion Is Laundered Per Year From Narcotics Trafficking, According to an Official Report]. <http://misionesonline.net/paginas/action.lasso?-database=noticias3&-layout=web&-response=noticia.html&id=11349&autorizado=si&-search>

Padilla Fredy, Nelson. "Los hombres de Osama bin Laden en Colombia" [The Men of Osama bin Laden in Colombia], *Cromos* [Bogota], no. 4, 364 (24 September 2001).

Palacios, Cesar, and Oscar Florentin. "Paraguay: Police Confiscate Arsenal from Gangster's Home," *Noticias* [Asuncion], 6 December 2002 (FBIS Document LA{20021206000030).

"Paraguay: Vice Interior Minister Confirms Presence of 'Dormant Islamic Terrorist Cells,'" *ABC Color* [Asuncion], 4 May 2001 (FBIS Document 20010505000002).

"Paraguay: 'Strong Ties' Seen Between Hong Kong Mafia, Tri-Border Based Hizballah," *ABC Color* [Asuncion], 22 November 2002 (FBIS Document LAP20021122000059).

Pardo, Rafael. "Colombia's Two-Front War," *Foreign Affairs*, 79, no. 4 (July/August 2000).

Portes, Alejandro, and Kelly Hoffman. "Latin American Class Structures: Their Composition and Change during the Neoliberal Era," *Latin American Research Review*, 38, no. 1 (2003).

"El prontuario de Fernandinho" [Fernandino's Handbook], *El Tiempo* [Bogota], 21 April 2001.

Rabasa, Angel, and Peter Chalk. *Colombian Labyrinth: The Synergy of Drugs and Insurgency and Its Implications for Regional Stability*. Santa Monica, California: Rand, 2001.

Rauber, Guido. *Lavado de Dinero: Triple Frontera*, [Money Laundering in the Triborder Region], Ministry of Public Health, Misiones Province, Argentina, *Working Paper* no. 1, 31 December 2000.

Reeve, Simon. *The New Jackals: Ramzi Yousef, Osama bin Laden and the Future of Terrorism*. Boston: Northeastern University Press, 1999.

Regulatory Reform in Mexico: Government Capacity to Assure High Quality Regulation. Paris: Organisation for Economic Cooperation and Development, 1999.

Ribeiro Jr., Amaury, and Sonia Filgueiras. "Sieve of Impunity," *Istoé* [São Paolo], 5 February, 2003 (FBIS Document LAP20030203000075).

Richani, Nazih. *Systems of Violence: The Political Economy of War and Peace in Colombia*. Albany, New York: State University of New York Press, 2002.

Richard, Amy O'Neill. "International Trafficking in Women to the United States: A Contemporary Manifestation of Slavery and Organized Crime," report for Center for the Study of Intelligence, Director of Central Intelligence, Central Intelligence Agency, April 2000. <http://usinfo.state.gov/topical/global/traffic/report/homepage.htm#contents>

Richards, James R. *Transnational Criminal Organizations, Cybercrime, and Money Laundering: A Handbook for Law Enforcement Offices, Auditors, and Financial Investigators*. Boca Raton, Florida: CRC Press, 1999.

Robinson, Jeffrey. *The Laundrymen: Inside Money Laundering, the World's Third-Largest Business*. New York: Arcade, 1996.

Rogers, Bill. "Arabs Accuse Paraguay Police Of Extortion," *Middle East News Online*, 4 October 2001.

Rohter, Larry. "Argentine Judge Indicts 4 Iranian Officials in 1994 Bombing of Jewish Center," *New York Times*, 10 March 2003.

Rohter, Larry. "Iran Blew Up Jewish Center in Argentina, Defector Says," *New York Times*, 22 July 2002.

Rohter, Larry. "Terrorists Are Sought in Smugglers' Haven," *New York Times*, 27 September 2001.

Rotberg, Robert I. "Failed States in a World of Terror," *Foreign Affairs*, 81, no. 4 (July/August 2002): 127-140.

Rotberg Robert I., ed. *State Failure and State Weakness in a Time of Terror*. Washington: Brookings Institution Press, 2003.

Rotella, Sebastian. "Jungle Hub for World's Outlaws," *Los Angeles Times*, 24 August 1998.

Royal Canadian Mounted Police. "RCMP Fact Sheets, 2000-2001: Fact Sheet No. 9: Organized Crime." www.rcmp-grc.gc.ca/pdfs/facts_2001_e.htm#factsno9

Rubio, Mauricio. "Violence, Organized Crime, and the Criminal Justice System in Colombia," *Journal of Economic Issues,* 32, no. 605 (June 1998).

"The Russian Connection," *Cambio 16* [Madrid], 6 October 1997 (FBIS Document 98L01001A).

Safford, Frank, and Marco Palacios. *Colombia: Fragmented Land, Divided Society*. New York: Oxford University Press, 2002.

Salot, Jeff. "Graham Defends Policy on Hezbollah," *The Globe and Mail* [Toronto], April 19, 2002 (FBIS Document EUP20020419000396).

Sánchez, Gonzalo. "The Violence: An Interpretive Synthesis," Pages 75-123 in Charles Bergquist, Ricardo Peñaranda, and Gonzalo Sánchez, eds., *Violence in Colombia: The Contemporary Crisis in Historical Perspective*. Wilmington, Delaware: Scholarly Resources, 1992.

Sanford, Wendell. Consul of Canada, Remarks for an Address: "Canada Post 9/11 – The New True North Strong and Free." University of California, Berkeley, Oct. 9, 2002.

Serrano, Mónica. "Transnational Crime in the Western Hemisphere." Pages 87-112 in Jorge I. Domínguez, ed., *The Future of Inter-American Relations.* New York and London: Routledge, 2000.

Serrano, Mónica, and María Celia Toro. "From Drug Trafficking to Transnational Organized Crime in Latin America." Chapter 12 in Mats Berdal and Mónica Serrano, eds., *Transnational Organized Crime and International Security: Business as Usual?* Boulder, Colorado, and London: Lynne Rienner, 2002.

Shelley, Louise, "Corruption and Organized Crime in Mexico in the Post-PRI Transition," *Journal of Contemporary Criminal Justice,* 17, no. 3 (August 2001): 213-31.

Silva, Ruy Gomes. *Effective Measures to Combat Transnational Organized Crime in Criminal Justice Processes.* Asia and Far East Institute for the Prevention of Crime and the Treatment of Offenders, *Resource Material Series* [Tokyo], no. 58 (December 2001). <http://www.unafei.or.jp/pdf/58-00.pdf>

Sweig, Julia E. "What Kind of War for Colombia?" *Foreign Affairs*, 81, no. 5 (September/October 2002): 122-141.

"Surveillance System on Friendship Bridge," *A Gazeta do Iguaçu* [Foz do Iguaçu], 6 November 2002 (FBIS Document LAP20021121000006).

Sweeney, Jack. "DEA Boosts Its Role in Paraguay," *Washington Times*, 21 August 2001.

Takeyh, Ray, and Nikolas Gvosdev. "Do Terrorist Networks Need a Home?" *Washington Quarterly*, 25, no. 3.

Thompson, Ginger. "Migrants to the U.S. Are a Major Resource for Mexico," *New York Times*, 25 March 2002.

Thoumi, Francisco. *Economía política y narcotráfico* [Political Economy and Illegal Drugs in Colombia]. Bogotá: Tercer Mundo, 1994.

"Three Sailors Sentenced for Smuggling Chinese Migrants," *National Post* [Toronto], 31 October 2002.

Timmerman, Kenneth R. "Likely Mastermind of Tower Attacks: Imad Mugniyeh," *Insight on the News,* 17, no. 49 (31 December 2001).

Tollefson, Scott D. "National Security," Chapter 5 in Rex A. Hudson, ed., *Argentina: A Country Study* (unpublished manuscript, Federal Research Division, Library of Congress, 1999).

Turbiville, Jr., Graham H. "Mexico's Multimission Force for Internal Security," *Military Review*, July-August 2000.

Turbiville, Jr., Graham H. "U.S.-Mexican Border Security: Civil-Military Cooperation," *Military Review*, July-August 1999.

United States. Office of the President. *International Crime Threat Assessment*. Washington, D.C.: 2000. http://clinton4.nara.gov

United States. Congress. 106th. House of Representatives. Committee on Appropriations. Hearing Before the Subcommittee on Immigration and Claims, "The Threat to the United States," 26 January 2000.

U.S. Department of Justice. Drug Enforcement Administration. *Mexico Country Brief*, July 2002. <http://www.usdoj.gov/dea/pubs/intel/02035/02035p.html>

U.S. Department of State. *Country Reports on Human Rights Practices 2001*. <http://www.state.gov/g/drl/rls/hrrpt/2001.htm>

U.S. Department of State. *Patterns of Global Terrorism 2000*. <http://www.usis.usemb.se/terror/rpt2000/index.html>

U.S. Department of State. *Patterns of Global Terrorism 2001*. <http://www.state.gov/s/ct/rls/pgtrpt/2001/html/10246.htm>

U.S. Department of State.*Trafficking in Persons Report 2002*." <http://www.state.gov/g/tip/rls/tiprpt/2002>

U.S. Department of State. Bureau for International Narcotics and Law Enforcement Affairs. *International Narcotics Control Strategy Report 1999*. <http://www.state.gov/g/om;/rls/nrcrpt/1999>

U.S. Department of State. Bureau for International Narcotics and Law Enforcement Affairs. *International Narcotics Control Strategy Report 2001*. <http://www.state.gov/g/inl/rls/nrcrpt/2001>

U.S. Department of State. Bureau for International Narcotics and Law Enforcement Affairs. *International Narcotics Control Strategy Report 2002*. <http://www.state.gov/g/inl/rls/nrcrpt/2002>

U.S. Department of State. Bureau for International Narcotics and Law Enforcement Affairs. *International Narcotics Control Strategy Report 2003*. Washington, D.C., 2003.

Van de Velde, James R., "The Growth of Criminal Organizations and Insurgent Groups Abroad Due to International Drug Trafficking," *Low Intensity Conflict & Law Enforcement*, 5, no. 3 (Winter 1996).

Webster, William H., Arnaud de Borchgrave, Robert H. Kupperman and Erik R. Peterson, Gerard P. Burke, and Frank J. Cilluffo. *Russian Organized Crime: A Report of the Global*

Organized Crime Task Force. Washington, D.C.: Center for Strategic and International Studies, 1997.

Weinberg, Michelle, et. al. "The U.S. Mexico Border Infectious Disease Surveillance Project: Establishing Bi-national Border Surveillance," *Emerging Infectious Diseases*, 9, no. 1 (January 2003).

Weintraub, Sidney. "Disrupting the Financing of Terrorism," *The Washington Quarterly*, 25, no. 1 (Winter 2002).

Weyland, Kurt. "The Politics of Corruption in Latin America," *Journal of Democracy,* 9, no. 2 (April 1998).

Wilcox, Jr., Philip C. "International Terrorism in Latin America," testimony to the U.S. House of Representatives, Committee on International Relations, September 28, 1995.

Wills Herrera, Eduardo, Nubia Urueña Corté, and Nick Rosen. "South America" in Transparency International, *Global Corruption Report 2003.* <http://www.globalcorruptionreport.org>.

www.ingramcontent.com/pod-product-compliance
Lightning Source LLC
Chambersburg PA
CBHW080243290526
45790CB00005B/1687